MW00653554

Praise for *Loosing the Lion*

"Leroy Huizenga gives us the resurrected Aslan in his exciting book *Loosing the Lion*. For too long Mark's Gospel has been the little kid bullied on the playground of biblical scholarship. Derided by scholars who think it a literary disaster or a hodgepodge collection of disconnected Jesus stories, Dr. Huizenga shows the multileveled complexity and subtlety of Mark's dynamic account of Jesus—the hero who defeats the devil. Not just a scholarly treatise, *Loosing the Lion* is a powerful and practical source for preachers of the Word. Although written by a Catholic, this book should be a resource for preachers of all traditions to present once more Mark's ever ancient, ever new drama of the world's redemption."

—Fr. Dwight Longenecker
Author of *The Mystery of the Magi:
The Quest for the True Identity of the Three Wise Men*

"Leroy Huizenga has composed a concise and informative entrée into the Gospel of Mark for preachers and teachers. He writes within the Catholic tradition, but his insights transcend denominations and theology as he introduces readers to the Gospel of Mark, why Mark matters, and why one should read this beautiful story. A superb resource for anyone who wants to get better acquainted with the Gospel of Mark."

—Michael F. Bird, PhD
Lecturer in Theology
Ridley Melbourne College of Mission and Ministry
Melbourne, Australia

"Dr. Huizenga's extremely readable *Loosing the Lion* is marked by deep learning, creativity, and verve. Rooted in historic orthodoxy and sensitive to the needs of the Catholic Church today, this book will serve well those who desire to teach and preach from the oft-neglected Gospel of Mark."

—JONATHAN PENNINGTON, PHD
Associate Professor of New Testament Interpretation
Director of Research Doctoral Studies
The Southern Baptist Theological Seminary
Louisville, KY

"For some time now, the first of the living beasts round the throne in heaven—the Markan Lion—has been kept in a cage by its academic zookeepers. They keep it around for exegetical tourism, but belittle it as short, haphazard, lacking in literary greatness, and wanting in theological complexity. What Huizenga sets out to do in this stimulating book is to set this Gospel-Lion free from our modern prejudices. He takes something precious, cleans it off, and gives it back to us to appreciate as if for the first time. The scholarship on which this book stands is impressive, but kept unobtrusive so as to be readable by laity and as a resource for preachers. Exegesis flows into liturgical preaching, confronting us with the awful beauty of the Cross."

—DAVID W. FAGERBERG, PHD
Professor of Theology
University of Notre Dame
Notre Dame, IN

LOOSING
THE LION

LOOSING
THE LION

PROCLAIMING THE
GOSPEL OF MARK

LEROY A. HUIZENGA

EMMAUS
ROAD
PUBLISHING

Steubenville, Ohio
www.emmausroad.org

Emmaus Road Publishing
1468 Parkview Circle
Steubenville, Ohio 43952

Library of Congress Cataloging-in-Publication Data
Names: Huizenga, Leroy Andrew, 1974- author.
Title: Loosing the lion : proclaiming the Gospel of Mark / Leroy A. Huizenga.
Description: Steubenville : Emmaus Road, 2017.
Identifiers: LCCN 2017039013 (print) | LCCN 2017041058 (ebook) | ISBN
  9781947792241 (ebook) | ISBN 9781947792227 (hardcover) | ISBN
  9781947792234 (pbk.)
Subjects: LCSH: Bible. Mark--Commentaries.
Classification: LCC BS2585.53 (ebook) | LCC BS2585.53 .H85 2017 (print) | DDC
  226.3/06--dc23
LC record available at https://lccn.loc.gov/2017039013

Nihil Obstat and Imprimatur
The Most Reverend David D. Kagan, D.D., P.A., J.C.L., Bishop of Bismarck
June 14, 2017

Cover image: © pimchawee / shutterstock.com

Cover design and layout by Margaret Ryland

To the Clergy of the Diocese of Sioux Falls and the Diocese of Bismarck and the Parishioners of the Cathedral of the Holy Spirit

Table of Contents

Preface

M ark has been the underdog among the four canonical Gospels until quite recently. Overshadowed by the Gospel of Matthew, the Church's favorite, the evidence we have suggests early Christians found the Gospel of Mark wanting. Papias of Hierapolis struck a defensive tone in the second century, implying that Mark's apparent lack of order didn't matter because it was ultimately a composite of St. Peter's recollections, while St. Augustine said it was a shorter summary of Matthew. Nearer our own day, Rudolph Bultmann, the great Lutheran scholar, said, "Mark is not sufficiently master of his material to be able to venture on a systematic construction himself"[1]—in other words, Mark was an incompetent who didn't know what he was doing and simply slapped random stories together (in the words of another German, Karl Ludwig Schmidt) like "a heap of unstrung pearls."[2]

In recent decades, however, scholars and literary critics have begun to see Mark's literary and theological genius. St. Mark tells a wild, crazy, impossible story at a breakneck pace with twists and turns that shock and surprise attentive readers, those with eyes to see and ears to hear the mystery of the kingdom of God that Jesus the Son of God brings.

My little book here is designed as a crash course in Mark's

---

[1] Rudolf Bultmann, *History of the Synoptic Tradition*, trans. J. Marsh (Oxford: Blackwell, 1963), 350.

[2] Karl Ludwig Schmidt, *Der Rahmen der Geschichte Jesu* (Berlin: Trowitzsch und Sohn, 1919), 281 (my translation).

Gospel, much as Mark's Gospel is a crash course in Jesus. My book grows out of talks I was invited to give on the Gospel of Mark to the clergy of the dioceses of Sioux Falls, South Dakota, in the fall of 2014, and Bismarck, North Dakota, in the spring of 2015, as well as my teaching of the Gospel of Mark to parishioners at the Cathedral of the Holy Spirit in Bismarck during 2015–2016. The book is keyed to the lectionary for Year B, in which Mark dominates, and it's designed to help clergy who will preach on Mark and congregants who will hear Mark understand the Gospel so that they might have an ever-deeper encounter with Jesus, that, like many characters in Mark's Gospel, they might see, hear, understand, believe, turn, and be forgiven, healed, and saved.

Mine is a substantive book, but homiletic in tone and light on footnotes, jargon, and academic debates, written like Mark's Gospel in an intense style that tries to capture Mark's dynamism and the oral energy of my talks (hence some of my language is punchy, and I include some personal reflections). It is not a proper commentary. It does not treat every verse or every technical issue; for those things one should consult critical commentaries. Like Mark's Gospel, it is proclamation, not apologetic: it asserts much more than it argues. That said, my treatments of Markan passages are not little sermons in themselves ready to be paraphrased or plagiarized; preachers will have to do their own work in taking what I provide here as food for thought and working it into their own homilies. The initial section on preaching isn't simply geared toward clergy but should also help laypeople better hear and heed homilies, as well as the Gospel of Mark, which itself is proclamation.

I hope this book will be a good resource for the text study groups many clergy engage in for their homily preparation, as well as for laypeople seeking to go deeper into Scripture in adult education and Bible studies. And, while I write as a Catholic and see Mark's Gospel as a deeply Catholic text thanks to its sacrificial emphasis on the Cross and Eucharist, Mark is a Gospel also congenial to Protestants, and so my hope is that my non-Catholic brothers and sisters will find much of value here as well. Indeed, the mentors who fired my love of Mark were Protestants: Dr. James R. Edwards, my undergraduate mentor at Jamestown College, later the Bruner-Welch Professor of Theology at Whitworth University; Dr. C. Clifton Black, the Otto A. Piper Professor of Biblical Theology at Princeton Theological Seminary; and the late Dr. Donald Juel, formerly Richard J. Dearborn Professor of New Testament Theology at Princeton Theological Seminary.

After a chapter on preaching, a chapter on how to read a Gospel, and a chapter introducing Mark's Gospel, the book follows the structure of Mark, for Mark tells a coherent story from start to finish. The lectionary for Sundays sometimes departs from the order of Mark's Gospel (indeed, the first reading from the Gospel of Mark in the liturgical year is Mark 13:33–37, the Parable of the Doorkeeper, appropriate for the apocalyptic season of Advent), and the Gospel readings for daily Mass follow their own schedule. It thus seemed advisable to follow Mark's story for the structure of the present book; the table of contents for part II will help locate Markan passages for particular Masses.

My thanks, then, to Bishop Paul J. Swain of the Diocese of Sioux Falls, Bishop David D. Kagan of the Diocese of Bismarck, Msgr. Thomas Richter, rector of the Cathedral of the Holy Spirit, and members of their respective staffs for their gracious invitations to teach Mark to their clergy and parishioners. Thanks also to the clergy and laypeople who heard my presentations with such eager attention and gave me such great feedback. I learned much from them. To all of them this book is dedicated.

Finally, my thanks to my wife, Kari, and my children, Hans, Miriam, and Max, for their patience, as they saw all too little of me in the spring while I was completing the manuscript.

April 25, 2017
Feast of St. Mark

PART I:

Preaching the Gospel of Mark

CHAPTER 1

The Shock Treatment of Beauty for an Age Gone Numb

Our age is numb. It's numb to beauty, to goodness, to truth, because it's numb to grace, and ultimately numb to God. And that means it's a good season for the preaching of Mark, because Mark is a Gospel that preaches well when understood, a radical Gospel for an age grown numb. I want to suggest that the shock of radical beauty one encounters in the liturgical proclamation of Mark's Gospel might rouse postmodern people to faith. In short, my advice is this: Give people the shock treatment of beauty in the Mass, in both Word and Sacrament. Liturgy and preaching should tell the shocking, beautiful story of the gospel in a beautiful way.

The Unbearable Numbness of Moral Therapeutic Deism

In our post-Christian culture, the gospel is no longer compelling, even in supposedly religious rural areas. The capitalistic media culture in which we live—in which everything from what's supposed to be hard news to hard-core pornography is packaged as entertainment for the sake of profit—affects Manhattan, NYC, as well as Medora, ND, thanks to the technology of the Internet, accessed through devices that fit in farm kids' pockets.

3

Where religion remains, it's become what Notre Dame sociologist Christian Smith famously calls "Moral Therapeutic Deism"[1]: moral, in that most people nowadays reduce religion to the morality of a mere ethics of consent; therapeutic, in that most people think the business of religion is to make them feel good; and deism, in that the God most people think they believe in is the grand watchmaker who set everything in motion but now stays aloof from our affairs. Moral Therapeutic Deism is a gossamer gruel, a sorry substitute for full-throated Christianity, in which the Triune God invades us to save us from ourselves and bring us to him forever.

Thus, ours is a culture grown numb to the gospel, content with counterfeits. The statistics are sobering, especially among the young. If you've read Christian Smith's *Young Catholic America: Emerging Adults In, Out of, and Gone from the Catholic Church*,[2] you know the picture isn't pretty.[3] It's the fruit of numbness. Christian churches of all sorts are complicit in their contribution to this numbness to the gospel, whether Catholic or Protestant. For too often, churches engage in accommodation, moralism, and gimmicks.

[1] Christian Smith and Melinda Lundquist Denton, *Soul Searching: The Religious and Spiritual Lives of American Teenagers*, repr. (Oxford: Oxford University Press, 2009). See especially chapter 4 (118–71).

[2] Christian Smith et al., *Young Catholic America: Emerging Adults In, Out of, and Gone from the Catholic Church* (Oxford: Oxford University Press, 2014).

[3] See Smith et al., *Young Catholic America*, 29–59, for statistics on acceptance of Catholic teaching and Mass attendance. Smith's work finds that Catholics 18 to 23 years old situated in the categories of "Completely, Mostly, and Moderately Catholic" have Mass attendance rates at 14% to 17% (64–65).

The Bland Alleys of Accommodation, Moralism, and Gimmicks

Accommodation is trying so hard to present the faith in the world's terms that the world's terms end up dominating, and so it then appears we're simply saying what the wider culture is saying. That's a recipe for Moral Therapeutic Deism. But we forget that the Bible from Genesis 3 to Revelation (and especially in the Gospel of Mark) reveals a conflict with the world, for the entire cosmos is fallen into rebellion and stands under the domination of the evil one. Without the Fall, there is no redemption, no gospel, no good news. Accommodation offers a false gospel of mere affirmation, not salvation. God doesn't affirm us; God saves us.

With accommodation comes mere moralism. Moralism ultimately has nothing transcendent to say and can only encourage people to try harder to fit whatever mold various spirits of the age have on offer. At best, it can only appeal to a certain nobility of spirit, and at worst, it devolves into divisive harangue.

Pope Francis rightly rails against this, as did Benedict before him. Much preaching today is merely moralistic, telling people what they must do, and as moralistic preaching is driven by the spirit of the age, usually what is preached is what they must do to be a good compliant bourgeois member of middle-class society. But in the Bible, God acts first and any moralism is a response to God's love expressed in saving actions. The particular God of Israel saves his people from Egypt, and then come the Commandments. The same God understood as Father, Son, and Holy Spirit saves his people in the life of Jesus Christ, and Christian morality flows from that.

The combination of accommodation and moralism leave churches with little to work with but gimmicks: a domesti-

5

cated, moralistic message of affirmation, slick marketing campaigns, and worship as entertainment.

Would That We Were Pagan

The result is a culture that thinks it knows the gospel but doesn't, and often doesn't rise to the dignity of paganism. I wish here to quote from a couple good Anglicans, C. S. Lewis and T. S. Eliot, who reflected deeply on the decline of Christian culture. In a pair of Latin letters from 1953, Lewis thought we needed a new paganism if we were to have a new age of Christian flourishing:

> What you say about the present state of mankind is true: indeed it is even worse than you say. For they neglect not only the Law of Christ, but even the Law of Nature as known by the Pagans. . . . They err who say: "The world is turning pagan again." Would that it were! The truth is, we are falling into a much worse state. Post-Christian man is not the same as pre-Christian man. He is as far removed as a virgin from a widow. . . . There is a great difference between a spouse-to-come and a spouse sent away.[4]

In a later letter, Lewis returned to the theme:

> But God who is the God of mercies, even now has not altogether cast off the human race. We must not despair. And among us are not an inconsiderable

---

[4] C. S. Lewis, Letter to Giovanni Calabria, March 17, 1953, in C. S. Lewis and Don Giovanni Calabria, *The Latin Letters of C. S. Lewis*, trans. and ed. Martin Moynihan (South Bend, IN: St. Augustine's Press, 1998), 82–85 (Letter 23).

number now returning to the faith. For my part, I believe we ought to work not only at spreading the Gospel (that certainly) but also to a certain preparation for the Gospel. It is necessary to recall many to the law of nature before we talk about God. For Christ promises forgiveness of sins, but what is that to those who, since they do not know the law of nature, do not know that they have sinned? Who will take medicine unless he knows he is in the grip of a disease? Moral relativity is the enemy we have to overcome before we tackle atheism. I would almost dare to say, "First let us make the younger generation good pagans, and afterwards let us make them Christians."[5]

For his part, T. S. Eliot suggested that a return to a religious sense of the holy was requisite:

We need to know how to see the world as the Christian Fathers saw it; and the purpose of re-ascending to origins is that we should be able to return, with greater spiritual knowledge, to our own situation. We need to recover the sense of religious fear, so that it may be overcome by religious hope.[6]

The Spirit of the Liturgy

Accommodation concerns not just content, but even the form of our faith, and that means attention to liturgy. Christians nowadays do not only think like the world, but worship like

[5] C. S. Lewis, Letter to Giovanni Calabria, September 15, 1953, in Lewis and Calabria, *Latin Letters*, 90–93 (Letter 26).

[6] T. S. Eliot, *The Idea of a Christian Society* (London: Faber and Faber Ltd., 1939), 62.

the world in worldly forms. And since *lex orandi lex credendi lex vivendi* (the rule of liturgical prayer is the rule of belief is the rule of life), they act like the world and drift away, for when churches accommodate to culture, they offer nothing distinctive over and against the culture. And then they empty: as it is said, a church that marries the spirit of the age becomes a widow in the next.

We Catholics shouldn't blame the Council. The Second Vatican Council, in its texts, gave us the theological and pastoral tools for mission in postmodernity. As Bishop Robert Barron often puts it, the goal of Vatican II was not to modernize the Church, but to Christify the world.

But a funny thing happened on the way to Christification. Vatican II was intended to drive a major missionary effort powered by the twin engines of Scripture and liturgy. But something went wrong in the implementation: instead of the compelling scriptural story of salvation history, we got the acid bath of positivist historical criticism; instead of compelling liturgy revealing the culmination of salvation history in the in-breaking of the eschaton at every Eucharist, we got something else.

The Second Vatican Council's *Sacrosanctum Concilium* was not a call to liturgical accommodation in matters of form, but a desire for people to see more clearly and participate more deeply in the Roman rite, precisely so that they might more deeply encounter the Triune God. *Sacrosanctum Concilium*'s call for the maintenance and priority of Latin, chant, and organ, for instance, reveals a deep desire for sacred liturgical beauty reflecting the beauty of God transcending the secular cultural forms trending in the 1960s and 70s.

So what do we do today? How do we "recover the sense of religious fear," as T. S. Eliot said, so that the Church and world may be overcome by religious hope once again?

I want to suggest the remedy of beauty: beauty in liturgy, which means beauty in both Word and Sacrament.

Why beauty? One reason is practical: this age is numb, if not hostile, to both truth and goodness, but beauty still grips people. Too often, we start with truth in the form of apologetics, or goodness in the sense of moralism. And people don't want to hear it. But beauty still has the capacity to shock, to awaken, to attract.

Another more profound reason is properly theological: God is beauty, as St. Augustine cried out in his confessions, "Late have I loved thee, O Beauty, ever ancient, ever new! Late have I loved thee!"[7]

Beauty thus facilitates an encounter with the God who is beauty. And that has implications for the preaching of Sacred Scripture in the liturgy.

Word and Sacrament on the Road to Emmaus

Indeed, the preaching of Scripture is liturgical, and the liturgy scriptural. The story of salvation history presented in Scripture continues in the time of the Church, made real in every Mass. The Old Testament is fulfilled in the New and realized in the Eucharistic liturgy. The Passover celebrates the exodus and prefigures the crucifixion, which is re-presented in every celebration of Jesus's new Passover ritual, the Eucharist. Every time Mass is celebrated, the past of salvation history and the future of heaven meet in our present, at the altar, as God enters in to give us his own divine life in the precious Body and Blood of his Son.

Both Pope Emeritus Benedict and Pope Francis love the story of the risen Jesus appearing to the two disciples on the

---

[7] Augustine, *Confessions* (hereafter *Conf.*), 10.27.38.

road to Emmaus in Luke 24. Pope Francis mentions it frequently in interviews and homilies as a model for how the Church can lead those in despair back to joy in an encounter with Jesus Christ. In *Verbum Domini* §24, Pope Benedict writes: "The profound unity of the word and Eucharist is grounded in the witness of Scripture (cf. John 6; Luke 24), attested to by the Fathers of the Church, and reaffirmed by the Second Vatican Council [see *Dei Verbum* §21 and §26]. . . . The presence of Jesus [with the disciples on the road to Emmaus], first with his words and then with the act of breaking bread, made it possible for the disciples to recognize him."

The story of Jesus's journey with the two disciples on the road to Emmaus in Luke 24 is profound. The disciples do not recognize it is Jesus who walks with them; their eyes "were kept" from recognizing him. They express confusion and despair regarding Jesus's Passion and their dashed hopes. But the risen Jesus (whom they cannot yet recognize) then preaches to them: he explains to them how the Scriptures of Israel point to him and the events of his Passion and Resurrection. It takes the crucified and risen Christ to make sense of Scripture.

And then it takes the Eucharist to make sense of Christ. The disciples do not recognize Jesus until the supper. St. Luke writes: "When [Jesus] was at table with them, he took the bread and blessed it, and broke it, and gave it to them. And their eyes were opened and they recognized him; and he vanished out of their sight" (Luke 24:30–31).

They recognize Jesus only in the Eucharistic ritual. And why does Jesus vanish from their sight? He doesn't, really. Luke is suggesting that Jesus is truly present in the elements of the Eucharistic bread and wine. And so Benedict writes in *Verbum Domini*: "The Eucharist opens us to an understanding of Scripture, just as Scripture for its part illumines and explains the mystery of the Eucharist. Unless we acknowledge the Lord's Real Presence in the Eucharist, our understanding of Scripture remains imperfect" (§55). Salvation history centers on Christ and culminates in each and every Eucharist as the fulfillment of Scripture's story of salvation history. But the divine Word is received not only in the liturgy of the Eucharist, but in the liturgy of the Word as well. The Second Vatican Council reminds us of this in *Dei Verbum* §21: "Especially in the sacred liturgy, [the Church] unceasingly receives and offers to the faithful the bread of life from the table both of God's word and of Christ's body." And in *Evangelii Gaudium*, Pope Francis observed, "The homily has special importance due to its Eucharistic context: it surpasses all forms of catechesis as the supreme moment in the dialogue between God and his people which lead up to sacramental communion" (§137).

The unity of ambo and altar is usually shown forth in Church architecture, and that unity should be manifest in our preaching. For preaching is a liturgical act, not something that happens in the middle of liturgy, but as an organic part of it.

The Beauty of the Word

So what is beauty, why does it matter, and what might it mean to preach beautifully in the context of beautiful liturgy? As St. Thomas Aquinas states, beauty consists in the threefold cord of integrity, consonance, and clarity.[8] Integrity is the ontological wholeness and perfection of a thing. Consonance (or proportion) is harmony of parts so that a thing might achieve its end. Clarity reveals the truth of a thing.

---

[8] See especially *Summa theologiae* [hereafter, *ST*] I, q. 39, a. 8, resp. See also *ST* I, q. 5, a. 4, ad 1, and *ST* II-II, q. 145, a. 2, resp.

Beauty matters because beauty attracts. If we are to attract numb postmoderns to the God who is beauty, liturgy ought to be beautiful, presenting the integrity of the Roman rite, doing so through the harmony of good order and execution, thus revealing truly the beauty of God in his heaven come to earth on the altar.

And so, the concern for beauty isn't an idiosyncratic fixation of the aesthete. Rather, beauty is a means by which the gospel advances. As Pope Francis teaches in *Evangelii Gaudium*: "Evangelization with joy becomes beauty in the liturgy, as part of our daily concern to spread goodness. The Church evangelizes and is herself evangelized through the beauty of the liturgy, which is both a celebration of the task of evangelization and the source of her renewed self-giving" (§24). Elsewhere in the encyclical, Pope Francis calls for "a renewed esteem for beauty as a means of touching the human heart and enabling the truth and goodness of the Risen Christ to radiate within it" (§167).

And so, ideally, in a given Mass, the liturgy itself, the homily, and everything involved in the celebration—the music, the architecture, the *ars celebrandi* of the priest celebrant—will come together in one harmonious whole.

Let's talk then about the particularities of beautiful preaching. How do we do it?

The Priority of Preaching

The first thing to say is that preaching matters. The homily is where clergy can have maximum impact. Doing the math, depending on the diocese, each clergyman is responsible for dozens, hundreds of families; hundreds, thousands of souls. Clergy cannot possibly meet with them all regularly, or even irregularly. But clergy can engage them—and they can engage the clergy—through the sacred pulpit. And so, given the greatness of the opportunity, preaching demands one's best energies.

Indeed, a Gallup poll released April 14, 2017 found that preaching matters most: "The content of the sermons could be the most important factor in how soon worshippers return. Gallup measured a total of seven different reasons why those who attend a place of worship at least monthly say they go. Three in four worshippers noted sermons or talks that either teach about scripture or help people connect religion to their own lives as major factors spurring their attendance."[9]

Second, preaching is an oral event, where preachers encounter real embodied people. Most people today spend their lives watching pixels, and so encountering a real orator is blessedly weird. In *Ecclesiam Suam* (1964), Pope Blessed Paul VI wrote of preaching: "No other form of communication can take its place; not even the enormously powerful technical means of press, radio, and television" (§90)—and today he would include the Internet in that list. Returning to the point a decade later in *Evangelii Nuntiandi* (1975), Paul wrote, "The fatigue produced these days by so much empty talk, and the relevance of many other forms of communication, must not, however, diminish the permanent power of the word, or cause a loss of confidence in it" (§42). Not only is this theologically true, but it is also true on the ground in practice. Orality is natural, whereas modern media are artificial. Thus, even in a technological age, an embodied oral

---

[9] Layla Saad, "Sermon Content Is What Appeals Most to Churchgoers," Gallup, http://www.gallup.com/poll/208529/sermon-content-appeals-churchgoers.aspx. Although the survey indicates that Protestants care more about preaching than Catholics, it also indicates that homilies that teach about Scripture and that connect religion to their lives remain the most important reason Catholics attend Mass.

event like preaching can cut through the noise and bring us back to our embodied personhood.

The Rhetoric of Preaching

Clergy therefore ought to be confident in the potential of their preaching, for in the homily they have an opportunity. As priests in particular, they are an embodiment of Christ really meeting people, speaking the word of God written about the Word of God incarnate. It's a real rhetorical event providing an opportunity for an encounter with Christ. So let's plunder the Greeks and turn to Aristotle for help with the rhetoric of preaching.

For Aristotle, the components of a speech are *ethos, logos,* and *pathos—ethos* being the speaker's self-presentation, *logos* the content of the speech, and *pathos* the audience's response. As preaching is an embodied oral event, *ethos* matters—vestments, posture, gestures, facial expressions, whether one stands at the ambo or somewhere else. Preachers would do well to memorize their homilies so they can stand and deliver them and be fully present in their bodies as they present the homily with every fiber of their being. Beauty here means that the homily is delivered well, every gesture making for integrity, consonance, and clarity.

Logos matters too, the content of one's homily. Beauty here means the content is composed well, that every word is clear and doing what it is supposed to do. But here, many preachers are subconscious Cartesians, wanting to make the faith a matter of the intellect, especially given the collapse of catechesis in prior generations and the questions surrounding the relevance of the Church's doctrine today. And so, many think the one thing a homily should do is teach. But a homily can do so much more; teaching is just one of the many rhetorical options. Homilies can challenge, console, comfort, afflict, condemn, save, and so on. Preachers ought to ask not so much what the texts for the day mean, but what the texts do, or better, what God wants to do through the texts—that is, ask after their intended rhetorical effects—and then craft their homilies toward the end of moving their people in the rhetorical direction of the texts.

This brings us to *pathos*, the reaction of the audience. What effects do the text, the homilist, and ultimately God wish the homily to have on the people of God? A focus on teaching as the mere transmission of doctrine doesn't always take root, for static didacticism can close people off. Dynamic rhetorical preaching, however, challenges people and draws them in, and thus can teach effectively. Preachers must decide what the rhetorical point of the homily should be so that the people do something, so that they change, so that they grow in grace. Challenge them.

On this point, leadership guru John C. Maxwell relates a story:

> President Abraham Lincoln, an incredible communicator, was known during the Civil War to attend a church not far from the White House on Wednesday nights. The preacher, Dr. Gurley, allowed the president to sit in the pastor's study with the door open to the chancel so he could listen to the sermon without having to interact with the crowd. One Wednesday evening as Lincoln and a companion walked back to the White House after the sermon, the president's companion asked, "What did you think of tonight's sermon?"

"Well," Lincoln responded, "it was brilliantly conceived, biblical, relevant, and well presented."

"So, it was a great sermon?"

"No," Lincoln replied. "It failed. It failed because Dr. Gurley did not ask us to do something great."[10]

Great things can seem small, but people will not attempt them unless challenged, unless invited through beautiful preaching that attracts them to God.

The Point of Preaching

Attraction to God means approaching him, and approaching him means holiness. Ultimately, preaching is one of the means the Church's ordained ministers have in their arsenal to fulfill the Church's chief mission: the making of saints who will share in God's own blessed life. There we find the ultimate challenge of preaching: moving people to sainthood and salvation. The very first paragraph of the Catechism teaches:

> God, infinitely perfect and blessed in himself, in a plan of sheer goodness freely created man to make him share in his own blessed life. For this reason, at every time and in every place, God draws close to man. He calls man to seek him, to know him, to love him with all his strength. He calls together all men, scattered and divided by sin, into the unity of his family, the Church. To accomplish this, when the fullness of time

---

[10] John C. Maxwell, *Everyone Communicates, Few Connect: What the Most Effective People Do Differently* (Nashville, TN: Thomas Nelson, 2010), 205.

had come, God sent his Son as Redeemer and Savior. In his Son and through him, he invites men to become, in the Holy Spirit, his adopted children and thus heirs of his blessed life. (*CCC* §1)

There is a well-known and poignant saying that is often attributed to the French poet and essayist Charles Péguy: "Life holds only one tragedy, ultimately, not to have been a saint." Sainthood is the point of life, and thus the point of preaching.

Preaching the Fourfold Sense of Scripture

Now, sainthood involves hearing Scripture rightly, and that means spiritual exegesis, or interpreting the Bible for the fourfold sense. For, unlike historical-critical approaches to the Bible that treat the texts as ancient artifacts of long-dead communities, the fourfold sense of interpretation the Church's Tradition received and developed from the Apostles to the contemporary Catechism is designed to make saints. The letter (the "literal" sense) presents the truth of the story of salvation history, and then the three spiritual senses rooted in the letter also move people to sainthood. In the allegorical sense, believers see the same God working in the same ways in both Testaments and the Church for our salvation, Jesus and the Church fulfilling Old Testament types, and, convinced that the events of the New Testament are true, they are inspired to write their lives into that story. In tropology, the moral sense, believers learn what they are to do to be saved. In the anagogical sense, which concerns the soul's progress to heaven, believers are confronted with their beatific destiny and are inspired to achieve it. In sum, the fourfold sense of Scripture makes saints.

Because the fourfold sense sees Christ at the center of

Scripture, it's not an outdated medieval relic, but rather most fully realizes conciliar and postconciliar teaching on Scripture. The Second Vatican Council teaches us in *Dei Verbum* §21 that "all the preaching of the Church must be nourished and regulated by Sacred Scripture," and more recently, in *Verbum Domini* §59, Benedict reminded us, "Generic and abstract homilies which obscure the directness of God's word [that is, Scripture] should be avoided, as well as useless digressions which risk drawing greater attention to the preacher than to the heart of the Gospel message. The faithful should be able to perceive clearly that the preacher has a compelling desire to present Christ, who must stand at the centre of every homily."[11] Putting Christ at the center of every homily means employing spiritual exegesis, the fourfold sense.

At root, this means attention to the patterns of salvation history. The people of God should see how the Old Testament texts are fulfilled in the New Testament texts and made real in our liturgy and lives today. There is continuity between a Gospel passage, which will center on Jesus Christ, and all the Old Testament texts it quotes or alludes to; that's essentially the allegorical and, thus, the Christological reading of the literal sense. Then the homily may engage tropology, shaping people into Christlikeness, and anagogy, moving them on the way of sainthood towards heaven.

I have found that this sort of Christ-centered spiritual exegesis really preaches. The Christian mind and spirit delight in such things. We humans are narrative by nature, and so we appreciate stories. We Catholics appreciate the parallels

---

[11] Pope Francis, for his part, like the last several popes, is deeply concerned for good preaching, dedicating a major section of his Apostolic Exhortation on the Proclamation of the Gospel in Today's World, *Evangelii Gaudium* (November 24, 2013) to it (§§135–44). The section is worth slow, sustained reading and reflection.

allegorical typology offers, especially when we are about to encounter in the Mass the same God who superintends salvation history from the exodus to the Last Supper and crucifixion, to the Eucharist we ingest, and to the heaven it portends.

That human beings are narrative by nature and that the Gospels are stories standing at the center of the story of salvation history have implications for homiletics. Above all, preaching connects when it's done in a narrative way. Good preachers are storytellers. That does not mean simply finding clever anecdotes as illustrative filler—often people come away remembering more about the anecdotes than the biblical texts—but retelling the particular point of the story of salvation history the lectionary texts provide on a given day in a lively, compelling way.[12]

Spiritual exegesis preaches. For one, it helps makes sense of the Old Testament, much of which is simply bewildering to modern Christians. Why not show how Catholic liturgy is rooted in the Torah's legal code? We have male priests who wear vestments and offer the sacrifice of the Eucharist in churches that resemble temples because ancient Israel had male priests who wore vestments and offered sacrifice in temples. For another, typology and allegory help Christians see the unity of Scripture in the one God whose Spirit inspired it when it can appear at first glance disjointed and random. And again, anagogy reminds the faithful of their ultimate hope, their heavenly destiny.

[12] See: Jeffrey Arthurs, *Preaching with Variety: How to Re-create the Dynamics of Biblical Genres* (Grand Rapids, MI: Kregel Publications, 2007); Joshua Genig, *Viva Vox: Rediscovering the Sacramentality of the Word Through the Annunciation* (Minneapolis, MN: Fortress, 2015); Eugene L. Lowry, *The Homiletical Plot: The Sermon as Narrative Art Form* (Louisville, KY: Westminster John Knox, 2000); and especially John W. Wright, *Telling God's Story: Narrative Preaching for Christian Formation* (Downers Grove, IL: InterVarsity, 2007).

In sum, homilies driven by spiritual exegesis are relevant without pandering because they affect the present lives and future destiny of those who hear them as they encounter Christ the Incarnate Word existentially in the Word and Sacrament, the homily and the Eucharist.

Preaching the Fourfold Sense in a Way that Sticks

As the four senses support each other, a homilist ought to tie them together in a memorable way. And so let's now get practical. Preachers ought to boil everything down to one theme, one point, a memorable and moving summary of what God is saying through the Gospel for the day, no more than seven words, three of which really matter, and repeat it a few times throughout your homily.

Advertising often works this way. Remember "Little. Yellow. Different."? It was an advertisement for Nuprin, a painkiller popular years ago. In another vein, I also remember a talk—and maybe one of two talks, actually—from college. North Dakota's poet laureate, Larry Woiwode, gave a talk on humility and the Gospels and repeated "The way up is the way down" again and again as he reflected on Jesus's words about the last being first and the first last, the humble being exalted and the exalted humbled. It's sealed in my memory to this day. Or a homily from a visiting priest I heard at Sacred Heart parish in Lombard, Illinois: several times he repeated, "Nothing changes if nothing changes." I've never forgotten, and I've called on that phrase when I've needed to discipline myself in prayer, in diet, in exercise, in family duties, in work habits. One final example: "Serious. Affordable. Catholic." (Feel free to refer your young people to www.cometomary.com.)

I've forgotten a lot of homilies and a lot of talks, a lot

of commercials and a lot of slogans. Those I've mentioned, however, I remember; the Woiwode talk and the homily inspire me to this day. I was given a takeaway that will drive me to holiness, to salvation.

Now, the Gospels in particular, and especially the Gospel of Mark, do more showing than telling. They don't always make the point obvious. So you need to learn to preach stories, to discern the possible points, and deliver them well. If you're a great storyteller, you can leave the point implicit. Most of us should make it explicit.

In short: Instead of offering the gimmicks that accommodation and moralism breed, find the theme of the Gospel for the day, interpret it according to the fourfold sense, determine through thought and prayer what effects God would have your homily work in your people, craft a short phrase summarizing the rhetorical point, and deliver your homily well.

The Gospel According to St. Flannery—or, Crucify Your Congregation

So what does this have to do with Mark?

Scripture is liturgical; the Gospels are liturgical; Mark itself is liturgical. In the second century, St. Justin Martyr noted that Scripture was read in the Mass "as long as time permits,"[13] which might mean the entirety of a Gospel like Mark was read in one Mass, and indeed, Mark itself may be a narrative homily. (Neither Mark nor Justin's priest had to deal with a football kickoff time, however, and they weren't going to the arena for the games—except as prey.)

The Gospel of Mark and the sacred liturgy are both escha-

---

[13] Justin Martyr, *First Apology* 67, in *Ante-Nicene Fathers* [hereafter, *ANF*], 10 vols., ed. Alexander Roberts and James Donaldson, repr. (Peabody, MA: Hendrickson, 2004), 1:186.

tological; they reveal the God who encounters us in them. In the Mass, the eternal beauty that is God, ever ancient, ever new, breaks into our time. Liturgy mediates the encounter of heaven and earth, of God and man. And that's what Mark's Gospel does; it tells of God breaking into time, invading the cosmos in Jesus to save it. In the liturgy, people should perceive heaven breaking into time, just like in Mark's Gospel, God breaks into time. Both Mark and the liturgy are eschatological, and both need to be understood and performed as such.

In an age numb to the gospel, the shock treatment of beauty is required. Mark is a beautiful Gospel that shocks. It's the Gospel Flannery O'Connor would have written, and so I want to close with a quote from her:

> Push back against the age as hard as it pushes against you. What people don't realize is how much religion costs. They think faith is a big electric blanket, when of course it is the cross.[14]

That's Mark's message in a nutshell. Mark is the perfect Gospel for an age grown numb, a people of the Internet with senses dulled by accommodation, moralism, and gimmicks. Like the liturgy, Mark's Gospel is about God mounting an invasion of love to rescue a hostage cosmos. Like O'Connor's writing, it's a brilliant, beautiful, shocking piece of literature, full of twists, turns, and surprises. Above all, it's about the grace of the Cross.

---

[14] Flannery O'Connor, *The Habit of Being: The Letters of Flannery O'Connor*, ed. Sally Fitzgerald (New York: Farrar, Straus, Giroux, 1979), 229.

Chapter 2

Sticking to the Story—or, How (Not) to Read a Gospel

The Gospel of Mark is both brute and beautiful. But most have missed its beauty, finding little but literary brutality. Until recently, Mark has been the underdog Gospel, overshadowed by the other three. In the ancient world, St. Augustine claimed Mark was an abbreviation of Matthew, suggesting that Mark imitated Matthew "like his attendant and epitomizer," with Mark providing little material of his own.[1] The implication is that Mark didn't matter much. In the modern world, the late great German scholar (and, as it happens, my dead nemesis) Rudolf Bultmann famously regarded Mark as mere folk literature lacking serious literary merit: "Mark is not sufficiently master of his material to be able to venture on a systematic construction himself."[2] The implication is that Mark was incompetent. And, of course, those who have studied the Gospels know that most scholars today believe Mark was the first Gospel written because it's just so bad— flawed Greek, deficient content, no structure.

Except that's all wrong. Recent readings of the Gospel

---

[1] St. Augustine, *Harmony of the Gospels* [hereafter, *Cons.*] 1.2.4, in *A Select Library of Nicene and Post-Nicene Fathers of the Christian Church*, 1st ser., 14 vols., ed. Philip Schaff, repr. (Peabody, MA: Hendrickson, 1994), 6:78.

[2] Rudolf Bultmann, *History of the Synoptic Tradition*, trans. J. Marsh (Oxford, UK: Blackwell, 1963), 350.

of Mark have upended such opinions and, finally, after all these centuries, unearthed Mark's literary beauty. However Matthew's and Mark's Gospels might be related—and for interpreting them, it doesn't matter if one is dependent on the other, for each author wrote an internally coherent story without drawing attention to any sources—Mark presents a crazy, compelling, beautiful story, a true work of literary art proclaiming Jesus the Christ as the crucified and risen Son of God.

To see that story, to get the most out of Mark, we need to know how to read a Gospel, and that means we need to know what a Gospel is. For reading something rightly requires knowing what sort of genre of literature it belongs to. Hijinks ensue when people jack up genre. We're familiar with contemporary literary art, from the novel to the sitcom, from the short story to the romcom, from cable series to the network procedural. We seldom pay conscious attention to questions of genre because we don't have to—until we come to ancient literature, where our unfamiliarity with it means we can make mistakes.[3]

I want to suggest to you that the Gospel of Mark is three things: *Bios*, Index, and Icon—an ancient biography, an index of Jesus, and a sacramental narrative icon. Mark follows the genre conventions of *bios* (plural *bioi*, and in Latin, singular *vita* and plural *vitae*), ancient biography, presents Jesus in continuity with the real historical Jesus, and makes Jesus Christ, the eternal Son of God risen and ascended, sacramentally present to his readers. The Gospel of Mark presents the One who entered the time of history from eternity. We have, then, in Mark's Gospel the meeting of time and eternity. Mark is

---

[3] For instance, it's better to read Genesis 1–11 according to the genre expectations of ancient cosmogony than modern scientific history. Genre slippage leads to fundamentalism on one side and liberalism on the other.

historical and heavenly, and so both historical tools and theological sensitivity are required for its interpretation.

The Gospels as Ancient Biographies

The Gospels are *bioi*, ancient biographies, which most scholars now recognize. Many giants of German academic genius once thought the Gospels didn't have a genre, being folk literature, while evangelicals and others have thought they might be a new genre *sui generis*, the idea being that a unique Savior needs a unique genre. But go home tonight and try to invent a new genre; good luck![4] And as for Bultmann's believing Mark an incompetent editor, reading the Gospel of Mark as a story in the genre of *bios* reveals its narrative brilliance.

In accord with earlier ideas about the Gospels' genre (or lack thereof), most clergy have been trained to read the Gospels using source, form, and redaction criticism. Editorial changes to a Gospel's presumed sources reveal the author's intent in addressing some situation in his own community long ago. But these approaches ignore the narrative form of the Gospels, taking passages out of their contexts in a Gospel to compare them to sources and passages in other Gospels. Further, they read the Gospels as surreptitious stories about the authors' communities rather than what the Gospels present themselves as—stories about Jesus.

Ironically, then, searching for authorial intention in this way reads the Gospels against the grain of their author's intention. The Gospel writers wrote narratives about Jesus and intended them to be read without attention to whatever

---

[4] Story and poetry, content and form, are the rough material of oral literature. Technology makes new genres possible, from stone and chisel and papyrus and the stylus enabling early writing, to the printing press making possible the novel, to the video camera making possible cinema and TV.

sources they may have used.[5] Put bluntly, St. Matthew and St. Luke probably didn't hand out copies of their supposed sources of Mark and "Q" to their first readers, nor would Mark have insisted his readers couldn't have understood his Gospel without whatever sources he used, and the writers wanted to promote faith in Jesus Christ, not reveal surreptitious secrets about their own pressing issues.

Most clergy have been trained in these methods, which involves the piecemeal reading of isolated pericopes estranged from their narrative context. Laypeople, too, have been taught to read the Gospels (and indeed all the Scriptures) in piecemeal fashion. We have children memorize Bible verses, and (to be honest) most people don't really read the Bible. Rather, they hear selections in Mass provided by the lectionary. The result is that most of us approach the Gospels and the broader Bible as a collection of verses and stories with no narrative thread. We know parts with little, if any, sense of the whole.

What was a *bios*, a "life," an ancient biography, and how does the genre help us read the Gospel of Mark?

Richard Burridge, an Anglican clergyman and biblical scholar, found it impossible that the Gospels should have no

---

[5] Literary theory has complicated the concept of authorship, with many contemporary critics and theorists holding as an article of faith that authors are irrelevant for the interpretation of literary works. The concern is twofold: (1) that biography becomes a surreptitious substitute for the work itself; and, more radically, (2) that interpreting for authorial intention ultimately leads to violence because it constrains a reader's freedom. The solution is to begin with the interpretation of the text of the work itself and then see it as the product of the "model" or "ideal" author, which stands in a direct, indexical relationship to the historical, empirical author; see Leroy A. Huizenga, *The New Isaac: Tradition and Intertextuality in the Gospel of Matthew*, repr., Novum Testamentum, Supplements 131 (Leiden: E. J. Brill, 2012), 21–41. In the present book, when I employ "Mark" as author, I mean the model or ideal author as could be inferred from a responsible reading of the text, but that author then reflects the real, empirical author, St. Mark.

genre or be a new genre, as did many scholars after the heyday of form criticism, and he proved to the satisfaction of most that the Gospels belonged to the category of Greco-Roman *bioi*.[6] For his work on the Gospels, he won the Ratzinger Prize. He writes:

> Any attempt to ask literary questions about the gospels, and in particular, their genre, is automatically precluded in advance. . . . The form critics' distinction merely has the effect of removing the gospels from any discussion of their context within the first century on the grounds that they do not share some predetermined literary aspirations. . . . Much more detailed and accurate study of the various genres, types and levels of first-century, and especially Graeco-Roman, literature is needed.[7]

He then provided the study he called for, comparing the Gospels to representative examples of Greco-Roman *bioi*, ancient biographies, and found the Gospels fit that genre rather well.

Ancient Greco-Roman biography focuses intensely on its subject to reveal his character and identity by words and deeds and is arranged chronologically as a continuous narrative. Burridge writes:

> The synoptic gospels are in prose narrative. . . . Furthermore, narrative is the best description of the prose: it is not drama, though there are some dramatic elements, nor dialogue, like Satyrus' *Euripides*,

---

[6] Richard A. Burridge, *What Are the Gospels? A Comparison with Graeco-Roman Biography*, 2nd ed. (Grand Rapids, MI: Eerdmans, 2004).

[7] Burridge, *What Are the Gospels?*, 11.

although dialogue is contained within the gospels. They are not speeches, like the *Evagoras*, or sermons, although they may exhibit some rhetorical, oral or proclamatory features. Finally, the narrative is mainly continuous; some of the links between sections may be vague or tenuous, but overall the narrative seems intended as a continuous whole. While the gospels may not be as continuous as *Lives* of statesmen or generals, like Agricola, they are more continuous than those of philosophers, like the *Demonax* with its string of unconnected episodes. Thus *the mode of representation of the synoptic gospels is prose narrative of a fairly continuous nature, like historiography or βίοι.*[8]

For most clergy and laypeople, then, reading and preaching the Gospels requires a paradigm shift. The Gospels are *bioi*, and they have the narrative character of story. How do we read the Gospels as stories?

Fortunately, it's not difficult to read the Gospels as stories. Again, human beings are narrative by nature. Narrative is the fundamental category for human epistemology and, therefore, human existence.[9] That's why all cultures in all times and places tell stories, from grand stories telling them who they fundamentally are to folk and fairy tales incul-

---

[8] Ibid., 193. Emphasis original.

[9] See Stanley Hauerwas and L. Gregory Jones, "Introduction: Why Narrative?" in *Why Narrative? Readings in Narrative Theology*, ed. Stanley Hauerwas and L. Gregory Jones (Eugene, OR: Wipf & Stock, 1997), 1–18. See also Walter R. Fisher, *Human Communication as Narration: Toward a Philosophy of Reason, Value, and Action* (Columbia: University of South Carolina Press, 1987), and Fisher, "Narration, Knowledge, and the Possibility of Wisdom," in *Rethinking Knowledge: Reflections Across the Disciplines*, ed. Walter R. Fisher and Robert F. Goodman, SUNY Series in the Philosophy of the Social Sciences (New York: State University of New York Press, 1995).

cating morals and wisdom in children. We're also, therefore, narrative by nurture: from fables to film, we've all engaged in stories and have learned to interpret them without a lot of reflection, and most people have learned the basics in literature classes in school.

Interpreting the Gospels as stories can be complex, of course, like any endeavor. We could discuss narratology and semiotics and reader-response theory and deconstruction. Or we can get on with it, using what we know of stories by nature and the basic formation we have had in reading literature. And God willing, we will do so.[10]

Reading the Gospels as stories involves attention to the basic story stuff: plot, characterization, setting, conflict, resolution. Readers or hearers of stories track these components and respond to the dynamics of the story.[11] Stories, like good homilies, are thus *rhetorical*: they don't simply teach morals or truths, but *move people*. The preacher's job, then, is to evoke the pathos the story would have people experience as they're carried along by the plot. Preaching, then, is retelling a Gospel's stories in the context of its fundamental story so

---

[10] For literary and narrative approaches to the Gospel of Mark, see: Ernest Best, *Mark: The Gospel as Story* (Edinburgh, UK: T&T Clark International, 1988); Robert M. Fowler, *Let the Reader Understand: Reader-Response Criticism and the Gospel of Mark* (Harrisburg, PA: Trinity Press International, 2001); Jack Dean Kingsbury, *The Christology of Mark's Gospel* (Philadelphia, PA: Fortress, 1983); Elizabeth Struthers Malbon, "How Does the Story Mean?" in *Mark and Method: New Approaches in Biblical Studies*, ed. Janice Capel Anderson and Stephen E. Moore (Minneapolis, MN: Fortress, 2008), 29–58; Francis J. Moloney, "The Markan Story," *Word & World* 26 (2006): 5–13; and Mark Allan Powell, *What Is Narrative Criticism?* Guides to Biblical Scholarship New Testament (Minneapolis, MN: Fortress, 1991).

[11] In the ancient world, literacy rates were low, perhaps 5–10%. And so, most Jews and Christians encountered their Scriptures aurally as they were read orally, while those who were literate would read texts—even private letters—out loud. In the present book, I'll generally speak of "readers" for simplicity's sake.

that people notice more clearly what's going on in the story's dynamics and have the "Aha!" moments that will grip them.

Think of any good piece of writing, or TV show, or film you've seen, and think through its progression. First, beginnings matter much. The beginning of a story will set up the characters and conflicts, raising questions for readers, hearers, and viewers about the possibilities for how the story will progress. What's the issue? What will the hero do? How will she handle her enemies? Will she succeed? Next, the bulk of a story reveals the plot, the unfolding of what the beginning sets up. Here a good, effective story pulls its readers, hearers, and viewers along for an interesting ride, full of twists and turns, keeping their attention. Finally, there is a resolution of the conflict that gives readers, hearers, and viewers a deep sense of catharsis—joy, despair, sadness, hope, or whatever experience the rhetoric of the story was aiming at. A good story, like good preaching, invites investment. It moves people. Mark does that.

So Mark's Gospel is a story, as are all the canonical Gospels. It's meant to be read and heard from start to finish. It's not a collection of random pearls on a string. The lectionary generally respects the order of a Gospel, but not always. Sometimes passages appear in the lectionary out of sequence, and for good reason. For example, Mark 13:33–37, the Parable of the Doorkeeper, is the Gospel for the first Sunday of Advent. Jesus tells three of his disciples to be like the vigilant doorkeeper and keep watch all the time because they don't know when he will come back and end the world. And so it's entirely appropriate to begin the liturgical year and the liturgical season of Advent with that passage. Advent isn't just about getting ready for the coming of little baby Jesus, but rather also about getting ready for the kingdom of God, and thus the end of the world. That's why early Advent presents so many readings about John the Baptist.

But beginning with Mark 13 breaks the order of Mark's Gospel. Similarly, the lectionary will sometimes omit certain verses from a passage, as on the twenty-second Sunday of Ordinary Time, which presents Mark 7:1–8, 14–15, and 21–23. Or, sometimes the lectionary will put hard sayings in brackets as options, or omit them altogether, as is the case with Mark 4:10–12. Of course, the Catholic deacon or priest must read what the lectionary provides, but I would suggest that preachers provide further context in the homily for passages from which the lectionary provides selections. It will help congregants if the preacher sets the passage in context in his homily by mentioning what has come before in Mark's Gospel and, if warranted, discusses portions of passages the lectionary has omitted. In this way, the preacher employs *lectio continua*—continuous reading—and engages his congregation in the particular dynamics of a Gospel's story.

The Gospels as Indices

As *bioi*, the Gospels bear a direct relationship to Jesus: the evangelists are presenting the real Jesus who walked around the Holy Land around AD 30. But the genre of *bioi* allows authors a lot of freedom in shaping their accounts. Material is arranged topically within the rough chronological structure, and without concern for modern "scientific history" as the nineteenth century would have it. That's why attempts at harmonizing the Gospels devolve into absurdity, with (for instance) Peter denying Jesus up to eight times to account for all the differences in the Gospels' accounts.[12]

---

[12] In his *Harmoniae Evangelicae* (Basel, 1537), Andreas Osiander posited that Peter denied Jesus eight times to account for supposed discrepancies in the Gospel accounts; see David Laird Dungan, *A History of the Synoptic Problem: The Canon, the Text, the Composition, and the Interpretation of the*

But Christian faith affirms that Jesus was one real human being, not a myth, subject to the realities of space and time. And so we need to have some adequate philosophical conception for how Jesus of Nazareth (who's also the Christ and Son of God) relates to the written Gospels. The way it stands now, many scholars engaged in the quest for the "historical Jesus" sort and sift the materials from the canonical and heretical Gospels, discard most of it by assigning it to the creative energies of some early genius, school, or sect, and then use a little of it to recreate a picture of their historical Jesus. But that's insufficient for Christian faith, which affirms that the Gospels aren't simply stories for our edification unmoored from Jesus of Nazareth, as the Catechism, quoting the Second Vatican Council's *Dei Verbum*, affirms:

> The Church holds firmly that the four Gospels, "whose historicity she unhesitatingly affirms, faithfully hand on what Jesus, the Son of God, while he lived among men, really did and taught for their eternal salvation, until the day when he was taken up." ... "The sacred authors, in writing the four Gospels, selected certain of the many elements which had been handed on, either orally or already in written form; others they synthesized or explained with an eye to the situation of the churches, the while sustaining the form of preaching, but always in such a fashion that they have told us the honest truth about Jesus." (*CCC* §126, quoting *Dei Verbum* §19)

Gospels, The Anchor Yale Bible Reference Library (New York: Random House, 1999), 305–6. More recently than Osiander, the evangelical Harold Lindsell, representative of modern fundamentalism, required only six discrete Petrine denials of Jesus to harmonize them in *The Battle for the Bible* (Grand Rapids, MI: Zondervan, 1976), 174–76.

How, then, might we conceive of the "historicity" of the Gospels and the "honest truth" which they tell?

I would offer the possibility of the "Index," one of the three major classes of signs that those who study semiotics (the science of signs) have offered.[13] For Christianity is semiotic; it's shot through with signs signifying invisible realities beyond them. Creation is a sign. Jesus is a sign. Sacraments are signs. Words are signs. And so the Gospels are signs.

Now, fundamentalists will conceive of the Gospels as what semioticians call an "Icon," another class of signs. In iconic mode, signs represent what they signify *directly*. The classic example is the photograph. But the problem here is twofold. First, given their differences, the Gospels can almost look like photographs of different people. They can't simply be direct presentations of exactly what Jesus did and said, for they cannot be harmonized on that level. Second, modern semiotics usually surrenders any metaphysics, so there's no participation of the sign in the signified in iconic mode. I am not in the photo on my driver's license, but the divine is present in Christian icons.[14]

Another possibility is the option taken by theologi-

---

[13] American polymath Charles Sanders Peirce developed this semiotic typology. See Peirce, "Logic as Semiotic: A Theory of Signs," in *Philosophical Writings of Peirce*, ed. Justus Buchler (New York: Dover Publications, 2011), 98–119. See also Peirce, "On a New List of Categories," *Proceedings of the American Academy of Arts and Sciences* 7 (1868): 287–98, which is a publication of an oral presentation on May 14, 1867, available in *The Essential Peirce: Selected Philosophical Writings Volume 1 (1867–1893)*, ed. Nathan Houser and Christian Klousel (Bloomington, IN: Indiana University Press, 1992), 1–10, and on the "symbol" in particular, see Peirce, "Upon Logical Comprehension and Extension," *Proceedings of the American Academy of Arts and Sciences* 7 (1868): 416–32, which is a publication of his oral presentation on 13 November 1867, available at http://www.iupui.edu/~peirce/writings/v2/w2/w2_06/v2_06.htm.

[14] Below I will suggest that the Gospels are like the traditional icons of Christian worship in that they make Jesus really present.

cal liberalism, the "Symbol." Symbols stand in an *arbitrary* relationship to that which they signify. Now, in theological liberalism, experience reigns supreme and even determines one's picture of Jesus, whether this means the experiences of contemporary individuals or groups or the supposed experiences of Jesus's disciples. And so, on this model, the Gospels symbolize not so much Jesus of Nazareth as they do what his disciples and the early Church made of him after their experiences of the Resurrection—whatever that impression was.[15] Thus, in practice, most liberal presentations of Jesus become projections of contemporary desires, with Jesus looking like a postmodern progressive.[16]

For Catholicism, continuity is the watchword. Catholics see the continuity between the Old and New Testaments, between Israel and the Church through the Jew Jesus, and between Jesus and the Gospels. Salvation history is a story of continuity with all foreshadowed in the Old Testament, fulfilled in Jesus, and made present in the Church. Think of how the crucifixion fulfills Old Testament sacrifices and how the Eucharist bears the crucifixion forth in our present. Continuity is why we have male priests wearing vestments offering the sacrifice of the Mass in churches that emulate the Temple.

As regards the Gospels and Jesus, then, we Catholics see them in continuity. Liberalism sees no real connection between Jesus of Nazareth and the Gospels, while fundamentalism sees them as crude direct presentations. Continuity is the true, salutary middle way. And so the category of the "Index" can help,

---

[15] The work of Rudolph Bultmann and Paul Tillich is representative of this position. For a more recent and accessible representation of this position, see Luke Timothy Johnson, *The Real Jesus: The Misguided Quest for the Historical Jesus and the Truth of the Traditional Gospels*, repr. (New York: HarperOne, 1997).

[16] See John Shelby Spong, *Biblical Literalism: A Gentile Heresy* (New York: HarperOne, 2016).

for it emphasizes continuity, as the index concerns cause and effect relationships. Modern semioticians will often use the example of smoke as an index of fire, while the ancients, especially the Stoics, were enamored of the symptom as an index of disease. I would suggest that the Gospels are indices: they are effects that stand in continuity with their cause, Jesus.

Further, a cause generates multifold effects in dynamic ways. Think of all the complex ways smoke rises and wafts from fire, or how the various symptoms of a single disease evolve and change. That means that everything in the Gospels, whether the short parables in the Synoptic Gospels or the long mystical discourses in John, can go back to the one Jesus in history while also allowing the evangelists great freedom under the aegis of the Holy Spirit to shape their Gospels in accord with their purposes. The index helps explain how the Gospels can be so different from one another on the one hand, and yet all go back to the one real Jesus Christ of history and faith on the other.

The Gospels, then, are *bioi* and indices with regard to history. They present Jesus of Nazareth faithfully in continuity with what he really said and did. But they also present Jesus as the Incarnation of the eternal Son of God, and thus, one more category is necessary to understand them fully: the classical liturgical (not semiotic) category of the icon.

The Gospels as Verbal Icons

Are the Gospels icons? Icons are images, but the Gospels are words.

But is it so simple? Jesus himself is the Word of God (John 1:1, 14) and the image, or icon (*eikōn*, Col 1:15), of the invisible God, who, St. John teaches, was, as Son of God, the agent of creation (John 1:3). God's creative word spoken in Genesis is identified as a person of flesh, the Son of God, in the Gospel of John. Read in light of John 1, the word through which God spoke creation into existence in Genesis 1:3—"Let there be light!"—is the Word of God, with God and God himself "in the beginning" (John 1:1–2), through whom "all things were made," and this same Word "became flesh and dwelt among us" (1:14), the Son of God revealing God's glory (1:14b) and God the only Son making God known (1:18).

St. John teaches, then, that God spoke a Person, the divine Son of God, who was made flesh in Jesus Christ. God's word isn't merely verbal, but personal. Jesus is the incarnate Word. And that becomes part and parcel of early Christian belief, such that St. Paul can write that Jesus Christ is the image (*eikōn*) of the invisible God (Col 1:15). In Jesus, word and image are one.

Icons and Scripture, then, both mediate the one divine Son of God. Indeed, it was the Incarnation of the Son of God in Jesus Christ taught in verbal Scripture that proved the decisive warrant legitimizing visual icons at the Second Council of Nicaea in AD 787, thus formally ending the iconoclastic controversy. St. John of Damascus rooted the legitimacy of icons in the Incarnation: "I do not worship matter, I worship the God of matter, who became matter for my sake, and deigned to inhabit matter, who worked out my salvation through matter."[17]

As icons and Scripture both flow from and point to Jesus Christ, similarities abound.[18] Icons, like Scripture, are

---

[17] St. John of Damascus, *On Holy Images*, trans. Mary H. Allies (London: Thomas Baker, 1898), 15–16. Telford Work observes, "The Second Council of Nicea found images and relics to be analogous in essence to the books of the Gospels. Iconic practice thus followed liturgical practices regarding the nature and use of Scripture" (*Living and Active: Scripture in the Economy of Salvation*, Sacra Doctrina: Christian Theology for a Postmodern Age [Grand Rapids, MI: Eerdmans, 2002], 3).

[18] Orthodox theologians observe the similarities. Consider Leonid Oupensky in "The Meaning and Content of the Icon," in *Eastern Orthodox Theology: A Contemporary Reader*, ed. Daniel B. Clendenin, 2nd ed. (Grand Rapids,

"written"—not "painted"—precisely because of their roots in the Incarnation. Icons, like Scripture, are thus written representations of the incarnate Word.[19] Many icons themselves illustrate this relationship, portraying Jesus and the saints holding Scriptures.[20]

Further, iconography is stylized according to the dictates of divine realities, the ultimate truth of an event an icon relates, and thus iconography involves not realism or perspective, but the revelation of heavenly realities.[21] So too, I would argue, do the Scriptures. Many of the stories St. Mark tells (to say nothing of the other evangelists) are not realistic, as if they were raw eyewitness accounts or now-dead scientific history, but rather iconographic, heavily stylized to reflect divine realities.[22]

MI: Baker Academic, 2003), 33–63: "The church has 'eyes to see' just as it has 'ears to hear'" (35); "Word and image point to one another" (45); "The icon is distinguishable from all other things, just as the Holy Scripture is distinguishable from all other literary works" (47); "If the word and the song of the church sanctify our soul by means of hearing, the image sanctifies by means of sight" (62); "By words and by image, the liturgy sanctifies our senses" (63). See also Markus Bockmuehl, *Seeing the Word: Refocusing New Testament Study*, Studies in Theological Interpretation (Grand Rapids, MI: Baker Academic, 2006), and Telford Work, *Living and Active: Scripture in the Economy of Salvation* (Grand Rapids, MI: Eerdmans, 2002).

[19] As the *kontakion* for the Feast of the Triumph of Orthodoxy states, "We confess and proclaim our salvation in word and images" (quoted in Oupensky, "Meaning," 34). Similarly, in his theology of images, St. John of Damascus orders words as a species of images.

[20] Work writes, "In these icons the figures bear Scripture to the viewer, pointing to the very texts whose messages point back to them" (*Living and Active*, 19).

[21] Here we see the crucial difference between an icon in the liturgical sense and the photograph as an example of the iconic mode in contemporary semiotics. The former is stylized, participatory, eternal, and revelatory, while the latter is a mechanistic representation of a moment of time.

[22] Consider Mark's treatment of the calling of the first disciples in Mark 1:16–20, discussed below on pp. 96–97.

Moreover, icons are beautiful. It's not just that they are aesthetically pleasing, but rather, being divine, they ultimately mediate God himself, who is beauty itself. The beauty of God is reflected in Jesus Christ, the incarnate Son of God and, thus, in the Gospel of Mark, which is an icon of Christ and so must be beautiful. Modern scholars who deny Jesus's divinity also deny the beauty of Mark's Gospel; perhaps seeing the Gospel of Mark as a verbal icon will enable us to see its beauty.

Finally, like Scripture, icons are prayed, meditated upon, and contemplated. Unlike mere works of visual art such as photographs and painting, icons are written in an attitude of prayer as an act of prayer, and they are, in turn, received as such, the faithful praying them in meditation and contemplation.

I've presented these parallels to suggest that Scripture is in fact Scripture, and not simply a disparate collection of textual artifacts bearing historical witness to long-dead Israelite, Jewish, and Christian communities. One might say that the historical-critical method, which many clergy and academics learn along the way as a matter of course, is a form of the heresy of iconoclasm. Scripture is coherent not only in presenting the story of salvation history or revealing the truths of Catholic doctrine, but chiefly in bearing witness to Jesus Christ, its center. The words of Scripture, then, and primarily the Gospels, which concern Jesus most directly, actually mediate the divine Son of God to us.

Seeing the Gospels as ancient indexical biographies and verbal icons solves problems. Supposed contradictions are no longer an issue, nor are complaints about Mark's supposedly incoherent structure, since neither ancient biographers nor iconographers concerned themselves with nineteenth-century conceptions of facticity and chronology belonging to "scientific history," itself the legacy of Newtonian science.

Rather, St. Mark uses the canons of *bioi* to write a verbal icon of the Son of God. Antedating Newton and von Ranke, St. Mark is not concerned for temporal chronology, but rather is writing the iconic story of the eternal Son of God who comes to us from outside time. And so, far from lacking mastery of his material, St. Mark shows himself a deft revelator of God in Christ in his written Gospel. Understanding the Gospel of Mark as an iconic biography allows us to read—nay, pray—the Gospel of Mark in ways revealing its brilliance and secrets and to encounter Jesus Christ thereby.

Indeed, icons shock like Mark's Gospel shocks, being signs of contradiction shattering the world's expectations. Leonid Oupensky writes:

> The strange and unusual character of the icon is similar to that of the gospel. For the gospel is a true challenge to every order, to all the wisdom of the world. . . . The gospel calls us to life in Christ; the icon represents this life. This is why it sometimes uses irregular and shocking forms, just as holiness sometimes tolerates extreme forms which seem like madness in the eyes of the world, such as the madness of those who are fools in Christ. . . . Madness for the sake of Christ and the sometimes provocative forms of icons express the same evangelical reality. Such an evangelical perspective inverts that of the world. The universe shown to us by the icon is ruled not by rational categories or by human standards, but by divine grace. . . . It reflects the ascetic effort and the joy of victory. It is sorrow transformed into the joy of the living God. It is the new order in the new creation.[23]

---

[23] Oupensky, "Meaning," 61–62.

Oupensky might as well have been writing about the Gospel of Mark. Now buckle up for a crash course in Mark's story and theology.

CHAPTER 3

A Crash Course in Mark's Gospel

The Gospel of Mark is a story, a narrative whose rhetoric is meant to grab its readers and hearers by constant surprise and, ultimately, bring them to the depths of despair and the heights of resurrection hope. Mark's Gospel delights serious readers and deserves its place among the world's great literature, having become a favorite of contemporary literary critics.[1] Why? Because Mark's literary artistry dazzles. While the Gospel is sometimes rough around the edges, Mark's literary and rhetorical devices surprise and delight his readers.

Yet Mark's story does have a message. Stories can have themes and make points. Sometimes the point is obvious or the storyteller will make the moral obvious. For instance, some, but not all, of Jesus's parables end with Jesus making his points explicit. But a story is prior to any points made. Stories are told to make whatever points much more dramatically than a letter or speech could make them, and points and themes can be determined accurately only once one exhausts the story.

Mark's story transcends itself and points readers to divine realities. Fundamentally, Mark's story is about apocalyptic holy war: In Jesus Christ, God himself invades a hostile cosmos

---

[1] See, for instance, Frank Kermode, *The Genesis of Secrecy: On the Interpretation of Narrative*, repr. (Cambridge, MA: Harvard University Press, 2006).

to liberate it from its satanic oppression. Mark matches the intensity of the theme with supreme intensity in how he tells the story. If we don't engage the contours of the whole story, but rather simply read piecemeal looking for simple points, we'll miss Mark's message.

Mark's Literary Dynamics

How is Mark's story written, then, and what themes does the Gospel of Mark deliver?

Intensity

First, the Gospel of Mark is *intense*. It's short—fifteen and a half chapters by our modern reckoning—and its very brevity generates the experience of intensity.[2] It's subtle and suggestive. Mark shows; he doesn't tell. Instead of spelling things out, Mark's use of editorial commentary is sparse and sparing, with the effect of inviting readers into the world of the story.

Mark's intensity means Mark is a Gospel of action. Although Mark portrays Jesus as a teacher much more than the other evangelists,[3] his Gospel presents much less content of Jesus's actual teaching. It doesn't present Jesus delivering long speeches like the Sermon on the Mount in Matthew or the great "I am" discourses in John. That would slow down the action. Mark presents Jesus giving extended teaching only in

---

[2]   Our modern system of chapters and verses was first employed in the English-language Geneva Bible in 1560. Our chapters and verses are thus an early modern editorial decision and often get in the way of profitable reading. Their existence suggests the Bible is a collection of discrete verses and encourages piecemeal reading. Nevertheless, they're not perfectly random and can be a rough gauge of how much an author spends on a topic or theme.

[3]   See Mark 1:21–22, 27; 2:13; 4:1–2, 38; 5:35; 6:2, 6, 34; 8:31; 9:17, 31, 38; 10:1; 11:17; 12:35, 38; 14:49.

two relatively brief chapters, a chapter of parables in Mark 4 and his predictions of the destruction of the Temple and the later end of the world in Mark 13, and in those chapters, it is secret teaching given only to insiders—Jesus's closest disciples and Mark's readers.

When Jesus teaches publicly, it's associated with his unique authority and expressed in exorcism. Jesus teaches in the synagogue, and the result is that "they were astonished at his teaching, for he taught them as one who had authority, and not as the scribes" (1:22). He then performs an exorcism, and the reaction is amazement: "And they were all amazed, so that they questioned among themselves, saying, 'What is this? A new teaching! With authority he commands even the unclean spirits, and they obey him'" (1:27). Mark's Jesus is about deeds, not words.

Further, things happen quickly: Mark employs the Greek term *euthus*—"immediately"—forty-one times.[4] "And immediately they left their nets and followed him" (1:18); "And immediately the leprosy left him, and he was made clean" (1:42); "And immediately the hemorrhage ceased; and she felt in her body that she was healed of her disease" (5:29). Mark's intensity (1) draws the reader into the story and (2) forces the reader to focus on the protagonist, Jesus.

Allusion

Second, in keeping with its subtlety, Mark's Gospel is *allusive*. Mark makes *intertextual* allusions to the Old Testament

---

[4] Some dynamic translations, for the supposed sake of variety, will translate this one Greek word with several phrases, like "at once," "just then," "right away," "without delay," and so forth. So too with Mark's phrase *en tē hodō*, "on the way," which gets rendered "on the road," "along the path," "along the road," etc. Such translations obscure the repetition and, thus, perception of key Markan phrases laden with significance.

much more than he quotes it. Readers must discern what Old Testament passages are in play, and many supposedly obscure passages in Mark's Gospel come into clearer focus when readers see parallels with them. Intertextual allusions tie Markan passages tightly to Old Testament antecedents and generate typological relationships. Moreover, Mark's Gospel alludes not to the Hebrew Old Testament (what becomes the medieval Masoretic Text) but rather to the Greek Old Testament—that is, the Septuagint, or "LXX."[5] That's important because there are often significant differences in many passages between the Hebrew Masoretic Text and the Greek Septuagint.[6]

Mark also makes many *intratextual* allusions to other passages in his Gospel through catchwords and catchphrases much more than the other evangelists, inviting readers to consider those passages and the personages in them in parallel, thus emphasizing themes by repetition. This, perhaps, is the most distinctive literary feature of Mark's Gospel, making for flashbacks and foreshadowing and setting readers up for the experience of surprise and irony.

Intercalation

Third, Mark makes use of *intercalation*. He often weaves two stories into each other, either as a sandwich in an A-B-A' pattern (e.g., Jairus's daughter and the hemorrhaging woman, Mark 5:21–43) or as a proper intercalation in an A-B-A'-B' pattern (e.g., Jesus's confession and Peter's denial, 14:53–72). And sometimes Mark will simply juxtapose two stories side

---

[5] Scholars speak of the Septuagint, or LXX, for the sake of convenience. In antiquity, several Greek versions of the Jewish Scriptures/Old Testament were in circulation. For our purposes, discerning which precise version Mark might have used is not important.

[6] See pp. 253–56 below on Mark 12:1–12, the Parable of the Wicked Tenants.

by side in an A-B fashion (e.g., Jesus's third Passion prediction with John and James's request for glory, 10:32–45). Whether simple juxtaposition, sandwiching, or formal intercalation, the effects are high drama, surprise, and irony.

Some scholars will assert that the point of a Markan A-B-A' sandwich is in the middle, the B section, much like the older understanding of chiasms. But this will not do: why would Mark include the outsides of a sandwich, the A sections, if they didn't matter? Every word of both stories in a sandwich matters. Sandwiches, like the more complex intercalations, are dramatic, building to a climax in the A' section, which focusing on the middle B section misses.

Indeed, if the Gospels may be compared to icons, as above, then Mark's juxtapositions, sandwiches, and intercalations may be compared to diptychs, triptychs, and tetraptychs of historic sacred art: not only surprising, jarring, or delighting the reader, but ultimately moving him or her to worship in an encounter with Jesus mediated by the verbal icon of the Gospel's text.

Irony

Fourth, Mark's Gospel employs the rhetorical device of *irony* throughout. Mark's intratextuality (the connections between passages within the Gospel) and intercalations often create the experience of irony, as the contrasts he generates in tying passages together jar the reader. James and John seek glory at Jesus's right and left hand right after Jesus makes a Passion prediction. The disciples, who should be insiders, all fail, while outsiders make themselves disciples. Jesus confesses his identity at the precise moment Peter denies him. The young man who proved apostate and fled naked in Gethsemane gets to announce the Resurrection at the empty tomb. Throughout the Gospel, those whom Jesus adjures to silence speak, but when the women at the empty tomb are commanded to speak, they remain silent.

Perception and Allegory

Finally, Mark is *metaphorical*, even *allegorical*. Some scholars are willing to concede that John's Gospel is allegorical but would refuse Mark that descriptor. But the strict delineation between figures such as metaphor, simile, analogy, and allegory hasn't always been so fine.[7] Concretely, Mark employs verbs of literal perception—seeing and hearing—metaphorically or allegorically to refer to spiritual perception (or most often lack thereof). In the third boat scene, Jesus asks the uncomprehending disciples, "Do you not yet perceive or understand? Are your hearts hardened? Having eyes do you not see, and having ears do you not hear?" (8:17–18a). The two levels of letter and spirit are operative in Mark's Gospel, if in a subtle way.

Further, Mark will employ in the story certain words and phrases in a literal way that also function as metaphors in an allegorical way to speak of spiritual realities, particularly the discipline of discipleship. Here the most significant are "follow" (*akoloutheō* or the pattern of verb + *opisō* + pronoun)[8] and "the way" (*hodos*) or more fully "on the way" (*en tē hodō*).[9] In the story, characters are to literally follow Jesus on the way

---

[7] St. Augustine, representative of the broader tradition, speaks in a twofold way of the letter and spirit of Scripture, and anything figurative, from simple metaphor to allegory, belongs, for him, to the realm of spiritual interpretation; see *Christian Instruction* (hereafter *Doctr. chr.*) 2.14–21, 23–26 and 3.9–24. For St. Thomas Aquinas, *allegoria* concerns what we might call typology, the phenomenon of Old Testament–New Testament parallels of persons (see *ST* I, q. 1, a. 10, resp.).

[8] See Mark 1:17–18, 20; 2:14–15; 3:7; 5:24; 6:1; 8:33–34; 9:38; 10:21, 28, 32, 52; 11:9; 14:13, 54; 15:41.

[9] See Mark 1:2–3; 2:23; 4:15; 6:8; 8:3, 27; 9:33–34; 10:17, 32; 10:46, 52; 11:8; 12:14.

of discipleship, like the no-longer-blind Bartimaeus in Mark 10:52, who then become metaphorical, allegorical exemplars of discipleship.

Finally, reading Mark's Gospel allegorically does not mean imposing a foreign grid on the story or (in preaching or in the present book) delineating each of the four senses for every passage. That could become pedantic and tedious. Rather, allegorical reading of Mark is natural and organic. It is natural because spiritual exegesis according to the fourfold sense simply emerged as a codification of the way believers naturally read their Scriptures for faith and life. It is organic because the four senses function together seamlessly. The letter links the Testaments, informs faith and morals, and moves souls towards heaven, all with Jesus Christ as the conceptual and spiritual center.[10]

The Role of the Reader

Finally, while it's true that the reader is simply necessary for literature and its analysis—no piece of literature, from a grocery list to a Shakespearean sonnet, reads itself—Mark's Gospel draws especial attention to the role of its readers in a conspicuous way.

First, literary theory and criticism has rightly paid attention to the role of readers in recent decades, as texts are written to be read and as readers read them. Some reader-response theory glories in a free-for-all where anything goes and no interpretation could be wrong or right. But more responsible reader-oriented theories pay attention to the structure and dynamics of a text itself, asking what a model or ideal reader might and must make of it for a correct interpretation. Such approaches avoid the difficulties of author-centered interpre-

---

[10] See the discussion of preaching allegory above on pp. 17–21.

47

tation while respecting the goal of discerning an objective meaning of a text. That's the approach employed in this book: instead of seeking the meaning of Mark's Gospel in its author's supposed edits of reconstructed sources, we read the text as the whole in the very form the author, St. Mark, actually composed it and ask what the model or ideal reader should make of it.[11]

Second, Mark's Gospel calls out to its readers implicitly and explicitly. In Mark 13, the audience for Jesus's teaching about the destruction of the Temple and the end of world comprises only the first four disciples called: Peter, James, John, and Andrew (13:3). At the end of the chapter, however, the conclusion of the Parable of the Doorkeeper emphasizes the need to keep watchful vigil in light of everyone's ignorance of the time of the End; Mark's Jesus says, "And what I say to you I say to all: Watch" (13:37). Jesus's words here admonishing "all" to "watch" imply a universal audience: not only the four but now everyone who reads Jesus's words is invited— commanded—to maintain perpetual vigilance.

Toward the beginning of Jesus's discourse in the chapter, Mark as narrator (or even Jesus himself, envisioning his words being written down?) states, as an aside, "let the reader understand," in the context of the mention of the "desolating sacrilege" (13:14). Like the four disciples hearing Jesus's words in the story, the reader is to understand that Jesus is discussing the destruction of the Temple, not the end of the world. More broadly, the aside indicates that the Gospel of Mark invites its readers' deepest involvement in the story.

---

[11] See Umberto Eco, *The Role of the Reader: Explorations in the Semiotics of Texts,* Advances in Semiotics (Bloomington, IN: Indiana University Press, 1979), and Leroy A. Huizenga, *The New Isaac: Tradition and Intertextuality in the Gospel of Matthew,* repr., Novum Testamentum, Supplements 131 (Leiden: E. J. Brill, 2012), 21–41.

Where does that leave the reader? Mark's Gospel is not neutral, and Mark does not write to satisfy curiosity, for entertainment, or simply for posterity. Mark's Gospel, like all the Gospels, makes claims and therefore refuses attempts at dispassionate analysis. That's why historical criticism, supposedly neutral and objective, often fails to interpret the Gospels rightly; a neutral posture assumes a stance against the grain of the text, against the receptivity of faith. Rather, Mark's Gospel calls readers to do just what Jesus calls characters in the story to do: repent and believe the gospel in light of the advent of the kingdom (1:14–15) and then follow Jesus (1:16–20) on the way of discipleship (8:22–10:56), the way of the Cross. Mark's Gospel positions its readers as implied disciples, as insiders privy to the mystery of the kingdom of God (4:10–12), faithful to the Cross, faithful to Jesus, Christ crucified.

Markan Motifs

The story of Mark's Gospel features three dominant and related motifs: secrecy, the distinction between insiders and outsiders, and the contrast of fear and faith.

Secrecy

The secrecy motif has enthralled interpreters because, at first glance, it's just so bizarre. Why would Jesus conduct certain healings and exorcisms privately, and why would he adjure many recipients of his mercy to silence? And why do so many of them break silence? The classic answer was given on historical grounds: Jesus didn't really claim to be the Christ/ Messiah, but after the disciples' experience of his Resurrection, whatever really happened, they believed Jesus to be the Messiah. Wrongly charged as a messianic pretender, Jesus was vindicated as Messiah by the Resurrection, and so the disciples realized Jesus had been the Messiah all along, even though he never claimed to be.[12] This thesis has rightly fallen on hard times. Historical approaches often fail to explain odd features of Mark's Gospel, and then historical critics turn around and charge Mark with incoherence. Literary approaches that take the Gospel's narrative form seriously, however, provide answers, producing compelling readings of Mark's Gospel that reveal its brilliance.[13] In Mark's story, the motif of secrecy serves discipleship and irony. It serves discipleship in that Jesus grants deeper revelation of his mission and identity only to those who come into his presence, who would be disciples close to him, with him. But then it serves irony, particularly the irony of discipleship failure, in that those commanded to silence often speak while those commanded to speak keep silence (16:8).

Above all, secrecy serves the theme of Jesus's divine Sonship. In fact, the "messianic secret" is a misnomer that misses much of the point. For, of all Mark's secrets, Jesus's secret identity as the divine Son of God is the one most closely kept: human characters in the story aren't privileged to know it. Readers of Mark's story, on the other hand, are given priv-

---

[12] This line of interpretation starts with William Wrede's writing on the "messianic secret" in Mark in his seminal *Das Messiasgeheimnis in Evangelien: Zugleich ein Beitrag zum Verständnis des Markusevangeliums* (Göttingen, DE: Vandenhoeck & Ruprecht, 1901) and gave rise to the split between the Jesus of history and the Christ of faith that one finds in continental scholarship with figures such as Albert Schweitzer, Rudolph Bultmann, and Edward Schillebeeckx.

[13] For instance, most interpreters regard Jesus's mention of Abiathar in Mark 2:26 as an infamous error, because 1 Samuel 21 states Ahimelech was high priest during the episode Jesus mentions, in which David and his men consumed the Bread of the Presence. But if one digs deeper into the Old Testament and sees certain parallels, Jesus's reference to Abiathar makes sense. Literary readings that pay significant attention to allusion and the typologies allusions establish can resolve inconcinnities that, at first glance, appear troublesome. See below on Mark 2:23–28 on pp. 115–120.

ileged knowledge of Jesus's status as the divine Son of God because they read the first verse (1:1), read what the demons exclaim about Jesus's divine Sonship (1:24, 3:11, 5:7), and read the centurion's sardonic utterance (15:39). With this privileged knowledge, Mark invites readers to become insiders. Perhaps the secret isn't that Jesus is the Christ, but that Jesus as the Christ (as Peter confesses at Caesarea Philippi in 8:30) is also the divine Son of God (as the centurion speaks in 15:39).

Insiders and Outsiders

Mark sets up a distinction between insiders and outsiders, and secrets are for insiders. Insiders are those in the story physically close to Jesus who receive revelation not available to outsiders. The disciples are called to "be with him" (3:14). Those "about him" (*peri auton*) are his true family (3:32, 34) and, with the disciples, receive the mystery of the kingdom of God (4:10–12). Insiders press in close to him and receive healing, like the hemorrhaging woman (5:25–34), and follow him on the way of discipleship, like Bartimaeus (10:46–52).

Outsiders, on the other hand, stand removed from Jesus and are either curious, or unbelieving, or hostile. Outsiders like the curious crowds receive parables obscure on their surface, like the Parable of the Sower (4:11), while insiders receive the ultimate meaning of the parables through Jesus's own direct revelation (4:13–20; contrary to the conclusions of mainstream modern scholarship, then, in Mark's Gospel at least, parables are allegorical). Others will disbelieve Jesus and mock him and find themselves outside, like those who doubted Jairus's daughter was only sleeping (5:39–40). Still other outsiders are hostile, and they reject and oppose him and seek to destroy him (see 3:6 and 8:11–13, 15).

Mark establishes the distinction between insiders and outsiders decisively in 3:31–4:34 after Jesus encounters increasing hostility and a murderous conspiracy in 2:1–3:30. At the end of chapter 4, Mark writes explicitly, "With many such parables he spoke the word to them, as they were able to hear it; he did not speak to them without a parable, but privately to his own disciples he explained everything" (4:33–34).

But as soon as he sets up the distinction in Mark 4:33–34, Mark begins breaking it down: he immediately presents the reader with the first of three boat scenes in which Jesus's disciples show themselves ever duller. They lack insight into Jesus's identity (4:41: "Who then is this, that even wind and sea obey him?"); they miss a theophany thanks to their great fear and hardened hearts (6:45–52); and they misunderstand Jesus totally, their hardened hearts making them fail to see, hear, and understand the meaning of the loaves (8:14–21).

While the disciples are failing and falling away, thus looking like outsiders, Mark presents examples of those who should be outsiders—a demoniac, blind men, a deaf mute, a bleeding woman, little children—as insiders.

Fear and Faith

The difference between outsiders and insiders is fear versus faith. Insiders exercise faith in coming into Jesus's very presence. They're with him, close to him, either brought to him by others in faith, like the paralytic and like the children whom Jesus blesses, or seeking him themselves with persistence in spite of impossible odds, like blind Bartimaeus, the hemorrhaging woman, and Jairus the synagogue ruler, father of a dying and then dead daughter. Faith in Mark's Gospel involves making oneself an insider by pressing into Jesus's presence, often in the face of situations otherwise hopeless.

Fear is the opposite of faith. Those who have fear, like the disciples, find themselves ever more on the outside, their senses dulled, and they risk missing healing and revelation. In the first boat scene, Jesus asks the disciples, "Why are you afraid? Have you no faith?" (4:40). But fear and faith can be mixed in Mark's Gospel. After seizing Jesus's garment and obtaining her healing, the hemorrhaging woman falls before Jesus in *fear* and tells him the whole truth, but Jesus responds by commending her *faith*: "Daughter, your faith has made you well" (5:33–34). Likewise, there is the anguished cry of the father of the demon-possessed boy: "I believe; help my unbelief!" (9:24).

For Mark, then, insiders exercise faith in coming into Jesus's presence and receive healing and revelation. Outsiders, on the other hand, run the range from indifferent or curious to hostile, and they often suffer fear, remain removed from Jesus, and at best receive only parables.

But parables are not nothing, and the boundary between insiders and outsiders is permeable. Even though Jesus turns inward to insiders after Mark 3:30 because of the hostility he's encountered in his public mission, the way to him remains open. Parables are offered as enticing mysteries inviting hearers to go deeper and come into Jesus's presence where they might receive the whole truth.

Mark's Theological Themes

Mark's literary dynamics and motifs serve his theological claims. Stories make points; points are sketched in stories. Stories deliver themes, and themes are often claims. Mark's theological claims are revealed in the stories he tells and, consistently, through the broader story of his entire Gospel.

Mark's Gospel is a Gospel, a story, neither a letter nor a work of systematic theology, but Mark's Gospel does offer much for reflection about classical theological topics like

Christology, soteriology, ecclesiology, and theology proper. It does so subtly, however, through the form of story. And thus, it will not do to regard St. Paul's letters as theological masterworks while restricting the Gospels to the moral sphere, as if they exist simply to provide Jesus as an exemplar. The Gospels are narrated theology.

Stories are rhetorical; they suggest and imply, as well as make direct, explicit theological claims through the narrator or characters. Mark's suggestions and implications, however, aren't mere options open for discussion. What Mark suggests and implies is meant as the truth. But Mark's Gospel makes theological truth claims through narrative, through story, not through direct propositions (although characters in stories will make propositional claims). Indeed, the form of story is more rhetorically effective than propositions. Stories involve readers and hearers, inviting them to cooperate, to raise subtle interpretive questions the story will later answer, to experience a range of emotions as they respond to the dynamics of a story in real time.

All that is to say that Mark makes theological claims that can be discerned and understood only by careful reflection on the story, or, put the other way, that the story conditions theological topics like Christology, and only when we achieve the end of the story are Mark's theological claims finally clear—if we have eyes to see and ears to hear!

So, when Mark's Gospel employs titles for Jesus—like Christ, Son of God, Son of man, Son of David—the content of those titles can't simply be imported wholesale from their understanding in Judaism. While certain understandings dominated, Jews had varying opinions among themselves about what such titles might mean. Their meaning is determined for Mark's readers by Mark's own Gospel. He appropriates, shapes, and interprets the import of those titles through the very dynamics of the story. The story reveals to us the truth about God, Jesus, the cosmos, and man as we are carried along in despair and hope, fear and faith, death and resurrection.

It's best, then, to encounter Mark's theological claims in the context of the flow of his story. We'll begin first with a short summary of Mark's major theological themes and then run through the Gospel in outline, showing how they emerge in the story.

Christology

We ended the prior section with reflections on fear and faith. In Mark's Gospel, faith isn't intellectual assent to the truths of propositional theology (as important as that is for Christian faith as a whole system of belief and practice), but rather radical trust in the person of Jesus, the sort of trust that persists in seeking Jesus in spite of impossible odds.

So, who is Jesus? The scholarly commonplaces of "low" and "high" Christology can't contain Mark's Jesus. Mark's Jesus is both God and man, and the most striking feature of Mark's Christology is his dynamic, three-dimensional picture of Jesus: he displays a range of passions and a vulnerability beyond other Gospels.

Further, while Mark's Gospel draws on figures and titles from the Old Testament and their interpretation in later Jewish tradition, Mark does not simply claim that Jesus is this or that figure and import the content wholesale. Rather, Mark's Jesus defines and transforms the figures and titles Mark applies to him. Mark's Jesus may be the Christ, but he's a dying one. Mark's Jesus may be the Son of man, but the Son of man must suffer many things. Mark's Jesus may be the Son of God, but he's a crucified one.

What titles and figures, then, are significant for Mark's Jesus?

First, Mark's Gospel presents Jesus as the Spirit-empowered Christ/Messiah, the ultimate, end-time son of David (another way of saying Christ or Messiah). But Jesus is a weird son of David, an ironic Christ, given the dominant Jewish expectations of the day. Instead of saving his people by killing for them in a violent revolution overthrowing Rome, Jesus the Christ redeems them by dying for them, going the way of the Cross, undergoing crucifixion at the hands of the oppressors.

Second, Mark's Gospel presents Jesus as "Son of man." It's a third-person reference Jesus employs of himself that evokes the eschatological, divine son of man of Daniel 7:13–14:

> and behold, with the clouds of heaven
> there came one like a son of man,
> and he came to the Ancient of Days
> and was presented before him.
> And to him was given dominion
> and glory and kingdom,
> that all peoples, nations, and languages
> should serve him;
> his dominion is an everlasting dominion,
> which shall not pass away,
> and his kingdom one
> that shall not be destroyed.

In this passage, the "son of man" is a figure alongside God, the "Ancient of Days," and he is given everlasting dominion and kingdom. Now, Jesus alludes to Daniel 7:13 in Mark 13:26: "And then they will see the Son of man coming in clouds with great power and glory." Jesus also quotes from it when answering the high priest at the Sanhedrin's hasty trial: "You will see the Son of man . . . coming with the clouds of heaven" (14:62b). Christ/Messiah and Son of man are similar, if not identical, especially when found in the same person, Jesus. Both titles point to Jesus's everlasting reign.

Third, Mark's Gospel presents Jesus as Son of God. Indeed, Jesus's identity as Son of God is the strictest secret of Mark's Gospel. The demons confess him as "Son of God" (3:11) and "Son of the Most High God" (5:7), but the only human in Mark's Gospel to call Jesus "Son of God" is the centurion who crucified him, and he does so sarcastically. Why? Because Mark insists that Jesus cannot—must not—be understood as "Son of God" apart from the crucifixion, lest Christians settle for a mere superstar.

In fact, Mark keeps the secret of Jesus's identity as Son of God so secret that no one at the Baptism of Our Lord save Jesus himself hears the heavenly voice of the Father saying, "You are my beloved Son; with you I am well pleased" (1:11), a reading that fits with the theme of Markan secrecy. In Matthew's scene of the Baptism, the heavenly voice speaks in the third person: "This is my beloved Son, with whom I am well pleased" (Matt 3:17); everyone hears. In Mark's version, the second person "you" indicates that God speaks only to Jesus, as a whisper. "Son of God" is absent from Peter's confession of Jesus as the Christ at Caesarea Philippi (8:30; cf. Matt 16:16).

Therefore, no human in the story knows Jesus is the Son (though demons will call him that and similar names, like Holy One of God in 1:24) until it's subtly revealed to Peter, James, and John at the Transfiguration (9:2–8), when the heavenly voice tells the three, "This is my beloved Son; listen to him" (9:7). In short, the major secret in Mark's Gospel isn't the so-called "messianic secret" about Jesus's Christhood, but the secret of Jesus's divine Sonship.

Jesus's Sonship also ties in to other titles and types Mark employs. For Jesus is Son of God as Son of David. The prophecy of a Davidic descendant who would establish an everlasting Davidic dynasty of throne and kingdom in Samuel 7:13–14a involves divine Sonship: "I will be his father, and he shall be my son." Further, Jesus is the "beloved Son" of God (1:11, 9:7), just as Isaac was the "beloved son" of Abraham (Gen 22:2, 12, 16). Sonship involves sacrifice.

Fourth, Mark's Gospel even presents Jesus as God himself come to earth. This is perhaps the greatest of Mark's secrets. Jesus's divinity is mediated subtly, largely through allusions that place Jesus in parallel with the LORD God in Old Testament stories (as in the second boat scene; see below on Mark 6:45–52, in the section in this chapter on Mark 4:35–8:21 ["Insiders to Outsiders, Outsiders to Insiders"], and chapter 4 of part II [covering the use of the 4:35–8:21 section of the Gospel in the lectionary]). And so, with their access to the very material of Mark's story, readers of Mark's Gospel are the ultimate insiders, in a position beyond the characters in the story to understand more deeply the fundamental identity of Jesus Christ: he is God come to earth.[14]

Given the identity of Mark's Jesus as Christ, Son of man, Son of God, and indeed God himself, we can see that Mark's Gospel emphasizes Jesus's supreme authority, and his authority in turn points to his true identity. If Jesus did the sort of

---

[14] Again, Markan Christology is dynamic. Perhaps more than any other Gospel, Mark's Gospel emphasizes in a multi-dimensional way the dynamic range of Jesus's person as fully human and fully divine. See Vincent Taylor, *The Gospel according to St. Mark* (New York: Macmillan, 1952), 121: "The sheer humanity of the Markan portraiture catches the eye of the most careless reader; and yet it is but half seen if it is not perceived that this Man of Sorrows is also a Being of supernatural origin and dignity, since He is the Son of God. . . . Mark's Christology is a high Christology, as high as any in the New Testament, not excluding that of John." On the worship of Jesus as God in the New Testament and early Christianity, see Larry Hurtado, *Lord Jesus Christ: Devotion to Jesus in Earliest Christianity* (Grand Rapids, MI: Eerdmans, 2005).

things he did in Mark's Gospel as a mere mortal, the scribes might be right to say Jesus is possessed (3:22).

The crowds are amazed because Jesus teaches with authority, unlike the scribes (1:22) and exorcises with authority (1:27). As Son of man, Jesus has authority to forgive sins (2:10). And Jesus delegates his authority to his disciples in teaching, healing, and exorcism (3:15, 6:7). To the crowds in the Gospel of Mark, Jesus's authority is striking because they encounter him as a man. To disciples and readers who perceive the mystery of Jesus's identity, however, it is no mystery. It's an expression of who he is. And who Jesus is, ultimately, is God—God come to earth.

Soteriology

So what's the problem, then? Why does God come to earth in Jesus? In terms of *soteriology*, the problem isn't primarily that individuals are sinners or that Rome is oppressing the Jews. Rather, the entire world stands under the domination of sin, death, hell, and the devil, Satan being the illegitimate *dominus* of the cosmos after the Fall. In Mark's Gospel, soteriology is cosmic; it's liberation of the cosmos from the powers that oppress it. Jesus doesn't deal with Rome; he deals with the satanic forces undergirding Rome. Jesus defeats Satan, the usurper, and begins to establish his rightful reign as Davidic Christ, as Danielic Son of man, as divine Son of God.

That's no mere moral program of human improvement or social program of justice. Rather, Mark's Gospel is ultimately a story of apocalyptic holy war: Jesus is the God of Israel invading the rebel cosmos to liberate it from sin, death, hell, and the devil. That's what the kingdom of God means in Mark's Gospel. The kingdom has come in the person of Jesus the liberator. And Jesus's ultimate stroke of liberation is his crucifixion. He comes "not to be served but to serve, and to give his life as a ransom for many" (10:45). Jesus wins the final battle of his holy war at Golgotha.

Now much soteriology has concerned itself with theories of sacrifice and justification, how Jesus's death deals with sin and reconciles sinners to God. Western Christians usually speak in terms of debt and guilt: We are sinners whose guilt incurs a debt we owe God but cannot pay, and so God sends Jesus to die and, somehow, pay that debt and forgive us from our objective status as guilty sinners.[15]

But the earlier and broader Christian tradition, rooted deeply in the New Testament, has seen another important dimension in soteriology: that of Christ the conqueror, *Christus Victor*.[16] It's the idea that the human race is not merely guilty, but also held in bondage, held captive by sin, death, hell, and the devil. *Christus Victor* should be seen as Mark's overarching soteriological model, as it involves the entire cosmos, as well as us in it, who, thanks to sin, are guilty, liable to death, worthy of hell, and vulnerable to the devil. We need not simply forgiveness, but also *liberation* from those hostile powers. Jesus, then, is both victim and victor, the victor by becoming the victim, the one who defeats sin, death, hell, and the devil not only by his death but also by everything he

---

[15] The *Catechism of the Catholic Church* bears subtle witness to the complexity of soteriology in "Christ's Redemptive Death in God's Plan of Salvation" (*CCC* §§599–623) in discussing the various ways in which Jesus's death saves. While coherent and reflecting the richness of the biblical witness and theological tradition, the Catechism settles on no one particular theory. The Catechism assumes the significance of the *Christus Victor* model in employing the language of ransom from Mark 10:45 in CCC §§601, 605, 608, and 622, and indeed by the very fact of teaching Jesus's death was a sacrifice, for in Judaism (as well as paganism), sacrifice was meant not only to please and propitiate God but also to drive away the demonic.

[16] See the classic modern treatment in Gustav Aulén, *Christus Victor: A Historical Study of the Three Main Types of the Idea of Atonement*, trans. A. G. Herbert (London: SPCK, 1931).

is and does from his Incarnation to Ascension.

This is how Mark's Gospel views salvation: Jesus's healings and exorcisms are battles in that great war of liberation, and Jesus gives his life as a "ransom" (10:45) on the Cross to liberate us from those hostile powers holding us captive as his final stroke sealing Satan's defeat.

Church and Eucharist

And that great war of liberation isn't fought by Jesus alone; his disciples fight with him in the Church, as Jesus called his disciples to be with him, to teach, and to exorcise (Mark 3:13–15), and the Eucharist is the Church's supreme secret weapon. For, as Jesus's sacrifice on the Cross seals the ultimate victory over sin, death, hell, and the devil, the Eucharist makes present that sacrifice in the time of the Church. Mark's Jesus founds the Church subtly in the suggestive calling of the Twelve in 3:13–15. While Mark doesn't use the word "church," as Matthew 16:18 does (*ekklēsia*, usually "congregation" or "assembly" of Israel in the Greek Old Testament), the concept is there in his choosing of the Twelve. Just as the twelve sons of Jacob (whom God later gives the new name of Israel, in Gen 32:28) are the founding fathers of the twelve tribes the congregation or assembly of the nation of Israel comprises, so Jesus chooses twelve Apostles to found his new congregation, his new assembly, his Church.

Mark's Gospel, then, operates with the concept of the Church. What might Mark suggest about the Eucharist?

Observers have long noted that John's Gospel presents profound reflection on the Eucharist in John 6 without providing any account of its institution. Mark's Gospel does provide an account of its institution in 14:22–25, but in a way perhaps analogous to John's reflection, Mark provides stories foreshadowing it before its institution in the Gospel and interpreting it for believers in the time of the Church after the Gospel. Mark, too, is a Eucharistic Gospel.

Mark's Gospel reveals its Eucharistic nature not only in its presentation of the institution of the Eucharist but also, more broadly, in what's called the "bread section" (6:33–8:26), in which *artos*, "loaf" or "bread," appears seventeen times. Most significant are the feedings of the five thousand (6:30–44) and four thousand (8:1–10), which are obvious signs of the Eucharist. In the institution of the Eucharist, Mark presents the rite as a Christian sacrificial ritual that will replace Temple sacrifices in the wake of Jesus's crucifixion and the Temple's coming destruction. In the feedings, Mark presents the Eucharist as the sacrificial meal that nourishes those who receive, strengthening them for discipleship and, indeed, spiritual battle—it's no accident that the numbers that Mark gives as the numbers of males (*anēr*, 6:44) present are approximately the numbers of a Roman legion. The Church is the true Rome, not civilizing the world by force of Caesar's arms, but liberating it by the power of Jesus the true *Dominus*.[17]

Cross and Discipleship

The root of the sacrifice of the Eucharist is Jesus's sacrifice on the Cross, which the Eucharist interprets and from which the Eucharist flows. Indeed, the theme of the cross is central to Mark's story. Jesus declares at Caesarea Philippi that "it is necessary" (*dei*) for him as Son of man to "suffer many things, and be rejected by the elders and the chief priests and the

---

[17] See Brant Pitre, *The Case for Jesus: The Biblical and Historical Evidence for Christ* (New York: Image, 2016), 102–18. Pitre suggests that Jesus fulfilled prophecies of Daniel when he brought the kingdom and founded the Church, and so the Roman Catholic Church ultimately fulfills the prophecies of Daniel's serial kingdoms as the last in the sequence of the empires of Babylon, Persia, Greece, and Rome. The Roman Church conquers the Roman Empire from within.

scribes, and be killed, and after three days rise again" (8:31). And then, in the cross, we find the essence of *discipleship*. Jesus calls those who would be his disciples to come to Jerusalem with him to suffer crucifixion: "If any man would come after me, let him deny himself and take up his cross and follow me" (8:34). Like the master, so the disciple; discipleship is cruciform.

That's why Peter freaks out and rebukes Jesus (8:32). He can't countenance a crucified Christ. (In his defense, Peter was a Jew and Jews simply didn't have a category for a crucified Christ; it's like a square circle or a feline canine. But he failed to submit, forgetting that Jesus the Christ is the one who gets to define what all things ultimately mean.) But Jesus ups the ante: not only must the Christ suffer and die, but if one wants to be a disciple, one must "follow" him "on the way" to Jerusalem, to go and die likewise. In the world of the story, it's a literal call to crucifixion. Allegorically, it's a call to spiritual mortification—and, for too many Christians in the wider world today, martyrdom.

Indeed, again and again in Mark's Gospel, one sees a contrast between a *theologia gloriae* and a *theologia crucis*, between a *theology of glory* and a *theology of the cross*.[18] Theologies of glory evade the cross; they're all gain, no pain, allergic to suffering. Theologies of the cross recognize the depth of human sin revealed and conquered in the crucifixion, necessary

---

[18] On the theology of the cross in a Catholic key, see: Joseph Ratzinger, *Principles of Catholic Theology: Building Stones for a Fundamental Theology*, trans. Sr. Mary Frances McCarthy, S.N.D. (San Francisco: Ignatius, 1987), 184–85; Ratzinger, *Introduction to Christianity* (San Francisco: Ignatius, 2004), 172–74 and 213–15. As Pope Benedict, he taught: "The theology of the cross is no theory; rather, it is the reality of Christian life. To live in faith in Jesus Christ, to live in truth and love, implies daily sacrifice; it implies suffering" (General Audience, November 5, 2008; my translation from the Italian at http://w2.vatican.va/content/benedict-xvi/it/audiences/2008/documents/hf_ben-xvi_aud_20081105.html).

for salvation. They recognize that Christianity is cruciform through and through, that suffering is redemptive.

The theology of glory is Peter's problem at Caesarea Philippi: he assumes Christhood involves glory, and Jesus teaches it requires the Cross. In fact, it's Peter's problem at the Transfiguration, too. He's overwhelmed by Jesus's proleptic resurrection glory, but the heavenly voice reminds Peter that Jesus is God's "beloved Son"—like Abraham's beloved Son Isaac (see Gen 22:2, 12, 16), Jesus is meant to be a sacrifice. And Peter is not the only disciple captured by fantasies of glory. Immediately after Jesus's final Passion prediction (10:32–24), Mark juxtaposes James's and John's jarring demand to sit at Jesus's right and left hands "in [his] glory" (10:37). It's as if their theology of glory blinded them to Jesus's theology of the cross. Thankfully, Mark's Gospel teaches there's hope for the blind!

Discipleship and Its Discontents

Discipleship, then, is cruciform. The cross is necessary for Jesus and also for his disciples. But all save Christ will fall away. We're not sure what happens to the hemorrhaging woman or Bartimaeus; they're not present at the crucifixion in any event. Jesus dies alone, forsaken by man and, apparently, for a time, by God. What is the point of Mark's theme of discipleship failure?

Among all the Gospels, Mark paints the bleakest picture of the disciples. In fact, shortly after the third boat scene, Jesus will call even Peter "Satan" (8:33), and unlike in the other Gospels, there is no explicit scene of reconciliation of the disciples with Jesus (though the young man at the empty tomb announces reconciliation in 16:7). Peter denies Jesus; in Gethsemane they all scatter; and Jesus dies alone, without any disciple keeping vigil. There is no great commission on the mountain, as in Matthew; no Resurrection appearances as in Luke and Acts; no command to Peter to feed Jesus's sheep, as in John. The disciples go away after the arrest and do not appear in Mark's Gospel again.[19] In Mark's Gospel, they fail to the uttermost. They become outsiders. But again, the boundary is permeable. As the disciples fail and fall further, readers encounter those who should be outsiders who, through the exercise of their persistent faith, make themselves insiders.

Divine Victory: The Grace of God

Many scholars have taken the easy way out, the way of moralism, and asserted that Mark presents the failing disciples as foils whose negative example is to be rejected. Rather, the idea goes, Mark's readers are to succeed, unlike the disciples, who failed.

Good luck with that. The disciples in Mark's Gospel knew Jesus and were directly chosen by him. They witnessed his teaching, miracles, and exorcisms. They were with him day and night for years. Yes, Mark recounts their failings, but it's the height of hubris to think we could do better where they failed. Something else is likely afoot.

That something, I think, is Mark's radical theology of *grace*. The point of the Markan theme of discipleship failure isn't the rank legalism of that raw moralism that tells us we can be better than the Twelve Apostles. Rather, it's this: We are like the Twelve in that we endeavor to follow Jesus in his war of liberation on the way of the cross, but we too fail, and sometimes spectacularly, like Peter. But thanks be to the God of mercy who in divine victory raised the crucified Jesus from the dead! Just as the young man announcing the Resurrection

---

[19] See the discussion of Mark 16:8 and the longer ending of Mark 16:9–20 on pp. 312–15.

(himself a restored apostate; see Mark 14:51–52) told the women that the disciples and Peter were to go to Galilee to see Jesus, we too are invited to go to Galilee, as it were, to see him once more. "But go, tell his disciples and Peter that he is going before you to Galilee; there you will see him, as he told you" (16:7). Men and women (see 16:8) prove faithless; God alone is faithful.

Return to Galilee

And so we may begin again. The young man's mention of Galilee loops readers back to the beginning where Jesus began his ministry in Galilee, preaching the Gospel, proclaiming the kingdom, and calling disciples (1:14–20).[20] We are brought back to Galilee to begin again and again. We as readers, as insiders, as Catholics, are written back into the story, brought into the perpetual loop of Mark's Gospel, where we will follow, fail, and find forgiveness, again and again, on our way of discipleship, pressing on to sainthood, till kingdom come.[21]

---

[20] The Gospels are designed to loop readers back to the beginning. They thus transcend their original audience and become Scripture for the universal Church. Scholars have long noted this phenomenon in the Gospel of Matthew in particular. At the Great Commission, Matthew presents Jesus instructing the Eleven to teach the disciples they will make from among the nations "to observe all that I have commanded you" (Matt 28:19–20). In doing so, Matthew subtly invites renewed consideration of what Jesus has, in fact, taught throughout the entirety of his Gospel.

[21] This in no way undermines the Catholic theology of cooperation with divine grace on the way to sainthood, as if Mark supported the idea of *simul iustus et peccator* (simultaneously justified and sinful) found in later Lutheran and Protestant orthodoxy. Rather, the saints are profoundly aware of their sins and failings. In *Catholicism: A Journey to the Heart of the Faith* (New York: Image, 2011), Bishop Robert Barron writes:

> G.K. Chesterton once remarked, "There are saints in my religion, but that just means men who know they are sinners." For the great English apologist, the relevant distinction is not between sinners and non-sinners, but between those sinners who know their sin and those who, for whatever reason, don't. The heroes of the

And the kingdom will come, like the mustard seed, which grows till all the birds of the air nest in its branches (4:30–32). For Mark's ultimate lesson is that God is on the loose, broken out of all that would limit him from entering our reality. At the baptism of Jesus, the Holy Spirit enters the world screaming through the tearing (*schizō*, 1:10) of the heavens. At the crucifixion, the Father departs the Temple sanctuary through the tearing (*schizō*, 15:38) of the veil. And at the Resurrection, the Son busts out of the tomb. All three Persons of the Holy Trinity are on the loose.

The Shape of Mark's Story

While other outlines are possible, following a perceived chiastic or geographical structure in Mark's Gospel, the outline I present here is (like Mark's Gospel) rough and ready, faithfully following the literary dynamics of Mark's narrative structure. It's appropriate, then, to offer a quick, intense overview of Mark's story.

Jesus Christ Superstar (Mark 1:1–45)

The first chapter presents Jesus Christ as a superstar. He appears on the scene like Melchizedek (see Gen 14:17–20 and Heb 5:1–10 and 6:20–7:28), without any genealogy or birth story, responding to John the Baptist's call to repentance

---

faith—the saints—are precisely those who are ordered toward God and who therefore have a keener appreciation of how far they fall short of the ideal. St. John of the Cross compared the soul to a pane of glass. When it is facing away from the light, its smudges and imperfections are barely noticeable, but when it is directed at the light, every mark, even the smallest, becomes visible. This explains the paradox that the saints are most keenly aware of their sins, even to the point of describing themselves as the worst of sinners. We might mistake this for false modesty, but it is in fact a function of a truly saintly psychology. (176)

and baptism, though he needs neither. He gets baptized in a Trinitarian scene: He, the Son, is possessed by the Holy Spirit who comes "into him" (my translation of *eis auton* in 1:10), and the heavenly voice of the Father deems him the "beloved Son" like Isaac (1:11 and Gen 22:2, 12, 16), thus giving him his sacrificial commission. Immediately, the Spirit casts him out (*ekballō*, 1:12), just like a demon(!), into the wilderness, where he bests Satan and restores Eden, establishing a beachhead of the new creation. From there, he calls disciples and gets on with his mission of teaching, healing, and exorcism. He becomes so popular that he "could no longer openly enter a town, but was out in the country; and people came to him from every quarter" (1:45).

Kingdoms in Conflict (Mark 2:1–3:35)

In chapters 2–3, however, Jesus encounters rising opposition as the kingdom of God and the kingdom of Satan come into conflict. He perceives the scribes complaining in their hearts about his forgiving the paralytic—Mark is clear that they're not whispering out loud, and so Jesus doesn't overhear them; he simply intuits what they're thinking in their hearts (2:6–8). By the end of the five stories, Jesus has become so unpopular with the religious authorities that the Pharisees conspire with the Herodians to kill him (3:6).

After seeing his popularity plummet in Mark 2:1–3:6, Jesus chooses the Twelve to "be with him" (3:14), and after that point, only those who are insiders get the fullness of Jesus's teaching and healing. Mark will establish the division between insiders and outsiders in 3:31–35, the A' part of a sandwich (3:19b–35). The sandwich concerns the possibility that Jesus is either insane or demon possessed (a distinction with little difference in Jesus's day). Jesus's friends come to take charge of him, for they're concerned he's crazy (3:21)

and the religious authorities think he's possessed by Beelzebul (3:22–30). Jesus is informed his family is "outside" the
house he's in, looking for him (3:31 and 32; "outside" is
mentioned twice to drive home the point), and he responds
by looking to those inside the house sitting around him and
declaring, "Here are my mother and my brethren! Whoever
does the will of God is my brother, and sister, and mother"
(3:34b–35).

Turning Inward to Insiders (Mark 4:1–34)

Having established the insider–outsider distinction at the
end of chapter 3, Mark cements it in chapter 4. Jesus tells the
Parable of the Sower to the crowds (4:1–9) but provides no
point, no explanation. Mark 4:10–12 is key:

> And when he was alone, those who were about him
> with the Twelve asked him concerning the parables.
> And he said to them, "To you has been given the
> secret of the kingdom of God, but for those outside
> everything is in parables; so that they may indeed see
> but not perceive, and may indeed hear but not under-
> stand; lest they should turn again, and be forgiven."

Jesus is alone with an insider group sitting around him with
the Twelve, who, as we've seen, have been commanded to
be with him (3:14). Jesus declares that they are the ones
who have been given the secret, or mystery (*mustērion*), of
the kingdom. But outsiders—note Jesus uses the very word
"outside"—receive only parables, whose meaning in Mark's
Gospel remains obscure to them.

But not to insiders, including Mark's readers. Jesus then
proceeds to explain the meaning of the Parable of the Sower to
these insiders (14:13–20), and Mark closes the chapter rein-

forcing the idea: "With many such parables he spoke the word to them [crowds of outsiders], as they were able to hear it; he did not speak to them without a parable, but privately to his own disciples he explained everything" (4:33–34).

One could read Mark here in a strict predestinarian fashion, as if he were asserting God chose some to be saved insiders and others damned outsiders, as if there were a fixed impassible chasm between insiders and outsiders. But irony! That's not what Mark does. As soon as Mark establishes the categories, he begins to break them down. The boundary between insiders and outsiders is permeable.

Insiders to Outsiders, Outsiders to Insiders (Mark 4:35–8:21)

Right after his statement that Jesus explained everything to his disciples privately, Mark presents the first of three mysterious boat scenes in which the disciples act ever more as outsiders. In the first boat scene, they indulge their fear instead of exercising faith (4:40: "Why are you afraid? Have you no faith?") and are confused about Jesus's identity: "Who then is this, that even wind and sea obey him?" (4:41). In the second boat scene (6:45–52), they mistake Jesus for a phantasm and are "terrified," being "utterly astounded" in their confusion, lacking understanding, and suffering hardened hearts—the worst biblical thing that one can say about someone.[22] In the third and final boat scene (8:14–21), the disciples misunderstand Jesus's warning about the yeast of the Pharisees and Herod as having something to do with literal bread. Jesus wigs out, accusing them in rhetorical questions of neither perceiving nor understanding (Jesus alludes to the language of

---

[22] Indeed, Pharaoh—the biblical exemplar of one having a hardened heart—was the chief invective term of derision in the Western rhetorical tradition until Adolf Hitler invaded Poland on September 1, 1939.

Isa 6 in Mark 4:10–12), of having hard hearts, of not seeing, hearing, remembering, or understanding.

As soon as Jesus does that, however, the insiders begin showing themselves to have the characteristics of outsiders. Even as Jesus the Son of God goes forth to war against sin, death, hell, and the devil with repeated exorcisms and healings, the disciples show themselves to be ever thicker and duller. In the three boat scenes, the disciples fail to understand who Jesus is and what he's about and find themselves described with language appropriate to outsiders. The pattern culminates with Peter being called "Satan" by Jesus shortly after the third boat scene (8:33). Meanwhile, however, outsiders like the hemorrhaging woman (5:24b–34) show themselves to be insiders by forcing their way to Jesus through their persistent faith in spite of impossible odds.

The Cost of Discipleship on the Way of the Cross (Mark 8:22–10:52)

Precisely at the moment of Peter's greatest triumph and tragedy—his recognition of Jesus as the Christ at Caesarea Philippi but immediate failure to recognize the necessity of Jesus's suffering (8:29, 32b)—Jesus issues his famous call to the cost of discipleship in Mark 8:34–38:

> And he called to him the multitude with his disciples, and said to them, "If any man would come after me, let him deny himself and take up his cross and follow me. For whoever would save his life will lose it; and whoever loses his life for my sake and the gospel's will save it. For what does it profit a man, to gain the whole world and forfeit his life? For what can a man give in return for his life? For whoever is ashamed of me and of my words in this adulterous and sinful generation,

of him will the Son of man also be ashamed, when he
comes in the glory of his Father with the holy angels."

Jesus's call to the cross here is the heart of Mark's Gospel.
It comes at the outset of the "discipleship section" (8:22–
10:52), in which Jesus teaches about discipleship by word
and deed while the disciples fail repeatedly. The section starts
with the weird two-stage healing of an anonymous blind man
(8:22–26). It's juxtaposed with Peter's confession of Jesus as
the Christ for a reason. Just as the man has half sight, Peter is
half right. He has the *form* of Christ correct, but not the material *content* of his necessary suffering. But like the blind man
is healed in two stages, the juxtaposition suggests that there is
hope for Peter that one day he will understand, that one day
he, like the other blind man, Bartimaeus, will faithfully follow
Jesus on the way (10:46–52).

O Jerusalem! (Mark 11–13)

Jesus now arrives in Jerusalem to fulfill his threefold Passion
prediction: here, he must go his way of the Cross. Yet, he
enters Jerusalem in messianic glory, the crowds that came
with him from Jericho (10:46) acclaiming him the Davidic
Christ in their shouts of hosanna (11:9–10). Yet, like Peter
at Caesarea Philippi, thanks to their theology of glory, the
crowds misunderstand the Messiah. He comes not to do battle
for Jerusalem and Temple but to judge them: the very next
thing he does after his triumphal entry is to enact a subtle
prophecy of the destruction of the Temple, the very sign of
the people's national identity and the presence of their warrior
God in their midst.

Mark 11:11–25[26] is an intercalation. The A sections
concern the Temple, while the B sections concern the cursed
fig tree. Jesus enters the Temple and looks around (11:11).

Then the next day he curses a fig tree because it has no figs to sate his hunger, even though "it was not the season for figs" (11:13b). Then we're back to the Temple (11:15–19): Jesus drives out those who buy and sell and turns over tables and chairs. He then quotes Isaiah 56:7 ("My house shall be called a house of prayer for all the nations") and alludes to Jeremiah 7:11 ("But you have made it 'a den of robbers'"). Then, the next morning, Jesus's disciples "saw the fig tree withered away to its roots" (11:20), introducing the second B section (11:20–25[26]).

Jesus isn't critiquing the commerce necessary for Temple sacrifice (one would need Jewish coinage to buy animals on site, as it was impractical to sail with them from, say, Brundisium), nor sacrifice as such, which was what the Temple was simply *for*, and in any case, Isaiah 56 speaks of the nations bringing sacrifices to Mount Zion. Rather, Jesus is enacting a prophecy of the destruction of the Temple. In the Old Testament, prophets sometimes enact prophecy, like Hosea marrying the prostitute Gomer to symbolize Israel's infidelity (Hos 1:2–9) or Ezekiel lying on his side in front of a model of Jerusalem to symbolize its siege and destruction, and the coming exile (Ezek 4:1–8).

So too Jesus in the Temple: his violent acts symbolize its coming destruction, and the allusion to Jeremiah 7:11 seals it. Just as Jeremiah prophesied the destruction of the first Temple to the unrighteous people of his day who thought they could take refuge in the Temple and, thus, treat it like the dens to which highway robbers would retreat, thinking they were safe in spite of their sins, so too does Jesus prophesy the destruction of the second Temple.

If the reader misses the clues in Mark 11, after several controversies in the very Temple recorded in Mark 12, including the Parable of the Wicked Tenants, which is Jesus's indictment of the Jewish leadership (12:1–12), Jesus predicts the destruction of the Temple plainly in Mark 13. The disciples are enamored of the Temple complex's edifices, and Jesus, ever the apocalyptic killjoy, states, "Do you see these great buildings? There will not be left here one stone upon another that will not be thrown down" (13:2). Chapter 13 is an intercalation, the A sections (13:1–23 and 13:28–31) dealing with the Temple's destruction and the B sections (13:24–27 and 13:32–37) dealing with the end of the world in the unknowable future. The Temple was, in fact, destroyed forty years later by the Romans in AD 70, and in the broader Synoptic tradition its destruction is divine recompense for the murder of God's Son.[23]

The Passion of the Christ (Mark 14–15)

Jesus's anti-Temple polemic leads directly to his death and thus the Passion narrative. Mark's Passion narrative is compact but pregnant. As in the Gospels in general, Jesus's Passover meal is presented subtly as an ongoing sacrifice that will be the sacrifice of his community, the Church, which will persist after Temple sacrifices cease with its destruction. And, through the depiction of the fulfillment of Jesus's prophecies, Mark shows

---

[23] Well-meaning scholars rightly concerned with longstanding anti-Jewish readings of the Gospels often neglect the fact that Jesus and his Apostles, as well as the earliest Christians, were themselves Jews (and it is quite possible that many diaspora Jews were assumed into the Church, especially after Constantine). Thus, the conflict the Gospels depict between the Jew Jesus, on one hand, and the Jewish leadership, on the other hand, is intramural. It is not as if a Gentile savior founds a Gentile Church to replace Jewish Israel. A better reading of the Gospels and Acts sees Jesus the Jew founding a Church open to Jews and Gentiles to continue Israel's mission as the light to the nations; see, in particular, Second Vatican Council, Declaration on the Relation of the Church to Non-Christian Religions *Nostra Aetate* (October 28, 1965), §4, at http://www.vatican.va/archive/hist_councils/ii_vatican_council/documents/vat-ii_decl_19651028_nostra-aetate_en.html.

that Jesus's prophetic words are reliable and, thus, that his movement will endure.

Chapter 14 begins with a conspiracy: the chief priests and scribes plot to have Jesus killed, but they wish to avoid a riot: "Not during the feast, lest there be a tumult of the people" (14:2). Irony: Jesus will be killed during the feast, and Pilate has him executed to avoid a riot as the people scream ever louder for Jesus's death (15:6–15). The conspirator's plot fails in its details, precipitating the very tumult they hoped to avoid.

Jesus, on the other hand, prophesies Judas's betrayal (though not by name, Mark 14:17–21), Peter's denial, and the apostasy of all the disciples (14:26–31). All come true. The fulfillment prophecy of Peter's denial is particularly poignant, and Mark makes sure readers can't miss it: "And immediately the cock crowed a second time. And Peter remembered how Jesus had said to him, 'Before the cock crows twice, you will deny me three times.' And he broke down and wept" (14:72).

Moreover, in the Parable of the Doorkeeper (13:32–37), Jesus had adjured the first four disciples, Peter, James, John, and Andrew (see 13:3; they're the only audience for Jesus's words in chapter 13), to keep watch: "Watch therefore—for you do not know when the master of the house will come, in the evening, or at midnight, or at cockcrow, or in the morning—lest he come suddenly and find you asleep" (13:35–36). But in the Garden of Gethsemane, after Jesus tells Peter, James, and John to watch ("My soul is very sorrowful, even to death; remain here, and watch," 14:34), the three fail to watch and are found sleeping three times (14:37, 40, 41).

But there's more. The Parable of the Doorkeeper sounds eschatological, and it is, but it's not just about the return of Jesus at the end of the world. It's about everyone's individual hour. Keen readers note that Jesus speaks of a four-watch schema *through the night*—"you do not know when the master of the house will come, *in the evening, or at midnight, or at cockcrow, or in the morning*" (13:35; emphasis mine)—not an entire day of twenty-four hours. Jesus's final night in Mark's Gospel proceeds according to that schema: he institutes the Eucharist in the evening; he agonizes in the Garden of Gethsemane at midnight; he is denied by Peter at cockcrow; and he is tried and condemned by Pilate at dawn.

Mark's point is the necessity of intense vigilance, of watchfulness. "And what I say to you I say to all: Watch" (13:37). It's as if Mark is saying to his readers that they need to be ready at all times, 24/7/365, for "that day or that hour," precisely because "no one knows, not even the angels in heaven, nor the Son" (13:32) when it will happen. *Your* hour, dear reader, may come suddenly; for Jesus, it came two thousand years ago. And because the disciples slept instead of keeping watch, they missed the hour: "It is enough; *the hour has come*; the Son of man is betrayed into the hands of sinners" (14:41b).

And when Judas arrives and his mob seizes Jesus, all fall away: "And they all forsook him and fled" (14:50), in spite of their prior protests that they would stay faithful to the end (14:31). Their apostasy fulfills Jesus's precise prophecy delivered back in 14:27: "You will all fall away; for it is written, 'I will strike the shepherd, and the sheep will be scattered.'" Will they return?

Maybe, but not at the crucifixion. In Mark's Gospel, Jesus dies totally alone, forsaken by man and God. Mark 15:16–20 depicts Jesus isolated from humanity. Jesus is mocked by the soldiers who will crucify him. He is mocked by the placard above his head, which reads "The King of the Jews" (15:26). He is mocked by passersby (15:29–30). He his mocked by the chief priests (15:31–32a). He is mocked even by those crucified with him (15:32b), who ironically take sides with their own executioners against Jesus the Christ, the one who could save them.

Mark 15:33–36 depicts Jesus cut off from God. Darkness covers the land, and Jesus cries out, "My God, my God, why have you forsaken me?" (15:33–34). Bystanders misinterpret his Aramaic *Eloi* as a cry for Elijah, who fails to come (15:35–36). And Jesus dies alone, the heavens having held their horrible silence. One final ironic mockery: The centurion, seeing Jesus die this horrible death, mocked, misunderstood, forsaken by man and heaven, in a short sarcastic snort, says, "Sure, this man was the Son of God" (13:39, my paraphrastic translation).

The Grace of God on the Loose (Mark 16)

Mark now toys with his readers like a cat with a mouse. He introduces a group of women watching Jesus's crucifixion from a distance who had followed him and ministered to him and come to Jerusalem with him (15:40–41), thus raising the reader's hopes that maybe one character group might yet prove faithful. Will the women succeed where the men failed? They see the tomb where Jesus is buried, sealed shut with a large stone (15:46–47).

But ultimately they too will fail. They've followed Jesus but have been "looking on from afar" (15:40), and they are seeking a corpse to embalm (16:1), even though Jesus had prophesied his Resurrection (14:28). They find the stone already rolled away from the tomb (16:3–4) and encounter "a young man sitting on the right side, dressed in a white robe," but they are "amazed" (16:5), never a good thing in Mark's Gospel. The young man informs them that Jesus is risen, and that they should tell Jesus's disciples and Peter to proceed to Galilee, where they will see him (16:6–7).

But the women fail: "And they went out and fled from

the tomb; for trembling and astonishment had come upon them; and they said nothing to any one, for they were afraid" (16:8). Mark's major themes merge at this moment: failure, fear, secrecy, all in service of irony. Amazed and afraid, they ironically fail to speak when commanded. Does the secret of Jesus's Resurrection stay buried?

You can't keep a good man down, as they say. The young man is the key: it's the same young man who fled Gethsemane naked (14:51–52). He stands in parallel to Peter: He failed when Peter did, but now, in place of the linen baptismal garment he left behind, he wears a white robe, sign of the saints, and from his perch sitting on the right side, the side of God's favor throughout the Bible and the Western rhetorical tradition, he announces not only the Resurrection but also Peter's restoration: "Go tell his disciples and Peter . . . you will see him, *as he told you*" (16:7; emphasis mine).

As he told you. As he promised the disciples (and ostensibly the women) in Mark 14:28: "But after I am raised up, I will go before you to Galilee." The young man, restored, forgiven, mentions Jesus's promissory prophecy, reminding them "you will see him, as he told you" (16:7). Jesus's prophecies never fail in Mark's Gospel, so here too, readers should envision that the women and the disciples will indeed see him. It doesn't happen in the world of Mark's story, but failure is forgiven.

That's the grace of Mark's Gospel: Not moralism, that we should succeed where everyone else in the Gospel failed, but grace, that even those who saw Jesus with his mighty works and words in the flesh failed but were restored, forgiven. And indeed, the mention of Galilee in 16:7 invites readers back to the beginning of the Gospel, to encounter Jesus again, to hear afresh his command, "Come, follow me!"

Albert Schweitzer was no orthodox Christian believer, and Christian faith cannot accept his Teutonic separation of the Jesus of history from the Christ of faith, but he nailed Mark's ethos of encounter with Jesus in the closing words of his famous tome:

> He comes to us as one unknown, without a name, as of old, by the lakeside, he came to those men who did not know who he was. He says the same words, "Follow me!," and sets us to those tasks which he must fulfill in our time. He commands. And to those who hearken to him, whether wise or unwise, he will reveal himself in the peace, the labours, the conflicts and the suffering that they may experience in his fellowship, and as an ineffable mystery they will learn who he is . . .[24]

Following him means participating in his ultimate victory, now assured, for God is on the loose. The Spirit has broken out of heaven, the Father has broken out of the sanctuary, and now the Son has broken out of the tomb. That's the ultimate proclamation of the Gospel of Mark, that which preachers should proclaim.

---

[24] Albert Schweitzer, *The Quest of the Historical Jesus*, trans. William Montgomery et al. (Minneapolis, MN: Fortress, 2001), 487.

PART II:

The Gospel of Mark in the Lectionary

Jesus Christ Superstar (Mark 1:1–45)

Mark 1:1–8: Second Sunday of Advent

In Advent, thoughts naturally turn to the birth of little baby Jesus and his Mother, the Blessed Virgin Mary. And yet, the lectionary readings for the first and second weeks of Advent feature quite a few stories about John the Baptist, either with John himself as the protagonist or with Jesus discussing John and his significance.

Why does John the Baptist figure so prominently in the earlier days of Advent? There are three reasons. First, Advent deals not only with Jesus's first coming as the babe of Bethlehem in the middle of salvation history but also with his Second Coming at the end of salvation history. Second, John the Baptist is the last of the old covenant prophets. Third, John the Baptist is Jesus's forerunner in birth, message, and death.

Advent means "coming," and it prepares for Jesus's coming. He came as a baby, God incarnate on earth. But, with the readings about John the Baptist in Advent, the Church is teaching us to prepare for his Second Coming. The Gospel texts about John the Baptist paint him as a fiery apocalyptic prophet convinced the mighty one coming after him, Jesus, would bring about the end of the world and usher in the kingdom of God. That's why the Church's lectionary for Advent also presents Gospel texts about Jesus preaching about the kingdom and healing. Advent is meant to help us get our spiritual lives tuned up so that we're ready when he comes back for good, for real, to conquer sin, death, hell, and the devil once and for all.

When they're grown, John and Jesus preach the same message, the message that Jesus is the agent of the coming kingdom of God, in which all diseases will be cured, all demons and the devil banished, all the oppressed released as oppressors suffer their punishment, and all death conquered as the saints are raised to eternal life.

It is thus no accident that John and Jesus suffer the same fate. John is beheaded and Jesus crucified at the whim of craven political rulers installed by Rome: Herod Antipas and Pontius Pilate. Both rulers, at the outset, hesitate to have John and Jesus executed, but when push comes to shove, they decide it's more expedient to kill them than to risk their own power, prestige, and position.

And so, Advent prepares us not merely to welcome and worship little baby Jesus, but to accept Jesus's call to us to take up the cross and follow him. Our lives may be marked by suffering and martyrdom, but ultimately, his coming and our salvation are certain.

Mark's Gospel begins with John the Baptist: no Virgin Birth story, no genealogy, no shepherds, no angels. Mark simply states, "The beginning of the gospel of Jesus Christ, the Son of God" (1:1). Secrecy rules in Mark's Gospel, so why would Mark tip his hand about Jesus's identity? Because readers are insiders, and Mark reveals to us precisely whom we're dealing with in Jesus Christ.[1]

---

[1] "Son of God" in Mark 1:1 is textually uncertain. It's easy to understand a later scribe adding it, as scribes tend to add titles to Jesus. It's also possible to imagine Mark not having written "Son of God" here to preserve its dramatic rhetorical impact when uttered by the centurion at the moment of Jesus's death (15:39). But Mark did not withhold "Christ" in Mark 1:1, even though Peter's exclamation of such at Caesarea Philippi is also dra-

The prophecies Mark presents in Mark 1:2–3 are from Malachi 3:1 (perhaps influenced in form by Exod 23:20) and Isaiah 40:3—not just from Isaiah, even though he is the only prophet Mark ostensibly credits. The practice of listing multiple prophecies under one dominant prophet, as Mark does here, was not unheard of in ancient Judaism.[2] More interesting is what Mark's story is doing rhetorically with these prophecies.

The first, Malachi 3:1, subtly establishes John the Baptist as Elijah, for Elijah was understood as the messenger of Malachi's mention. Indeed, Mark will allude to the story of Elijah's encounter with the ailing Ahaziah's messengers in 2 Kings 1:1–8. In that passage, Elijah is described as wearing a hairy garment and a leather girdle (2 Kings 1:8). In Mark 1:6, John is described as "clothed with camel's hair, and . . . a leather girdle around his waist." The allusion cannot be missed: John the Baptist is Elijah, a supposition Jesus will subtly confirm in 9:12–13: "Elijah does come first to restore all things; and how is it written of the Son of man, that he should suffer many things and be treated with contempt? But I tell you that Elijah has come, and they did to him whatever they pleased, as it is written of him."

---

matic, and readers learn Jesus is the Son of God early in the Gospel of Mark, at 3:11: "And whenever the unclean spirits saw [Jesus], they fell down before him and cried out, 'You are the Son of God.'" My own judgment is that Mark did write "Son of God" but that some early scribe omitted it accidentally thanks to the identical -*ou* endings of four words in sequence: *Iēsou Christou huiou theou*. Alternatively, it is perhaps possible that a scribe with commitments to a merely human Jesus, perhaps a formal Ebionite, eliminated it. In any event, whether original or not, reading "Son of God" in Mark 1:1 does not interfere with the narrative logic of the Gospel.

[2] Joel Marcus notes that the "conflation of OT texts is familiar from postbiblical Judaism, especially from the Dead Sea Scrolls, and is common in Mark" (*Mark 1–8: A New Translation with Introduction and Commentary*, Anchor Yale Bible Commentaries 27 [New York: Doubleday, 2009], 147).

Elijah's subtle presence puts readers of Mark's Gospel in an apocalyptic mood, for Malachi also prophesied that Elijah was to come "before the great and terrible day of the Lord" (Mal 4:5), with the land suffering utter destruction if his return didn't precipitate repentance. John the Baptist, then, fulfills Elijah's mission, "preaching a baptism of repentance for the forgiveness of sins" (1:4), and all come from Judea and Jerusalem to John in the Jordan River to confess their sins and undergo baptism (1:5). In Mark 1, both John and Jesus are wildly successful, but the Jewish leadership will turn on them, and so they will suffer, bringing about the divine consequence of utter destruction when the Romans besiege and raze Jerusalem and the Temple in AD 70.

John the Baptist is Malachi's Elijah heralding the end of the age, but he's the forerunner. Now, when the New Testament quotes the Old Testament, more is often in view than just what is quoted. In part-for-whole fashion, quotations (and allusions) may function as synecdoches. The whole background context might be in play—it depends on whether the background of the quote in the Old Testament helps make sense of a New Testament passage in question.

The quote from Malachi functions this way. What Mark doesn't quote but wants his readers to actualize is another part of Malachi 3:1: "And the Lord whom you seek will suddenly come to his temple." It foreshadows Jesus's predicting the destruction of the Temple during Passion week, the crescendo of Mark's story. So, Malachi 3:1 in Mark 1:2 follows a pattern: Elijah comes as John the Baptist, the final messenger before the Lord arrives.

So too the prophecy from Isaiah 40:3 in Mark 1:3: the voice of the messenger prepares the way for none other than the LORD. For John's part, he himself emphasizes that he is only the forerunner, that the one coming after him is mightier and much worthier than he, who will baptize not with water but the Holy Spirit (1:8).

The quotation of Isaiah also evokes the theme of Isaiah's "New Exodus,"[3] the central theme of Isaiah 40–66. As the Israelites of old passed through the sea, traversed the wilderness, and crossed the Jordan to enter the promised land, so too will the LORD lead his people, Israelites and now also the nations, on the way of the LORD to their final eschatological liberation. It's thus no accident that Mark is the Gospel of "the way," using the word repeatedly to signify discipleship (for instance, Bartimaeus, having been healed, "follows" Jesus "on the way" in Mark 10:52),[4] for Mark's Jesus launches this New Exodus.

The theme of these intense first verses, then, is the opportunity for repentance in light of God's coming judgment and promise of liberation. John fulfills Elijah's role, suggesting to readers the final judgment is imminent, to be administered by the LORD God himself, who will liberate his faithful people. And all the people respond, as they will to Jesus in Mark's first chapter, in which Jesus proves immensely popular. But these same people will begin to turn on him in chapter 2 and will ultimately call for his crucifixion.

But Jesus will soon show up, not God. Or does God? The prophecies speak of the LORD, Israel's God, the God of the Old Testament, YHWH (which the RSV translation always treats in this way, with LORD in "small caps"). The Gospel of Mark will soon suggest that Jesus is God come in the flesh.

---

[3] See Ricki E. Watts, *Isaiah's New Exodus in Mark* (Grand Rapids, MI: Baker Academic, 2001).

[4] See pp. 46–47 and footnotes notes 8 and 9 in chapter 3 of part I above.

Mark 1:7–11: First Sunday in Ordinary Time / Sunday after Epiphany / Option 1 for January 6 / Baptism of the Lord

The Baptism of Jesus in Mark's Gospel is short, but intense and potent. The lectionary provides John the Baptist's words introducing the coming of one mightier and worthier than John who will baptize not with water but with the Holy Spirit (1:7–8), which, in Mark's Gospel, is obviously Jesus, who shows up to be baptized.

The pace of the baptism ought to leave the reader breathless. In one verse (1:9), Jesus arrives and gets baptized. Before the reader can blink, Jesus is already popping up out of the water while the heavens are "torn open" (*schizō*, 1:10). The tearing of the heavens here is a violent image. They're not simply "opened" (*anoigō*), as in Matthew 3:16 and Luke 3:22. Rather, they're ripped apart, rent like the Temple veil before the Holy of Holies at Jesus's death (15:38), where Mark employs the word *schizō* as well: the Father will depart the sanctuary as the Spirit has departed heaven to invade the world.

And the Holy Spirit comes screaming like a paratrooper through this cleft in the cosmic boundary between heaven and earth to launch the invasion that will mean the liberation of the cosmos. That first means invading Jesus, however. In Mark 1:10, the Spirit doesn't just land "upon him" like a dove lighting on his shoulder, as in Matthew's and Luke's versions. Rather, in Mark's version, the Greek says the Spirit descended "into him," *eis auton*. It's like the Holy Spirit is possessing Jesus to empower him to liberate those possessed by demons.[5]

---

[5] Jesus retains his own human and divine nature, including both wills. The Holy Spirit does empower Jesus to do his miracles and exorcisms, however. Positively, it is fitting for the Spirit's power to be an agent of Jesus's miracles, thanks to his kenotic emptying of himself of the prerogatives of

Demons in the possessed are no contest for the Holy Spirit in Jesus.

The concept of divine invasion explains why Jesus gets baptized in the Jordan. In general, the Church has understood Jesus's baptism as his self-identification with sinners, as an example to follow, and a turning toward his public ministry (though, being sinless, he need not turn from sin). But Mark does more. Jesus's name in Greek is *Iēsous*, the name of "Joshua" in the Greek Old Testament. Jesus's very name, then, evokes the conquest of the enemies of God and his people. And Jesus is baptized in the very river Joshua crossed to commence the conquest. It is no accident that the Spirit will drive Jesus into the wilderness to face Satan immediately after his Baptism.

But the Son of God does not go forth to war alone; this divine invasion is a Trinitarian offensive. The scene of the baptism is the first revelation of the Trinity in Scripture. The Son receives the Holy Spirit descended from heaven, and the voice from heaven announces the Father's pleasure in him. By the end of Mark's Gospel, God will be on the loose. All three Persons of the Trinity will have broken out: the Spirit from heaven, the Father from the sanctuary, and the Son from the tomb. And the war launched in Mark's Gospel will eventually be won.

The voice not only announces the Father's pleasure in Jesus the Son but also informs Jesus of his sacrificial commission: "You are my beloved Son" (1:11). Many people assume

divinity (see Phil 2:6–7), and because all three Persons of the Trinity work together in all operations of the economy of salvation. Negatively, assigning the power of Jesus's miracles and exorcisms to his divine nature would run the opposite risks of docetism and Nestorianism by estranging the two natures: Christian faith does not speak of either of Jesus's natures doing something, but rather his entire person, fully human and fully divine. For more, see St. Thomas Aquinas, *ST* III, q. 13, a. 2, esp. ad 3, and III, q. 43, a. 2–4.

Jesus just knows that he's to be a sacrifice, but being fully human means having the limitations of human knowledge, and if any Gospel emphasizes Jesus's humanity, it's Mark's. Jesus hears in the heavenly voice the allusion to Genesis 22:2, 12, and 16, in which Isaac is described as the beloved son. And, of course, the most significant thing about Isaac is that he was to be sacrificed by his father for redemptive purposes.

So too Jesus: he, the beloved Son, is to face sacrifice like Isaac, the original beloved son. The heavenly voice here is an omen of death. Indeed, that the sacrifices of these beloved sons are in view is confirmed by the fact that the only human to call Jesus "Son of God" in Mark's Gospel is the centurion at the precise moment of Jesus's death. Mark means to drive home the point that Jesus's divine Sonship means sacrifice.

Jesus hears; no one else present at his baptism hears the heavenly voice. In Matthew's version, the heavenly voice comes in the third person: "This is my beloved Son, in whom I am well pleased" (Matt 3:17), as the Father reveals Jesus Christ's nature and identity to everyone. But in Mark's version, the voice whispers in the second person: "You are my beloved Son; with you I am well pleased" (1:11). Readers of Mark are privileged with this insider information, but no character at this point in the story is, save Jesus. It fits Mark's theme of secrecy, which again is tied to his theme of faith: only those who press in to Jesus's very presence will receive revelation, particularly revelation of his ultimate identity.

In the baptism, then, we have the staging point for the Holy Trinity's invasion of the hostile yet hostage cosmos. Jesus is sent forth by the Father in the power of the Spirit to make war on sin, death, hell, and the devil. He'll face that final enemy in the very next story.

Mark 1:12–15: First Sunday of Lent

And so begins the war. The language is intense and violent: the Spirit that just came into Jesus (*eis auton*), possessing him at the baptism, now immediately drives him out into the wilderness. It's the same word used in Mark's Gospel for driving out demons, *ekballō*. While Jesus recapitulates Israel's experience in the wilderness here—the forty days alluding to Israel's forty years of wanderings—the emphasis in Mark's version falls on Eden. Jesus, the New Adam, confronts Satan where the old Adam failed to (Gen 3). He's not simply "tempted" (our English word from the Latin *tentatio*), which suggests a desire for the sin of some base pleasure, but "tested," a better translation of the Greek *peirazō*. Jesus here wrestles with Satan in an ordeal or trial not unlike a contestant in an athletic contest, and he bests him.

The "wild beasts" Mark mentions have suggested to some the spectacle of Christian martyrdom in the Circus Maximus, as if Mark were writing to encourage Roman Christians facing mortal persecution. Perhaps. But another option that makes sense on a literary, narrative level is to see Jesus here as the New Adam restoring Eden. He is with the wild beasts, as was Adam, having bested Satan, and now (in principle) restoring Eden. The wilderness (*erēmos*) is now pacified, and Jesus will feed the people with a Eucharistic miracle there in the feeding of the five thousand (6:30–44).

Satan having suffered an initial defeat, Jesus now advances and takes the message public: "The time is fulfilled, and the kingdom of God is at hand; repent, and believe in the gospel" (1:15).

Mark's opening raises apocalyptic expectations to a fever pitch, first with the coming of Elijah, and now with these, Jesus's first words. It sounds as if Jesus is predicting the imminent end of the world. Elsewhere, he seems to sound a similar refrain: "Truly, I say to you, there are some standing here who will not taste death before they see the kingdom of God come with power" (9:1). It's not for nothing that many have rejected Christian faith on the grounds that Jesus and the earliest Christians were wrong about the End.

So, we need to unpack Jesus's words here, as they may suggest to the reader that the End is at hand, but that's not ultimately the case.

First, Jesus himself displays rank uncertainty about the End elsewhere in Mark's Gospel: "But of that day or that hour no one knows, not even the angels in heaven, *nor the Son*, but only the Father" (13:32).[6] In fact, as apocalyptic as it is, Mark's Gospel discourages the seeking of signs of the End. The classic example is Jesus's prediction of the destruction of the Temple in 13:2. The disciples assume that means the end of the world, so Jesus has to disabuse them of that. In 13:3–8, he warns them not to be led astray by what seem to be portents of the End, for "the end is not yet" (13:7b). He also speaks of the necessity of speedy flight and its difficulties in 13:14–23 when the "desolating sacrilege" is erected—a reference to the destruction or desecration of the Temple (see Dan 11:31 and 12:11, as well as 1 Mac 1:54).

Jesus tells the four disciples (13:3) and readers with understanding (13:14) that the desolating sacrilege is the sign that it's time to head for the hills: "Let those who are in Judea flee to the mountains" (13:14b). Flight will need to be quick, so one should neither enter one's house nor return first from the fields before running away (13:15–18). Now, if this is the end of the world, there's nowhere to run to, nowhere to hide. But Jesus advises flight to the mountains, so the End is not here in view.

---

6 Emphasis added. On Jesus's knowledge, see footnote 6 of chapter 4 below.

In Mark 13:1–23, Jesus is talking about the destruction of the Temple and Jerusalem, not the end of the world. He's telling his four disciples and Mark's readers that the fight for Jerusalem is not their fight, that they don't want to get caught between the Roman legions and the walls of Jerusalem or its Temple. By contrast, when the world ends, it will be obvious, and so there's no need to look for obscure signs of the apocalypse: "But in those days, after that tribulation, the sun will be darkened, and the moon will not give its light, and the stars will be falling from heaven, and the powers in the heavens will be shaken. And then they will see the Son of man coming in clouds with great power and glory" (13:24–26). Then the angels will gather the chosen (13:27).

Jesus's point is that the End will be obvious. Which is good, because no one knows when it will happen—not the angels, not the Son, only the Father (13:32). So, instead of seeking signs of the End, disciples are to be vigilant at all times, precisely because they do not know the time of the End: "Take heed, watch and pray; for you do not know when the time will come. . . . And what I say to you I say to all: Watch" (13:33, 37).

I sometimes ask my students: If you knew the precise date of the end of the world, what difference would it make? Would you engage in debauchery and licentiousness and go clubbing in Minneapolis until, say, a week before, get your house in order, and then meet Jesus? No, of course not. We live as Christians out of love for God and gratitude for salvation, and we live in certain hope that the End will one day come.

What of Mark 9:1, in which Jesus promises some hearing him would not taste death until the kingdom of God comes with power? Mark himself shows the fulfillment of Jesus's words in the very next passage, the Transfiguration, in which Peter, James, and John witness Jesus blazing with Resurrection glory. There, they have seen the kingdom of God come with power.

Second, Jesus speaks of the *kingdom of God* being at hand. Jesus will describe the kingdom in parables in chapter 4, and three of the parables he employs are parables of growth: The Parable of the Sower (4:1–9, with its explanation in vv. 10–20), the Parable of the Growing Seed (4:26–29), and the Parable of the Mustard Seed (4:30–32). Now, parables of growth imply a longer horizon of steady development, and so the kingdom of God is something that comes steadily, slowly, and, someday, certainly. Parables of growth cut against the idea that Jesus thinks the kingdom he proclaims is imminent.

Third, Jesus speaks of the kingdom of God being *at hand*. Or does he? Translation is interpretation. You can't translate something until you have a sense of the whole of its meaning in its original language. And so, in light of Jesus's agnosticism toward the timing of the end of the world and the parables of growth, we can ask whether translations of Mark 1:15 that suggest Jesus proclaimed an imminent end of the world are correct.

The Greek word translated "at hand" is *eggizō*. It can mean "come near" or "draw near" in a spatial sense. In fact it's used precisely that way in Mark 11:1 ("when they drew near to Jerusalem") and 14:42 ("my betrayer is at hand," when Judas comes with his mob to seize Jesus). And so, the kingdom is not so much imminent, but immanent; it's a matter of space, not time.

The perfect tense Mark employs, *ēggiken*, "has come near," reveals this. The kingdom is already here, already present. The kingdom has come near in Jesus Christ. It's centered on him. It persists and grows through time in, with, and through the Church he founded. The last days aren't in the future, but have already begun and remain now in the age of the Church. They began with Jesus's life, death, and Resurrection, and will be completed at his Second Coming.

I find two analogies from C. S. Lewis many people are familiar with help them understand the biblical concept of the kingdom. The first is from his fiction, the liberation of Narnia in *The Lion, the Witch, and the Wardrobe*.[7] Narnia is frozen over, dominated by the diabolical figure of the White Witch. But then Aslan goes "on the move," and at the midpoint of the story surrenders himself to her, enduring execution on the stone table. After tending to his corpse, the children later find the table cracked and encounter Aslan resurrected, returned to his full leonine glory. Then the liberation begins: the snows begin melting, spring begins advancing. Eventually there's a great final battle in which the White Witch is slain. Glorious summer ensues, Aslan and his army having achieved Narnia's liberation.

A nonfiction example is the invasion of Normandy and the conquest of Nazi Germany. Landing about 150,000 men on D-Day, the allies have almost one million soldiers in northern France by the end of June 1944. At that point, it's a matter of math: with the Soviets pressing from the East and the allies now coming from the West, not even Albert Speer's logistical genius could save the Reich. The war is over *in principle* with D-Day. But it still takes eleven long months of brutal warfare to reach *Stunde Null*, zero hour, on May 8, 1945, when the German High Command finally surrenders. Then the European war is over *in fact*.

So too, then, with the kingdom: Jesus's baptism in the Jordan launches the invasion, but the kingdom will grow steadily through the years of history, as Jesus in his Church continues to heal, to exorcise, to reconcile enemies to each other and men to God.

---

7 C. S. Lewis, *The Lion, the Witch, and the Wardrobe* (New York: HarperCollins, 2004; originally 1950).

The kingdom's presence in Jesus fits well the Markan theme of Jesus as the Son of God leading the Trinity in an apocalyptic holy war to liberate the cosmos, for the kingdom of God ultimately is God's reign, where the cosmos is reconciled to Him. Where Jesus is present, there demons and disease flee. And so, the kingdom has its advent with Jesus, the coming one whom John the Baptist announced. The proper response is repentance, joining God's army to be liberated, and once liberated, advancing the liberation of the whole cosmos, which, ultimately, is the content of the gospel Jesus calls us to believe in. Liberation is coming. Join the resistance.

Mark 1:14–20: Third Sunday in Ordinary Time / Monday of Week 1

Having dealt with much of Mark 1:14–15 immediately above, we now deal with the call of the first disciples in 1:16–20. Important context is provided in 1:14, however. First, there is mention of Galilee, Jesus's home (1:9). Jesus returns there from the wilderness to launch his ministry, and the Gospel will have readers recall this passage when the young man at the empty tomb tells the women to go tell Jesus's disciples to go to Galilee, where they will see Jesus—in effect, inviting them to return again to the beginning and begin the journey on the way of discipleship with Jesus all over again, to respond to Jesus's call readily as the first disciples did.

Second, there's the theme of threat in Mark 1:14. John the Baptist's arrest sounds an ominous note, suggesting dark things for John, as well as Jesus. It also subtly suggests the dangers of discipleship, as there's a chain running from John to and through Jesus to the disciples. John has been arrested, a most serious matter in the ancient world, and so also might Jesus and those who follow him face such a threat.

And so Jesus invites others to join him in battle, calling two pairs of brothers on the shores of the Sea of Galilee (1:16–20). The scene is stylized, a verbal icon representing the ideals of discipleship. Jesus calls, and the disciples drop everything and go. They've never met Jesus and have no idea who he is, but they respond to his call immediately. All four leave their fishing gear, and thus their livelihoods, behind— and in the case of James and John, even their very father—to follow a stranger they have never met.

No one in real life acts like that, simply dropping everything, even one's very father, to follow someone they have never once met. The shocking way Mark has portrayed the call of the first disciples is a verbal icon representing the heavenly truth of the situation: the presence of the kingdom in Jesus the divine Son of God demands decisive response. Jesus calls, you go. Now. It's intense.

For many of us, fishing is a hobby—a hobby in which some have invested hundreds and indeed thousands of dollars. Were I to embark on such a major life change, I'd have a rummage sale and recoup some of that money and, of course, give it to the poor and provide for my family. And, for the two pairs of brothers, those nets are their livelihood in an age when people lived hand to mouth, where life was chiefly about survival.

The particular response of James and John (1:19–20) is even more striking. For Mark relates that they left their very *father* in the boat. The disciples are Jews, Asians, living in an age already marked by extreme filial piety backed among Jews by God in the Fourth Commandment.

In this verbal icon, Mark is portraying the radical response required by Jesus's call: the presence of the kingdom in Jesus Christ demands decisive response. Jesus calls, you go. Immediately.

Mark 1:21–28: Fourth Sunday in Ordinary Time / Tuesday of Week 1

Jesus's triumphs in teaching and exorcising in Capernaum make him a superstar as the crowds marvel not just at his power but his authority, so unlike the scribes. One might get the impression the scribes were ineffective, staid conservatives and Jesus a radical who got things done. And so, crucial for understanding the passage are the subtleties of Jesus's relationship to Judaism.

Christianity, and especially Catholicism, is Judaism plus Jesus. Though nineteenth-century Germanic scholarship was embarrassed by Jesus's Judaism and sectors of early-twentieth-century scholarship tried to erase it,[8] Jesus was a Jew, inheriting the Scriptures, traditions, and culture of Judaism. Jesus as Christ and Son of God, then, becomes the authoritative interpreter of the legacy of Judaism for the Church. Some things, like the dietary laws that kept Israel separate from the nations, are inappropriate for the Church, in which Jewish and Gentile believers are to be one.[9] Other things, such as laws pertaining to sacrifices, are fulfilled in Jesus's crucifixion and Eucharist. Moral things, especially regarding sexual morality, are kept and even interiorized and intensified.[10]

---

[8] See Susanna Heschel, *The Aryan Jesus: Christian Theologians and the Bible in Nazi Germany* (Princeton, NJ: Princeton University Press, 2010).

[9] See, for instance, Matt 28:16–20 and Eph 2:11–22.

[10] See, for instance, Matt 19:3–9, in which Jesus adverts to Gen 1 and 2 in denying divorce. Similarly, in Acts 15, the early Church adopts four basic rules for Gentiles who wish to be Christians, rules rooted in the Old Testament as rules for those who wish to sojourn in Israel. Each has to do with either theology or anthropology, or both—that is, fundamental truths about God and man. And so, idolatry is forbidden, as is meat from strangled animals and "blood," all of which probably have to do with pagan sacrifice. The injunction to refrain from "sexual immorality," *porneia*, in Acts 15 probably involves the maintenance of Levitical sexual ethics concerning

Catholicism in particular emphasizes continuity from the Old Testament through Jesus into the Church. For instance, the exodus grounds the feasts of Passover and Unleavened Bread, which become the framework for Jesus's Last Supper and crucifixion, which in turn become the Eucharist that the Church celebrates as its unbloody sacrifice. And, of course, Catholic continuity with Judaism and the Old Testament is seen in the sacrifice of the Eucharist celebrated by an all-male priesthood wearing vestments in Churches reflecting the Old Testament temples. Catholicism is weird in the modern world precisely because it's rooted in the Scriptures and traditions of Israel, thanks to Jesus the Jew, the Christ and Son of God.

The Gospel of Mark is often thought to have been written for Gentiles, but even if that's true (and there is no consensus nowadays on the original audiences of the Gospels), Mark's story sets itself deeply in Judaism. It begins by telling readers it's about Jesus the Christ (1:1) and then provides two quotes straight from Malachi and Isaiah (1:2–3). John appears as the great prophet Elijah fulfilling Jewish apocalyptic expectations (1:4–8). Mark may not be Matthew, but like all the New Testament documents, Mark's Gospel is thoroughly Jewish.

And so, we must attend to the subtleties of this passage. Jesus doesn't forsake the synagogue, but rather attends it and teaches there (1:21). But, as Christ and Son of God, his teaching is authoritative (1:22). This indicates no chasm here between Jesus and Judaism. Rather, the point is that Jesus is not merely an inspired prophet or skilled interpreter like the scribes (religious experts trained in interpreting the law), but rather, the One with ultimate authority over the law, demons,

---

not only the forbidden degrees of consanguinity but also the Levitical prescriptions regarding the normativity of heterosexual marriage, for they go to anthropology, the truth of the human person. As Church history shows, much of the Old Testament retains direct relevance to Christians.

and (once we get to miracles proper) even nature, given his identity.

When Jesus teaches publicly, it's associated with his unique authority and expressed in exorcism. On one hand, the exorcisms buttress his divine authority. On the other hand, they display the liberating nature of Jesus's teaching: in both word and deed, Jesus frees people held hostage from captivity to sin, death, hell, and the devil. Teaching and exorcism both flow from his divine authority.

Here, the exorcisms also reveal his identity, the ultimate ground of his authority. In the exorcism in the synagogue (1:23–26), the demon freaks out, blowing an unholy gasket: "What have you to do with us, Jesus of Nazareth? Have you come to destroy us? I know who you are, the Holy One of God" (1:24). The title the demon speaks is equivalent to "Son of God," and so, here again, we find the theme of secrecy. Knowledge of the ultimate truth about Jesus requires divine Revelation. Demons and angels have such knowledge, as do readers of Mark's Gospel (which is after all divine Revelation), but characters in the story do not.

Jesus commands the demon to be silent (1:25) for the usual reasons. First, Mark insists that Jesus's divine Sonship be understood in terms of the crucifixion, where the centurion calls Jesus—publicly!—Son of God. Again, a chief concern of Mark's story is to counter lazy theologies of glory with the rigors of the theology of the cross, and so the only time a human calls Jesus Son of God is at the moment of his death on the Cross. Second, knowing the truth about Jesus requires the sort of persistent faith with which one presses in to Jesus's presence. Thus, it would not do for Jesus's identity to be revealed here, now, at this point in the story, lest characters in the story assume one can assent to Jesus's identity apart from that persistent faith that would carry one even to the Cross.

The crowd reacts with amazement (1:27). In Mark's Gospel, being "amazed" (or "astonished" or similar) is not a good thing. For instance, the disciples are "amazed" at Jesus's words regarding the difficulties the rich will have entering the kingdom (10:23–24)—they're confused. Or again, in 10:32, in the context of the third and final Passion prediction in the discipleship section, those with Jesus on the way to Jerusalem are not only "amazed" but also "afraid." And again in 16:5, the women are "amazed" when they encounter the young man at the empty tomb who then tells them in 16:6 to *not* be amazed. The young man's white robe and position on the "right" side indicate his representation of the divine perspective, while the amazement the women experience is always a negative marker in Mark's Gospel.

Amazement, then, in Mark's Gospel, whichever Greek word is employed,[11] is not positive but, at best, neutral. It indicates surprise, perplexity, confusion, and even insanity (as in Mark 3:21). The crowd in 1:27 is certainly impressed after a fashion, but ultimately its members lack understanding. Further, they ask a question: "What is this?" In Mark's Gospel, asking questions (save Jesus's own questions to others) indicates lack of understanding. Consider the disciples in 4:41: "Who then is this, that even the wind and the sea obey him?" Or again, the women in 16:3: "Who will roll away the stone for us?"

The crowd, then, is not so much responding with faith to Jesus's mighty works as they are marveling at the specta-

---

[11] Mark employs three different Greek words in different passages, *thambeō* (1:27; 10:24; 10:32), to be astounded or amazed; *existēmi* (2:12; 3:21; 5:42; 6:51), to be confused, astounded, amazed, even to lose one's mind or senses; and *thaumazō* (5:20; 6:6; 15:5; 15:44), to be extraordinarily disturbed, amazed, or astounded, or to marvel or wonder. See the entries in Walter Bauer, F. W. Danker, W. F. Arndt, and F. W. Gingrich, *Greek-English Lexicon of the New Testament and Other Early Christian Literature*, 3rd ed. [BDAG] (Chicago: University of Chicago Press, 1999).

cle. The question, then, is whether any of them will press in beyond the borders of the theater of these signs and wonders and, through seeking Jesus in faith, come to understand who he is (the Christ and Son of God) and what he is about (liberating creation by bringing the kingdom of God's reign, ultimately through his death and Resurrection). This too, in fact, involves the Markan opposition of the theology of glory to the theology of the cross. Will the crowds, and we, understand Jesus Christ as a wonder-working superstar, the route taken by so much American Christianity, so allergic to suffering, or will they, and we, understand him as the suffering, crucified Son of God?

The answer is not given in the passage, which simply raises the question for the reader. And so Jesus's fame spreads throughout Galilee (1:28) as he continues his tour.

Mark 1:29–39: Fifth Sunday in Ordinary Time / Wednesday of Week 1

Jesus now takes his first four disciples to Simon's house, where Simon's mother-in-law[12] lies sick with a fever (1:29–30). In our antibiotic age—less than one hundred years old—fevers aren't that big of a deal. If they get too far north of 100 degrees, we go to the doctor for Amoxicillin or Zithromax. But, in the ancient world, an infection was usually as good as a death sen-

---

[12] Generally, it has been believed that St. Peter's wife died before his calling. But Eusebius cites Clement of Alexandria's claims from *Stromata* 7.11 that Peter bore witness to his wife's martyrdom in Rome; see Eusebius, *Ecclesiastical History* 3.30.1–2. Clement writes: "They say, accordingly, that the blessed Peter, on seeing his wife led to death, rejoiced on account of her call and conveyance home, and called very encouragingly and comfortingly, addressing her by name, 'Remember thou the Lord.' Such was the marriage of the blessed, and their perfect disposition towards those dearest to them" (*ANF*, 2:541).

tence. And so, when Jesus "takes" Peter's mother-in-law "by the hand" and "raises" her (*egeirō*, a word used for resurrection throughout the New Testament) in 1:31,[13] it's a sign of resurrection. He's raised her from the as-good-as-dead.

Note also two other locations where the resurrection motif is more obvious: (1) in Mark 5:41, Jesus "takes" the corpse of Jairus's daughter "by the hand" and commands it to "arise" (*egeirō*); (2) in 9:26–27, Jesus "takes" the almost-dead possessed boy (whom Mark says was "like a corpse" and regarded as dead by most of the crowd) "by the hand" and "raises" (*egeirō*) him too. Here, then, Mark suggests that Jesus can not only teach and exorcise but also raise the dead. Moreover, receiving resurrection life—as we all do at Baptism—issues forth in service to the Lord and his Church: "and the fever left her; and she served them" (1:31).

And, as the Resurrection of Christ is the beginning of the eschaton, the event that, for two thousand years, has been revivifying the cosmos, so too here does redemption spread. The whole city comes at evening (which, suggestively, will be the time of the Eucharist, 14:17–25) to Simon and Andrew's house, and Jesus heals and exorcises all who need it (1:32–24).

Jesus then departs to pray in the morning, alone (1:35, as he does in 6:46). But note the theme of pursuit: Simon and others "followed him," suggestive of discipleship, find him, and inform him, "Every one is searching for you" (1:36–37). Instead of returning, however, Jesus states his desire to move on to other towns to "preach there also" (1:38). And he does so in all of Galilee's synagogues, exorcising as well.

The passage, then, displays Jesus's authority over demons and death as he continues his apocalyptic war to liberate the

---

[13] In Mark's Gospel, *egeirō* means resurrection in 6:14, 16; 12:26; 14:28; and 16:6—as well as in 16:14 in the longer scribal ending.

cosmos, and it continues to raise the question for the reader of just how to view Jesus, as superstar or sacrifice.

Mark 1:40-45: Sixth Sunday in Ordinary Time / Thursday of Week 1

Mark's story of the healing of the leper is short but rich, involving many Markan motifs. It presents the height of Jesus's rock star status and hints at conflict to come while revealing more of Jesus's identity.

The leper models insider behavior: he comes into Jesus's presence with firm faith that Jesus can heal him of his leprosy (1:40). Mark then reveals something about Jesus: he can be moved, and emotionally at that: "Moved with pity, he . . . said to him, 'I will; be clean'" (1:41).

Mark, above all other evangelists, presents a dynamic Jesus, powerful beyond measure, but also emotional and vulnerable. Not only is he fully God and man, but he also displays a full range of passions and emotions to a degree unusual not only in the Gospels but, indeed, in all ancient literature. He is exhausted (*katheudōn*) in the boat in Mark 4:38, dead tired like the little dead girl in 5:39 (*katheudei*). He's not in control of his healing powers in 5:28-30 when the hemorrhaging woman gets zapped by touching the hem of his garment. Jesus finds the lack of faith he encounters in his hometown of Nazareth disturbing in 6:6. Jesus is disappointed in 8:12, groaning or sighing deeply (*anastenazō*) at those Pharisees who seek signs. He is indignant in 10:14 when the disciples hinder the little children from coming to him. Jesus displays rank passion and anger in the cleansing of the Temple in 11:15-17. He declares he is ignorant of the time of the End in 13:32. Jesus is overwhelmed with sorrow in Gethsemane (14:34). And

Jesus's death in 15:33–39 portrays a pitiful, pathetic, vulnerable figure whose death in Mark's Gospel is far from the triumphal image portrayed by John.

And so, moved with pity, Jesus cleanses the leper. This is more than a mild rash. Biblical leprosy included several different diseases, some of which, like Hansen's disease, were disfiguring and even deadly. The leper's healing isn't cosmetic. As he did with Peter's mother-in-law, Jesus here saves someone from creeping death. And like the hemorrhaging woman, who has menstrual impurity, and Jairus's daughter, the little dead girl, who has corpse impurity, the leper is an outsider. Leviticus 13:45–46 commands lepers to keep their garments torn and heads bare, to live outside the camp, and to cry out "unclean, unclean" should they encounter anyone. Levitical law thus excluded lepers from Temple and synagogue rites and, moreover, effectively cut them off from social contact.

Mark's Jesus restores such outsiders to full fellowship with Israel's God not only by healing them of that which excludes them from worship but also by later declaring all foods clean (7:19). Certainly, restoration to the social sphere is important, but the major point isn't simple inclusion for the sake of tolerance or diversity, a very postmodern read of Jesus's mission, but restoration to liturgical worship of Almighty God (which is why Jesus the Jew has the leper go to the priest in 1:44), through the person of Jesus himself, on his powerful authority.

Jesus here remains Jewish, committed to restoring creation to God and the sick and sinners to Israel. Hence, he's quite happy to have the leper return to the Temple and synagogue, and so he commands him to offer what Moses commanded for the cleansing of leprosy. As in Matthew and Luke, the break comes later, when Jewish resistance to the Jew Jesus leads him to form a remnant community within Israel, which will later include Gentiles.[14]

Why does Jesus command the leper to secrecy? First, although Jesus has healed many, many people, in sending the leper to the priest, there's a new element of risk involved: the healing may arouse unhelpful messianic expectation. Jesus has come to save his people by dying for them as a new Isaac (see Mark 1:11), not by killing for them, which is what most Jews expected the Christ to do.

Second, it sets up the irony at the end of the story, when the women are commanded to speak and remain silent. The leper here is commanded to remain silent but speaks, and Mark describes his speaking in evangelical terms: he began to "preach" (*kērussō*) and spread "the word" (*ton logon*, 1:45a). Third, the leper's disobedience might make him miss Jesus's true identity: the sacrifice for cleansing from leprosy in Leviticus 14:3-7 involves taking two birds, slaughtering one, smearing its blood on the other, and setting that other free, much like Jesus's blood sets free those who participate in his Body and Blood, his Eucharist (14:22-25). Obedience leads to understanding, and understanding involves knowing Jesus's true identity and mission.

Thanks to the leper's preaching, Jesus's popularity soars, and even when he hides in the country, people come to him from everywhere (1:45b). The first chapter, then, presents Jesus Christ Superstar. But in what follows, Jesus's popularity will sour.

---

[14] Acts follows the same pattern: Jewish resistance to the early Church, which was exclusively Jewish in Acts 1-7, leads to the inclusion of Gentiles (Acts 8 and 10 and following).

CHAPTER 2

Kingdoms in Conflict
(Mark 2:1–3:35)

Something is rotten in the district of Galilee, as in Mark 2–3 Jesus encounters increasing conflict culminating in a murderous conspiracy (3:6), after which he will turn inward to those who truly want to be with him, and then the religious leadership will judge him possessed and his friends and family will think him insane.

Mark 2:1–3:6 consists of five stories tied tightly together in a chiasm (A-B-C-B'-A') through which runs the thread of rising tension, with a hint of the crucifixion right in the middle: "The days will come, when the bridegroom is taken away from them, and then they will fast in that day" (2:20). Some older biblical critics, seemingly loath to regard Mark as more than a moron, have suggested Mark simply borrowed this chunk of text wholesale. Whatever Mark's sources, if any besides Peter,[1]

---

[1] Eusebius thus records the words of Papias of Hierapolis: "This also the presbyter [John the Elder] said: 'Mark, having become the interpreter of Peter, wrote down accurately, though not indeed in order, whatsoever he remembered of the things said or done by Christ. For he neither heard the Lord nor followed him, but afterward, as I said, he followed Peter, who adapted his teaching to the needs of his hearers, but with no intention of giving a connected account of the Lord's discourses, so that Mark committed no error while he thus wrote some things as he remembered them. For he was careful of one thing, not to omit any of the things which he had heard, and not to state any of them falsely'" (in Eusebius, *Ecclesiastical History* 3.39.15, in *A Select Library of Nicene and Post-Nicene Fathers of the*

a better judgment is that the weaving of these stories reveals the literary genius of Mark's story.

In good chiastic fashion, the first story, the healing of the paralytic in Mark 2:1–2 (A) stands in parallel to the last story (the fifth in this passage), the healing of the man with the withered hand in 3:1–6 (A'). The question in each concerns lawful healing. But the stories contrast with each other as well. In the first, the scribes do not whisper out loud, but merely question "in their hearts" (2:6), and Jesus thus doesn't overhear them, but "immediately perceiv[es] in his spirit" that the scribes "questioned within themselves" (2:8). The conflict is muted. In the fifth story, however, the conflict is open. The congregation is looking to accuse Jesus (3:2), and Jesus responds by provoking them: he confronts them by calling the man with the withered hand up front and center (3:3) and asking a rhetorical question about life and death (3:4). Angry and grieved at their hardness of heart, Jesus heals the man (3:5). Finally, the reaction is different at the end of each story. In the first story, those witnessing the healing of the paralytic glorify God (2:12). In the fifth story, the Pharisees witness the healing of the man's withered hand, depart, and conspire with the Herodians to eliminate Jesus (3:6).

The second story, which concerns Jesus calling Levi and then his eating with tax collectors and sinners in Mark 2:13–17 (B in the chiasm), stands in parallel to the fourth, which concerns Jesus's disciples plucking heads of grain on the Sabbath in 2:23–28. The question in each concerns lawful eating. Yet here too, the stories contrast with each other. In the second story, the scribes and Pharisees ask the disciples about Jesus's behavior. In the fourth story, the Pharisees ask Jesus

Christian Church, 2nd ser., 14 vols., ed. Philip Schaff, repr. [Peabody, MA: Hendrickson, 1994], 1:172–73).

about the disciples' behavior. And as there's no punctuation in Mark's ancient Greek, it's possible that they're not asking a question but making an accusation: "Look, your disciples are doing what's not lawful on the sabbath!" An accusation would be in keeping with the rising conflict in the sequence.

And in the middle story of the chiasm, the third, stands a hint of Jesus's death. He and his disciples are feasting while the disciples of John the Baptist and the Pharisees are fasting. Jesus explains the time will come when the bridegroom will be taken away, at which time fasting will be appropriate (2:19–20).

Mark 2:1–12: Seventh Sunday in Ordinary Time / Friday of Week 1

Jesus returns home from the country to Capernaum, preaching in his house. A swarm of bodies inside and out crush him as he preaches the word to them. The scene is again intense. The crush of the crowd is so great that the men bringing the paralytic for healing must have to body surf their way to the roof, and in a radical move surely striking fear in the heart of every homeowner, they make a hole in the roof and simply drop the dude down in front of Jesus (2:4).

Jesus responds to their faith and pronounces the paralytic's sins forgiven (2:5). This verse has provided long-standing warrant for the practice of infant baptism, in which the parents and the community provide the requisite faith for the baby's forgiveness of sins. Something else is going on here as well. Jesus now, for the first time, mentions forgiveness of sins, precisely that which defines John the Baptist's ministry in 1:4. Presumably both the paralytic and his friends wanted the man healed, but Jesus goes deeper here to the root issue, the eternal before the temporal, the spiritual before the corporal. Better to enter heaven lame than walk into hell.

The scribes question in their hearts—not out loud whatsoever—why Jesus thinks he can pronounce forgiveness, as that's God's prerogative alone, accusing him in their hearts of blasphemy (2:6-7). Modern scholars enamored of the striking human dimensions of Mark's Jesus downplay the high Christology the passage presents, but it's indeed here. Mark is equating Jesus with God, as he will do elsewhere.[2] Jesus confronts them, simply knowing in his supernatural way what they were thinking (2:8). And having asked the rhetorical question of whether words are easier than deeds (2:9), he proves his divinity by healing the paralytic by his very command (2:11-12).

"Son of man" in Mark 2:10 is no negation of this identification as divine. First, "Son of man" is Jesus's way of referring to himself in the third person, but it's not just an oblique phrase referring to his humanity, as it's sometimes used in the Old Testament (see, for instance, Ps 8:4 or the Lord's repeated use of it to address the prophet Ezekiel). It is, second, a title taken from Daniel 7:13-14, which prophesies a semi-divine figure who will rule the cosmos in glory at the end of time. Jesus will advert to that very verse at his trial in Mark 14:62, which then gets him condemned for blasphemy in 14:63-64, which is exactly what the scribes are accusing Jesus of here.

Mark 2:13-17: Saturday of Week 1

In this story of the call of the tax collector Levi and Jesus's eating with tax collectors and sinners, Jesus breaks two com-

---

[2] See, for instance, the second boat scene in Mark 6:45-52, in which allusions to the Old Testament make the scene a theophany in which Jesus intends to reveal his divine glory to the disciples and in which Jesus subtly takes the divine Name on his lips, discussed on pp. 170-171.

monplaces of Judaism. First, he's feasting, not fasting, which was one of the traditional three pious practices of Judaism, the other two being prayer and almsgiving (see Tob 12:8); Catholics are familiar with the same three (see Matt 6) and practice them especially during Lent. Second, he's not just feasting, but feasting with lowlifes like Levi. Tax collectors were considered as good as traitors, rapacious rascals who took money from Jews and gave much of it to Rome, keeping a lot for themselves.[3] (Did you ever wonder if Jesus left Levi and Simon the Zealot[4] alone together? Levi's lucky to have been left alive.) The "sinners" Jesus feasted with weren't simply sinners like everyone since Adam and Eve are sinners, born into original sin. Rather, "sinners" in the Gospels are people who have basically given up their Judaism altogether and live degenerate lives of debauchery and licentiousness.

Like the first four disciples Jesus called (1:16–20), Levi obeys immediately here, with the text giving no indication of any questions, any considerations, any hesitation. Levi simply rises and follows him (2:14). And the scandal compounds, for now Jesus eats with him and others mired in notorious sin. Now, in our day, like many things, eating has become casual. From TV dinners of a prior era to the drive-thrus of today, eating has become a matter of individual and often solitary indulgence. But traditionally, and often still today, eating is an occasion of friendship and intimacy. Indeed, it's said that eating with someone is the second-most intimate thing you

---

[3] On the roundly negative Jewish estimation of tax collectors in the Mishnah and the Babylonian Talmud, see m. 'Abot 3:17, b. Sanh. 25b, m. Tehar. 7:6, m. Ḥag. 3:6, and m. Ned. 3:4, and James R. Edwards, *The Gospel According to Mark*, Pillar New Testament Commentary (Grand Rapids, MI: Eerdmans, 2001), 82–83.

[4] In Mark 3:18, however, Simon is not named "the Zealot," but rather "the Cananaean." Mark's Gospel distances Jesus from all mundane revolution. See footnote 12 in chapter 6 below.

can do with another person. And so, certain Pharisaic scribes protest, asking Jesus's disciples, "Why does he eat with tax collectors and sinners?" (2:16).

Jesus's response is radical: "Those who are well have no need of a physician, but those who are sick; I came not to call the righteous, but sinners" (2:17). Now a certain reading of this assumes Jesus is engaging in a sort of irony: since none are righteous, thanks to original sin and as evidenced in many verses of Scripture stating that everyone is a sinner, Jesus means here that only those who recognize their sin—unlike the scribes and Pharisees—will wish to come to him. Another reading is possible, concordant both with Judaism and Catholicism, that assumes that it is indeed possible to be righteous in this world and that Jesus is reaching out to the unrighteous— those mired in notorious sin who have effectively given up on their religion and relationship with God—to reconcile them to Israel and, thus, to God. In either case, the scribes stand apart from Jesus, whether they refuse to recognize their own sin or simply reject Jesus as God's agent of reconciliation.

More important are the parallels the passage suggests. In the prior story, Jesus has declared his power to forgive sins and proven it by healing the paralytic, and now, in this first eating story, Jesus shares table fellowship with sinners. Indeed, in the prior story, Jesus linked healing from sickness with forgiveness of sins just as he here speaks of sickness and healing in parallel with sin and forgiveness. And so too is the pattern with the Eucharist. The Eucharist, the sacrificial meal in which Jesus's blood of the new covenant is poured out for many (14:24), is for the forgiveness of sins and is the privilege of forgiven sinners. In the first and last meals in Mark's Gospel, forgiveness culminates in a communion meal with Jesus himself.

Mark 2:18–22: Eighth Sunday in Ordinary Time / Monday of Week 2

In the prior story, Jesus calls a tax collector to be one of his disciples and eats with tax collectors and sinners. In doing so, he has broken two common pious practices of Judaism: he's feasting, not fasting, and he's associating with known sinners. Now, in this passage, Jesus continues his feasting, but in doing so, he is also breaking with his predecessor's practice: John the Baptist, along with his disciples, was fasting (2:18). And so, the question gets raised: What's with the partying? Elsewhere in the Gospels, Jesus reports he's been accused of being a drunk who eats too much (see Matt 11:7–19 and Luke 7:18–35).

Jesus's answer is really suggestive for those with eyes to see. He responds that the presence of a bridegroom at a wedding party means it's time to feast; fasting would be wholly inappropriate. And, in suggesting he's the bridegroom, he's alluding to the overarching concept describing God's relationship with his people in the Old Testament: marriage.

For, in the Old Testament, and of course continuing in the New, God's relationship to his people is presented in familial, indeed marital, terms. God is the husband of Israel (see Isa 54:5), and idolatry is thus spiritual adultery. The LORD even tells Hosea to marry a prostitute to symbolize Israel's infidelity (Hos 1:2–9), but he also has Hosea promise the people: "I will betroth you to me forever. I will betroth you to me in righteousness and in justice, in steadfast love and in mercy. I will betroth you to me in faithfulness. And you shall know the LORD" (Hos 2:19–20). Perhaps "know" here even refers to the marital consummation. Jeremiah too, for his part, uttered a prophecy in which the LORD speaks of his people having broken faith with him, their *husband* (Jer 31:32), in the context of the famous promise of the new covenant (31:31–34).

And so, when Jesus suggests he's the bridegroom, he's announcing not only that he's the mediator of the marital relationship God has with his people but also that he's in fact God himself, come in the flesh.

But an ominous note sounds. The heavenly voice at the baptism (1:11) has already suggested Jesus is to be a sacrifice like Isaac, and the scribal suspicion that Jesus is blaspheming (2:7) effectively accuses him of a capital crime. Now, the reader encounters Jesus declaring that a day will come when the bridegroom is "taken away" (2:20). In and of itself, it's ominous, especially for those who know how the story ends, with Jesus dying horribly on a cross. But there's more. The word for "taken away" here is *apairō*, while in Isaiah 53:8, the suffering servant is also "taken away," *airō*. There is only one word in common, and Mark appends the preposition *apo* to *airō*, but it may just be that Mark's readers are to pick up the allusion and hear a hint of the suffering servant and, thus, Jesus's sacrificial, propitiatory death.

Jesus the Jew fulfills Israel's Scriptures, and Catholicism is Judaism plus Jesus. Yet Jesus also brings newness in bringing fulfillment, which his words about the folly of mending an old garment with new cloth and pouring old wine into new skins emphasize. Fulfillment means radical change of belief and practice. That's the low-hanging fruit here. But there's more. Could it be that, in fulfilling the old by bringing the new covenant of the heart of which Jeremiah 31:31–34 speaks, Jesus's mention here of garments and wine looks forward to the robe of saintly resurrection righteousness the young man at the tomb wears (16:5) and the Eucharistic wine of the new covenant (14:23–24)?

Proving St. Mark the ancient author intended to foreshadow these things beyond a shadow of a doubt is a fool's errand, as any student of literary theory knows. But the text is there, having its effects. The Holy Spirit can intend meanings unknown to authors—did the writers of the Old Testament know that Jesus and the Church would fulfill so much of what they wrote?—and interpreters can find all sorts of such meanings in the Scriptures so long as they do not violate the constraints of the text and the Church's rule of faith.[5]

Mark 2:23–3:6: Ninth Sunday in Ordinary Time (2:23–3:6 or 2:23–28) / Tuesday of Week 2 (2:23–28) / Wednesday of Week 2 (3:1–6)

The sequence of Mark's five chiastic stories of rising conflict culminates in Jesus's declaration of his authority over the Sabbath as the ultimate son of David, final priest, and Son of man, and in the Pharisees and Herodians' conspiracy to murder him.

Here, Jesus's disciples do not so much break the law as offend the Pharisees' interpretive sensitivities. They're snacking like many farm kids do, chewing on a little grain as they walk through the fields. The Pharisees in the Gospels really are all about the letter of the law: work is forbidden on the Sabbath in the fundamental law given by God at Sinai, and so they avoid absolutely anything that could possibly be regarded as work. Now, harvesting grain is undoubtedly work (it's neither a hobby nor play), so the Pharisees aren't going to get into the niceties of whether snacking counts.

It's interesting that Jesus doesn't here simply talk about the spirit of the law versus the letter, or, since they're snacking, simply say, "Really, guys?" He appeals to the precedent of David breaking the law on one occasion, but the appeal works only in light of his own authority rooted in his identity. He's

---

[5] See St. Augustine, *De doctrina christiana* 3.2.

the new David, the Christ, and so he can call on David's precedent. He's also Lord of the Sabbath as the Son of man, and so can determine what goes. There's no need here to best them in debate (though he does on other occasions, usually for the benefit of others present).

So much more is going on, though, that we might not notice had Mark not made a minor error—if it's an error at all.

Jesus's mention of Abiathar is often regarded as a Markan mistake, for, as is often observed, Ahimelech was actually high priest during the episode Jesus mentions, David and his men eating the Bread of the Presence (1 Sam 21:1–9).[6]

The critical explanation usually involves pointing out that "Abiathar" would have been the heading in the section of the scroll in which the Old Testament story was found. (A similar approach is often employed to explain why Mark mentions Isaiah when he quotes from both Isaiah and Malachi in Mark 1:2–3.) But, as St. Augustine and Origen and many other Fathers taught, apparent problems and contradictions in Scripture are actually occasions of the Holy Spirit telling the reader to think harder and go deeper and find something of grander significance.

In Greek, the only words are *epi Abiathar archiereōs. Epi* is a preposition, and prepositions are the trickiest little things, as every linguist and sacramental theologian knows. The most important dictionary for the New Testament and early

---

[6] Scholar Bart Ehrman, once a fundamentalist evangelical but now an agnostic, famous for his best-selling popular books on the New Testament and Christian origins and his appearances on *The Colbert Report* and John Stewart's *The Daily Show*, began to lose his faith thanks to Mark's supposedly mistaken mention of Abiathar in this passage; see his *Misquoting Jesus: The Story Behind Who Changed the Bible and Why*, repr. (New York: HarperOne, 2007), 8–9. Reading the Bible as the Fathers and the Church would have us read—using the fourfold sense and seeking deeper spiritual meanings—provides satisfying answers to apparent conundra and contradictions in Scripture.

Christian literature lists no fewer than eighteen options for its possible functions, and I would suggest that the eighth possibility given there is in the one in view here, that *epi* in Mark 2:26 functions as a "marker of perspective": "in consideration of, in regard to, on the basis of, concerning, about."[7] Mark isn't saying the episode happened when Abiathar was high priest, but that the reader should consider what relevance Abiathar's priesthood might have for understanding Jesus.

In this passage Jesus presents himself acting as David did when threatened by Saul. Jesus has his disciples with him, like David had his warriors with him. And just as David and his men were permitted to eat the holy Bread of the Presence contrary to Mosaic law, so too could Jesus's disciples eat grain on the Sabbath.

But think now about the historical context of Mark's story. The wicked Herod Antipas, who would later have John the Baptist executed, was ruling Galilee during Jesus's life. Herod Antipas is like Saul, the king who pursued David to kill him. John the Baptist, who baptized Jesus as the royal Davidic Christ, stands in parallel to Samuel, who anointed David to be king and confronted Saul. Abiathar was descended from Eli, under whom Samuel received his call, and Abiathar was the final priest in the ancient line, removed ultimately by Solomon: "So Solomon expelled Abiathar from being priest to the Lord, thus fulfilling the word of the Lord that he had spoken concerning the house of Eli in Shiloh" (1 Kings 2:27).

That prophecy concerning the end of Eli's line was delivered in 1 Samuel 2:27–36 and involved words fulfilled ultimately by Jesus: "And I will raise up for myself a faithful

---

7 "ἐπί," in Walter Bauer, Frederick W. Danker, W. F. Arndt, and F. W. Gingrich, *Greek-English Lexicon of the New Testament and Other Early Christian Literature*, 3rd ed. [BDAG] (Chicago: Chicago University Press, 1999), 365.

priest, who shall do according to what is in my heart and in my mind; and I will build him a sure house, and he shall go in and out before my anointed for ever" (1 Sam 2:35).

So Jesus speaks of Abiathar not to point to a section in some old scroll, but rather to compare the Jewish priesthood of his day to the situation during the time of Abiathar. Just as Abiathar once warned David that Saul had murdered certain priests of the LORD (1 Sam 22:20–21), so too will Herod Antipas, the new Saul, murder John the Baptist and threaten Jesus. It's no accident that the Pharisees conspire with the Herodians (supporters of Herod Antipas) to murder Jesus in Mark 3:6, or that Jesus warns the disciples of the leaven of the Pharisees and Herod Antipas in 8:15, or that the Pharisees and Herodians try to trap Jesus regarding the payment of taxes to Caesar in 12:13–17.

And just as Abiathar's priesthood ended, and with it the ancient lineage of priests, so too will the Jewish priesthood of Jesus's day end (note that this fits well with Mark's theme of the coming destruction of the Temple). And just as the LORD raised up David as king, so too will he raise up Jesus the ultimate messianic son of David (see Mark 12:35) as the everlasting king to fulfill the promises regarding David's everlasting dynasty (see 2 Sam 7:4–16). And Jesus does so not only as messianic king but also as the faithful priest whose dynastic house, the Church, is built by the LORD (1 Sam 2:35).

The Bread of the Presence (literally, *panim*, "of the face" of God) was first established as a communal offering in Exodus 25:30, and Leviticus 24:5–6 informs us that there were twelve loaves, obviously symbolic of the twelve tribes. Jesus, of course, will have the Twelve Apostles as he founds his Church to continue Israel's work of redemption in the world. The Bread of the Presence that Jesus mentions in Mark 2:26 thus suggests that Jesus, the final priest, will also provide the new Bread of the Presence, the Eucharist.[8]

The long form of the reading for this week, the Ninth Sunday in Ordinary Time, includes Mark 3:1-6, Jesus's healing of the man with a withered hand. Given that it's the culmination of this five-story sequence of rising conflict and the closing of the chiasm and that it's tied tightly to the prior passage, it ought to be read. Preachers concerned for time are welcome to eliminate a joke or two from their homily.

In the prior story, Jesus went big. Whatever is going on with Abiathar, kingship, priesthood, showbread, and Eucharist, Jesus certainly declared his total authority over Jewish law, even over one of the Ten Commandments. And now in this story, as hostility toward Jesus comes to a climax, the question concerns not his disciples' behavior but his own.

Jesus enters the synagogue as he has again and again. And "they"—the antecedent is probably the Pharisees from Mark 2:24—watch Jesus, waiting to see if he'll heal the man with the withered hand, "so that they might accuse him" (3:2b). They're spoiling for a fight. This passage presents parallels with the prior: in each, the Pharisees are concerned for precise and proper fidelity to the law, while Jesus is concerned for the welfare of men. So it should be no surprise that Jesus throws down the gauntlet.

He calls the man forward, telling him to "rise" (*egeirō*) into the middle, using the word for his own Resurrection (see Mark 14:28 and 16:6), which suggests supernatural healing

---

[8] The first extant patristic reference relating the Bread of the Presence to the Eucharist is found in Origen in his thirteenth homily on Leviticus (*Hom. Lev.* 13.3.3); see Origen, *Homilies on Leviticus 1-16*, trans. and ed. Gary Wayne Barkley, Fathers of the Church 83 (Washington, DC: Catholic University of America Press, 1990), 237, and Mike Aquilina, *The Mass of the Early Christians* (Huntington, IN: Our Sunday Visitor, 2007), 25-27.

is at hand. Indeed, *egeirō* has been used already in 1:31 to describe the raising of Simon's mother-in-law from her fever, and thrice in 2:9–12, with reference to the paralytic's rising healed from his mat.

In the prior passage Jesus declared that the Sabbath was made for man, and so here, Jesus asks the rhetorical question about the purpose of Sabbath law: "Is it lawful on the sabbath to do good or to do harm, to save life or to kill?" (3:4).

Silence.

Rabbis, scribes, Sadducees, and Pharisees, any ancient Jews with an interest in the law, were good at debate, as the Mishnah and the Talmudim attest. Stories are recorded of rabbis debating not only each other but even God himself, and besting him on occasion.[9]

But here, silence. It indicates the Pharisees consider the matter closed. Having surrendered reason and cunning, they're preparing for violence. And so it's appropriate that Jesus gazes at them with divine anger (less a statement of Jesus's emotional state and more a reference to God's righteous anger in Exod 32:10), for they are displaying hardness of heart (Mark 3:5a)—the worst thing that can be said of someone in the Bible. Pharaoh, for instance, had a hardened heart and, before the rise of Adolf Hitler, was considered in the Western tradition the worst person in the world.

Jesus answers his own question by healing the man (3:5b), but the Pharisees answer his question by conspiring with the Herodians to kill him (3:6). For Jesus, the law serves mankind, while for the Pharisees, mankind serves the law.

---

9. The Babylonian Talmud, in b. B. Meṣ. 59b, records the claim of certain sages that Moses's words about the law not being in heaven (Deut 30:12) means they now have final authority over its interpretation on earth, with God laughing in response, "My sons have defeated me, my sons have defeated me!"

Jesus initiates this healing. He came to the synagogue, and he called the man out, unlike in other healings and exorcisms where individuals and crowds pursue him. Indeed, whenever Jesus initiates healing in the canonical Gospels, it's expressly on the Sabbath. Why? The phenomenon is a sign of the new creation. Before the Fall, the Sabbath meant profound harmony: God, man, woman, and nature were at perfect peace and rest. Thus, Jewish and Christian imagination has seen the Sabbath as a symbol of the new creation, when that peace and rest will once more be achieved—and transcended.[10] And so Jesus, the Lord of the Sabbath, heals on the Sabbath to signify that coming peace.

Mark 3:7–12: Thursday of Week 2

Right after the conspiracy in Mark 3:6, Mark informs readers that Jesus "withdrew" (3:7), marking the inward turn. Jesus retreats, but in this passage, Mark's brief reprise of chapter 1, Jesus remains popular and pursued by crowds from Galilee and Judea, as well as from Jerusalem, Idumea, the region east of the Jordan river, and Tyre and Sidon (3:8). Note well that many of those place names suggest newfound Gentile interest in Jesus, and so, here, we see a common pattern evinced in all four Gospels and in Acts: Jewish resistance to Jesus leads to Gentile inclusion. It's indeed ironic that Jesus turns inward just as the range and number of the crowds crescendo.

Jesus seeks retreat; he has his disciples prepare a boat for him in case he needs to escape the crush of the crowds (3:9) who are falling all over him to simply touch him (3:10, much like the hemorrhaging woman in chapter 5), but he nevertheless heals and exorcises many (3:10–11). It's like Jesus is a live

---

[10] See St. Augustine, *Confessions* 13.

wire who can zap people for healing if they simply touch him, and it's therefore ironic that he feels the need to retreat and escape. It's as if his mission is careening out of control and he might not be able to hold on. If the crowds here have any fault, it's that they're more interested in getting their own needs met than seeking to know Jesus himself, as in chapter 1.

One thing Jesus does control, however, is the demonic. The demons know who he is—they exclaim "You are the Son of God" when encountering Jesus (3:11)—and again, Jesus forbids them from making him known (3:12). Again, the secrecy motif has several functions. Jesus, and ultimately Mark, doesn't want "Son of God" separated from the Cross; in the world of the story, Jesus doesn't want to feed the crowd's desire for a superstar. Nor does Jesus want any more grief from the Pharisees and scribes, who have already reckoned him a blasphemer and lawbreaker worthy of death. Finally, there's irony in readers sharing the knowledge of who Jesus is when the characters in the story don't, almost as if Mark is saying knowledge of Jesus's person doesn't suffice; even the demons know he's the Son of God and shudder. Rather, what counts is the kind of faith that draws near to Jesus's person.

The passage, then, recapitulates in summary fashion the themes of Jesus's power, authority, and popularity from chapter 1, as well as the theme of secrecy, and marks Jesus's turn inward. Jesus continues the turn in choosing the Twelve to be his closest associates.

Mark 3:13–19: Friday of Week 2

Jesus responds to his rejection by the religious leaders and popularity with the crowds by taking control: he forms a remnant community within Israel, the Church, consisting at first of a small band to help him carry out his work of redemption.

Here we have Jesus as a new Moses forming a new Israel and giving them a new (if brief) law. Jesus goes up the mountain (*to oros*, not "hills," as some translations have), like Moses, and chooses the twelve he wants (3:13–14), just as Moses ascended Mount Sinai and forged the twelve tribes into one nation under the LORD God.

In fact, Jesus has already been carrying out the New Exodus. After Mark opens his Gospel with a quote from Isaiah signifying the New Exodus, Jesus crosses the Jordan and begins his spiritual war of liberation, besting Satan, healing, and exorcising. Like Moses, then, Jesus forges his ragtag band of refugees into a people on a mountain.

He gives them not the Ten Commandments but three profound tasks. First and foremost, they are to be with him (3:14a). In Mark's Gospel, nothing matters more than being with Jesus, in his very literal presence. Those "inside" with him sitting around him are his family (3:31–35); those inside with him sitting around him get revelation (4:10–20); those who press in to his presence get healing (see 5:25–34 and 10:46–52).

The application is obvious: for us today, drawing close to Jesus means sacraments and sacramentals, as well as probing the depths of the interior life. And here, in Mark's Gospel, we see a crucial, time-tested principle: *Nemo dat quod non habet*—you cannot give what you do not have. Or, in St. Bernard's words, we need to be reservoirs, not canals; we need to fill up with Christ so that we share out of abundance.[11]

---

[11] In one sermon St. Bernard preached:

> The man who is wise, therefore, will see his life as more like a reservoir than a canal. The canal simultaneously pours out what it receives; the reservoir retains the water till it is filled, then discharges the overflow without loss to itself. He knows that a curse is on the man who allows his own property to degenerate.... Today

Only then could the disciples hope to fulfill the next two charges: to preach and to have authority to exorcise demons (3:14b–15). Indeed, their success in these endeavors derives from their faith in Jesus's power in them, and it's no accident then that Jesus later exclaims, "O faithless generation" (9:19), when the disciples fail to exorcise a severely possessed boy (9:14–29). The boy's father, on the other hand, has partial faith ("I believe; help my unbelief!" 9:24b), and so Jesus exorcises the boy (9:25).

The names of the Twelve follow in Mark 3:16–19a. Simon stands first; here, as everywhere else in the Gospels, he is first among the Apostles. Mark mentions that Jesus named Simon "Peter." Changes of name in the Bible come at significant moments in which God reveals someone's role in the divine plan, as when Abram is named "Abraham," the father of many nations, or Jacob is named "Israel," he who wrestled with God. Simon becomes "Peter," "rock," and the irony is that Peter will prove anything but granite when push comes to shove comes to cross.

Most of the disciples play little role in the Gospels or Acts; they're present to fill up the number of Twelve. The first three, however, Peter, James, and John, sometimes along with Andrew as a fourth, form an insider group within the insiders. The three witness the Transfiguration (9:2–8) and accompany Jesus in Gethsemane (14:32–42), while, with Andrew, they

---

there are many in the Church who act like canals, the reservoirs are far too rare. So urgent is the charity of those through whom the streams of heavenly doctrine flow to us, that they want to pour it forth before they have been filled; they are more ready to speak than to listen, impatient to teach what they have not grasped, and full of presumption to govern others while they know not how to govern themselves. (Sermon 18.3a, on the Song of Songs, in *Bernard Of Clairvaux: Sermons on the Song of Songs*, vol. 1, trans. Kilian Walsh, Cistercian Fathers 4, The Works of Bernard of Clairvaux, vol. 2 [Collegeville, MN: Liturgical Press, 2008], 134).

receive Jesus's prediction of the destruction of the Temple and discourse on the end of the world (ch. 13). These four have been with Jesus longest (1:16-20), and so make up his closest associates.

One other disciple merits mention, Judas Iscariot. Mark relates that Judas "betrayed him [Jesus]" (3:19). Whether readers are assumed to know the end of the story or not, it's a dark, ominous statement, especially in light of what the disciples are called to do. They are called above all to "be with him." It is terrifying to think that someone called to such intimacy with Jesus, the Christ, Son of God, could turn on him and turn him in. It also suggests that being with Jesus involves being with him as one follows all the way to the Cross. But the disciples won't, and Mark's remark about Judas's betrayal of Jesus is the first hint of discipleship failure.

Mark 3:20–35: Tenth Sunday in Ordinary Time / Saturday of Week 2 (3:20–21) / Monday of Week 3 (3:22–30) / Tuesday of Week 3 (3:31–35)

In the Gospel of Mark, Jesus is misunderstood by all men (demons, as we have seen, understand perfectly—and shudder). In two places, characters identify Jesus correctly with regard to form but fundamentally miss the significance. At the crucifixion, the centurion rightly calls Jesus "Son of God" but does not mean it. At Caesarea Philippi, Peter rightly calls Jesus the Christ but rejects the necessity of his suffering. Reacting to the stilling of the storm, the perplexed, confused disciples had earlier asked, "Who then is this, that even wind and sea obey him?" (4:41).

Misunderstanding Jesus's identity is a major Markan theme. And we see it in this pair of passages, which most commentators recognize as the first Markan sandwich. In the A section, Mark 3:19b–21, Jesus is again crushed by a crowd, this time at his home. Jesus's friends or associates ("those with him," *hoi par' autou*) come to seize him, fearing he's gone insane. The B section is 3:22–30, in which the scribes claim Jesus is possessed by Beelzebul, no minor thing, considering that they're from Jerusalem and thus represent the religious leadership. The A' section is then 3:31–35, in which Jesus's mother and brothers seek him from outside the house.

Given the link between demon possession and insanity assumed in the ancient world, Jesus's scribal opponents and friends think the same fundamental thing about him, and thus get his identity precisely backwards. And yet, Mark also distinguishes the groups. The scribes come in for heavy fire, being accused of blasphemy of the Holy Spirit (3:29), while Jesus's friends and family are not described negatively in any way. Further, Mark distinguishes the "friends" or "associates" in the A section from Jesus's mother and brothers in the A' section. Not only are "friends" and "associates" simply different from family, but it's only the former that Mark describes as thinking Jesus is insane.

In response to rumors of his possession, in the B section (3:22–30), Jesus both shows the scribal claim is itself insane, and then, positively, hints at the apocalyptic war he is waging and winning. Note how Mark tells the story: the scribes are spreading rumors that Jesus is (1) possessed and (2) casts out demons by the prince of demons. Jesus confronts them directly about it, calling them to him (3:23a). Jesus will then respond in reverse order, dealing with the question of the power by which he casts out demons (2) and then the charge that he is possessed (1).

Now Mark tells us Jesus responded by speaking to them in parables, the first time the word, or the phenomenon, of "parable" appears in Mark's Gospel. Thanks to older, Enlightenment-influenced scholarship, most people think Jesus teaches in parables to use the commonalities of the culture to be clear and make a simple point. Mark, living before Descartes decided everything needed to be clear and distinct, employs parables in the opposite way. They're meant not to enlighten, but to darken and harden: "For those outside everything comes in parables; so that they may indeed see but not perceive, and may indeed hear but not understand; lest they should turn again, and be forgiven" (4:11b–12; see the following section on 4:1–20).

Jesus has here quoted Isaiah 6:9, from Isaiah's commission of hardening, in which Isaiah is called to proclaim judgment and destruction to the people. Parables thus concern judgment, and Jesus says they are for outsiders, not insiders, to whom revelation and explanation is given directly (4:10–11a, 13–20). And so it's interesting here in 3:23–30 that Mark describes Jesus speaking in parables to exemplary outsiders: the scribes who think Jesus is possessed by Beelzebul, Satan himself.

Jesus first responds to the charge of possession. He implies it's insane (note the paradox, as the passage concerns whether Jesus is insane) to think that Satan would work against his own purposes by exorcising his own demons; it'd be like deliberately raining artillery on one's own infantry. Jesus says Satan's house and kingdom would be divided, like Jesus's friends have come to believe he has a divided mind. Through the sandwich, Mark is showing the scribes are insane, not Jesus.

But Jesus suggests the scribes are also more right than they know: "And if Satan has risen up against himself and is divided, he cannot stand, but is coming to an end" (3:26). Jesus has set up what we might call the "Parable of the Strong Man": "But no one can enter a strong man's house and plunder his goods, unless he first binds the strong man; then indeed he may plunder his house" (3:27). Jesus has mentioned Satan's own "house" and "kingdom," which Jesus intends to end as he himself advances the kingdom of God (1:15). Satan is the strong man whose house Jesus will plunder and destroy.

And Jesus will do so in the power of Holy Spirit. The scribal charge of possession is not only insane; readers of Mark, insiders, know that it's flat wrong. Jesus is possessed not by Satan, but by the Holy Spirit, who came directly "into him" at his Baptism (1:10). And so, the scribes are guilty of blasphemy of the Holy Spirit (3:28–30). In their hatred of Jesus Christ, they have become so twisted that they look upon Jesus's works, done by the very power of the Holy Spirit who possesses him, and attribute them to Satan. It's a total confusion of the satanic and the holy, perfect evil and pluperfect good. There is no return from that point, and so forgiveness is impossible.

But again, the way Mark tells the story, Jesus's friends and family are in a different situation than the scribes, and also in a different situation from each other. While insanity and possession are linked, Jesus's friends, and then family, show concern for him—and justified concern, given what often happened to those in the ancient world thought insane and possessed.

Further, in most Markan sandwiches and intercalations, there's simple equivalence of characters and settings in the A–A' sections, such as "ruler" and "daughter" in both Mark 5:22–23 and 35, or "Jesus" and "the chief priests" in 14:53 and 55, the A–A' sections of Peter's denial, and "Peter," "courtyard," and "fire" in 14:54 and 66, the B–B' sections. But, in this sandwich here in 3:19b–30, there's a shift from Jesus's "friends" or "associates" in the A section (3:21) to "mother and brethren" in the corresponding A' section (3:31). It's the former, Jesus's friends, who think he's insane. Mark does not attribute the assumption of insanity to Jesus's mother and brothers. Is Mark protecting Jesus's family? Is he protecting Mary, the mother of Jesus, the Mother of God?[12] Possibly.

And it's also possible here to see Jesus's tender mother reaching out in concerned love for her Son. Yet, Mark uses her and Jesus's brothers[13] as the first example in his Gospel of outsiders: they are "standing outside" the house (3:31) while Jesus is inside with the crowd sitting "about him" (*peri auton*, 3:32a) in his very presence, so important in Mark's Gospel. Informed his mother and brothers are outside, Jesus then redefines family. He asks, "Who are my mother and my brethren?" (3:33). Mark tells us Jesus looked at those who sat "about him" (*peri auton*, 3:34) and declared, "Here are my mother and my brethren! Whoever does the will of God is my brother, and sister, and mother" (3:34b-35).

In Mark's story, the division between insiders and outsiders occurs first here and precisely here, not only after the Pharisees' conspiracy with the Herodians to kill Jesus (3:6), but especially after the scribes from Jerusalem, representing the highest religious authority, accuse him of possession by Satan. But there are outsiders and then there are outsiders.

---

[12] The title is wholly appropriate for the Markan mother of Jesus, since Mark presents Jesus as fully divine. See pp. 55-59 above on Christology and pp. 170-171 below on Mark 6:45-52.

[13] Either Jesus's cousins or kinsmen (which *adelphos* can certainly mean in Greek, especially the Greek Old Testament; see the classic treatment of the question in Jerome, *Against Helvidius*), or, as early Eastern Christianity suggested, Jesus's step-brothers from Joseph's prior marriage; *adelphos* certainly means half-brother or step-brother in Mark 6:17. It's also possible that Mark calls Jesus "the son of Mary" in Mark 6:3 to distinguish Jesus from James, Joses, Judas, and Simon, his step-brothers from Joseph's prior marriage. See Richard Bauckham, "The Brothers and Sisters of Jesus: An Epiphanian Response to John P. Meier," *Catholic Biblical Quarterly* 56 (1994): 686-700, at 698-700, and Epiphanius, *The Panarion of Epiphanius of Salamis: Books II and II (Sects 47-80, De Fide)*, trans. Frank Williams (Leiden: E. J. Brill, 1994), 607; Epiphanius, *The Panarion of Epiphanius of Salamis*, trans. Frank Williams 2nd ed. (Leiden: E. J. Brill, 2013), 36.

Not all outsiders are hostile or confused; some are simply curious. Again, the boundary between insiders and outsiders is permeable: those who persist in seeking Jesus in faith can come into his presence and receive healing, often metaphorical for spiritual revelation, as in the case with the blind men (see 8:22–26 and 10:46–52).

In this sandwich, then, there are actually three groups: (1) those inside the house with Jesus "about him," (2) the scribes from far away Jerusalem, so twisted that there's no hope for them, and (3) Jesus's mother and brothers, who, though outside, are near him and, indeed, seeking him. They come, send to him, and call him, seeking him (3:31–32). They are not far from the kingdom of God because they're reaching out to Jesus.

And yet the passage might make Catholics uncomfortable, for it implies the Blessed Virgin Mary was an outsider. A few considerations are important. First, as mentioned, she's seeking Jesus, coming to him, calling him, sending to him, just outside the house. Second, another Gospel, Luke, presumes that Mary grew in her understanding of her Son's person and work. In Luke 1:29, Gabriel's greeting troubles Mary and she reflects on what it might mean. In Luke 1:34, Mary asks an honest question about how she might bear the Savior when she's to remain a virgin. In Luke 2:19, Mary ponders the shepherd's report. In Luke 2:51, Mary keeps all things she's encountered in her heart. Mary (like Jesus, on an honest reading of the Synoptic Gospels, if not John) didn't know everything out of the gate. She had to learn the deeper significance of her Son and her role in his life. Maybe Mark portrays Mary as desiring to encounter her Son and understand him more deeply.

Third, Jesus presents motherhood as the model of discipleship: "Whoever does the will of God is my brother, and sister, and mother" (Mark 3:35). "Mother" remains an example here—indeed, by position at the end of the sequence, the term of greatest consequence—of one who does the will of God, and thus the true Mary of the Church's Scripture and Tradition remains the ultimate model of a disciple who does the will of God.

That said, Mark's depiction of Jesus's mother and brothers standing outside is radical. But it's of a piece with his portrayal of the disciples, whom he paints so darkly. Anyone who surrenders to fear and withdraws from Jesus's presence can become an outsider and fall away. The Blessed Virgin Mary, by her free, lifelong, and perfect cooperation with divine grace, did not.

CHAPTER 3

Turning Inward to Insiders
(Mark 4:1–34)

The culmination of the rejection of Jesus in the murderous conspiracy prompts him to turn inward. Jesus turns away from the crowds and their perplexed amazement and away from Jewish authorities who have him in their sights and turns towards those who are willing to follow him closely.

Mark 4:1–20: Wednesday of Week 3

In Mark 3, Jesus has turned inward after scribes and Pharisees turn on him. He chooses the Twelve, begins telling parables to those hostile to him, and makes a subtle but substantive division between insiders and outsiders. Now, in chapter 4, the division hardens: outsiders get parables with no clear point, while insiders receive the revelation of the mystery of the kingdom.

Mark 4 begins with the famous Parable of the Sower as the chief example of Jesus's parabolic teaching, the key to all the parables, a parable of parables, the parable about parables: "And he taught them many things in parables, and in his teaching he said to them . . ." (4:2); "Do you not understand this parable? How then will you understand all the parables?" (4:13). And so Jesus presents a parable about a sower sowing seed in all types of soil, and the bad soils yield nothing while the good soil yields thirtyfold and sixtyfold and a hundred-fold (4:8). Jesus closes with a call to understanding: "He who has ears to hear, let him hear" (4:9).

Most moralize the passage: be good soil! But a moment's reflection reveals something else is afoot. As gardeners and farmers know, telling soil to change is daft. Soil is inert. Soil can be amended with anhydrous ammonia or Miracle-Gro, but the soil has no hand in that. Impersonal and inanimate, it has no hands. Of course, figurative language like that employed in parables can be stretched, but the idea that Jesus is encouraging hearers to be good soil owes more to the optimism of Enlightenment moralism than to St. Mark's story.

The meaning of a passage depends largely on its literary context. What is said depends on where it is said. And this parable comes right after the culmination of misunderstanding of and hostility to Jesus in Mark 3 and his inward turn. He's speaking to crowds, but if one just reads the parable in Mark 4:3–9 without assuming anything else, it's quite cryptic. Outsiders such as the crowds simply hear some odd words about some anonymous sower tossing seed around at random.

Familiarity breeds interpretive indolence, and so many miss just how random the sower's action is: no one farms or gardens like that. Seed is precious, especially in the ancient world, and inefficiency in planting it costs money. (So too today, and so farming involves hi-tech tractors sowing seeds with the utmost precision using GPS.) The sower's actions here are strange, inexplicable. But it's a parable. For those who have read Mark 1–3, it's obvious the sower is Jesus—the crowds in the story may or may not have been able to make that connection. Jesus himself has cast the seed of the word everywhere. Some soil has begun to produce great yield—others, not so much. And so, the parable explains what Jesus has been doing to this point and why he's encountered hostility and rejection: some people are bad soil who reject cooperation with divine grace.

Some commentators have tried to coordinate character groups with the various types of soil, noticing that the rocky soil (4:5) reminds readers of Simon's name of Peter.[1] Certainly the soils of the parable and the explanation in 4:14–20 reflect human response to the word of the gospel. But, in the interpretation of the parable, Mark's Jesus is breaking the walls, as it were, of what is expected in such an interpretation even within the Gospel's story as the reader has encountered it up until now, describing categorical potential responses to the gospel that are quite difficult to trace out among characters within the walls of Mark's Gospel.

So the crowd of outsiders on the seashore receives a cryptic parable that, in Mark's story, explains responses to Jesus prior and forever. But insiders receive more, much more. In Mark 4:10–12, Mark's Jesus gives Mark's theory of parables. Jesus is alone now, with those who are "about him" (*peri auton*) and the Twelve whom he had called in 3:14 to be with him. And they ask him about parables in general (see 4:2), of which the sower serves as example and key. In 4:11b–12 Jesus responds:

> To you has been given the secret ["mystery," *mustērion*] of the kingdom of God, but for those outside everything is in parables; so that they may indeed see but not perceive, and may indeed hear but not understand; lest they should turn again, and be forgiven.

Insiders receive divine revelation: They have been given the "mystery" of the kingdom of God.

---

[1] Chiefly Mary Ann Tolbert, *Sowing the Gospel: Mark's World in Literary-Historical Perspective* (Minneapolis, MN: Augsburg Fortress, 1996).

Now, when moderns use the word "mystery," they usually mean abstruse conundra wrapped in enigmas with creamy recondite filling. We throw up our hands and say, "Welp, it's a mystery to me!" For us moderns, mystery means something we can never know, never figure out, something confusing. The appeal to mystery is understood as the last refuge of those who can't explain something, like evil or faith.

But, in Christian tradition, mysteries are rock-solid realities. They can be understood, accepted, rejected, debated, and experienced. Doctrines and sacraments are mysteries. Theologians write big books on the Trinity or on Christology, and mysteries like the Eucharist and Marriage are so tangible that Catholics take them into their very bodies. It's the Enlightenment rejection of traditional Christianity with its dogmas and rituals that makes "mystery" something opaque and turbid beyond all human ken. For Christianity, however, mysteries are two things. First, mysteries are matters of divine revelation that human reason could never discover on its own. Second, while mysteries can be known, they are inexhaustible: one can always go deeper and experience more, until the Eschaton, when we see God face to face.

Readers of Mark, as insiders, know that the mystery of the kingdom of God of which Jesus speaks is no conundrum or riddle: it's that Jesus himself is God on earth advancing the kingdom against Satan's illegitimate dominion in his apocalyptic war of liberation. More briefly, Jesus is the kingdom's divine agent.

But to outsiders, whether hostile scribes (see Mark 3:23) or curious crowds, Jesus speaks in parables. He's gotten his hand bitten by the religious leadership and runs the risk of being misunderstood as a superstar by the crowds, so now, outsiders will receive nice little stories that will cause Jesus no grief. At the end of the section on parables, Mark summarizes along the

lines of the insider–outsider divide: "With many such parables
he spoke the word to them, as they were able to hear it; he did
not speak to them without a parable, but privately to his own
disciples he explained everything" (4:33–34).

As discussed in the prior section on Mark 3:20–35, most
assume Jesus's parables are simple, clear stories making one
simple point. But for Mark's Jesus, cryptic parables exclude
the hardened, even as his message hardens, as Isaiah's message
was meant to harden: "They may indeed see but not perceive,
and may indeed hear but not understand; lest they should turn
again, and be forgiven" (4:12, quoting Isa 6:9). And yet, the
parable is not predestinatory. Mark, like Jesus, is not a Calvin-
ist. The boundary between insiders and outsiders in Mark's
Gospel will prove permeable; the disciples will act as outsiders, finally falling away, while outsiders like the hemorrhaging
woman and blind Bartimaeus will make themselves insiders,
pressing in to Jesus and getting healed.

The point of the exemplary Parable of the Sower is that, in
order to understand that parable and indeed all parables ("Do
you not understand this parable? How then will you understand all the parables?" 4:13), one must be an insider. It's a
parable about hearing parables rightly. Satan steals the word
away; tribulation withers its roots; worldly cares choke it.
Perhaps one can become good soil after all: if one persists in
seeking Jesus, one can become an insider who, like the Twelve
and those about Jesus in 4:10, receives straight revelation.
After all, Jesus did issue an invitation to the crowds: "He who
has ears to hear, let him hear."

Mark 4:21–25: Thursday of Week 3

It's natural and appropriate to the narrative, then, that Jesus presents his insiders with a series of three parables. Being insiders,

they've received the explanation of the Parable of the Sower. Having ears to hear, they hear, and now they get to hear more.

But the parables that follow aren't clear and distinct. Although given to insiders, they're cryptic and mysterious enough to invite insiders ever deeper into the mysteries of Christ and kingdom. And (true to Markan paradox and irony), in the midst of all this mysterious secrecy, they promise public revelation one day, after the crucifixion and Resurrection. Only then, when the Son of God has completed his sacrificial calling and when God the Father will have restored, redeemed, and resurrected fallen Adam in him, when misunderstanding of Jesus's mission admits no excuse, will the world enjoy public proclamation (16:7).

And so, Jesus asks his insiders an absurd rhetorical question: "Is a lamp brought in to be put under a bushel, or under a bed, and not on a stand?" (4:21). Of course not! Secrecy is temporary, strategic. One day, everything will be manifested and all secrets will come to light (4:22). And, as he did to those who heard the Parable of the Sower, Jesus here issues the invitation to hear, this time to insiders: "If any man has ears to hear, let him hear" (4:23).

Insiders now are invited to go deeper, for no one can ever exhaust the depths of Jesus Christ. The invitation is also a transition to what comes next. One should not only hear and hear well, but also consider the law of measure for measure. In this context, unlike Shakespeare's famous play, the concern isn't forgiveness, but rather understanding achieved through persistent contemplation of Christ. If insiders endeavor to understand, if they are persistent in seeking Jesus, they will be given even more.

Jesus concludes with words of promise and warning, however, for the boundary between insiders and outsiders is permeable: "For to him who has will more be given; and from him who has not, even what he has will be taken away" (4:25). What one "has" in this context is not talents or opportunities, but knowledge of Jesus Christ that leads ever deeper into him.

Here Mark reveals his Gospel to be more Catholic than many commentators would concede, like much of the New Testament. We see Markan mysticism rivaling that of the Gospel of John. We also see an operative theology of cooperation in which faithful insiders must continue to cooperate with God's grace in seeking Jesus if they wish to be saved.

Mark 4:26–34: Eleventh Sunday in Ordinary Time / Friday of Week 3

Jesus continues instructing insiders in parables. We now come to a parable that only Mark provides, the Parable of the Growing Seed. The short parable is gravid, full of suggestive significance. Like the sower, the man in this parable scatters seed and leaves the results to processes outside of his knowledge and control, processes that eventuate in harvest. In the same way, the preaching of the word is ultimately a matter of God's grace; every priest and missionary knows results are beyond his or her control.

Harvest in the New Testament always has eschatological overtones. The kingdom comes fully at the end of time thanks to God's action; human attempts to erect some sort of kingdom on earth usurp God's prerogatives and (as history attests) end in mystery. Yet, cooperation is present here too: the sower sows, farmers nurture, clergy and laypeople do the steady work of the kingdom and trust God for the results. Fidelity, not obvious success, marks the evangelizing disciple.

For us on earth beset by temptation, suffering, and failure, tempted to question and even despair as we confront the mystery of iniquity in and outside the Church, Jesus offers the hyperbolic Parable of the Mustard Seed. The kingdom starts small, with an obscure Jew in an arid Roman backwater and his failing followers but, thanks to God's grace, grows inexorably into the greatest of trees. Moreover, the tree attracts through its loving beauty, offering refuge for all the birds of the skies, an allegorical reference to those from every tribe, tongue, and nation who will come from east and west and recline at table in the eschatological kingdom of God.

But these glories are for insiders, for those who would be his disciples. Mark closes the parables chapter with a summary coda informing readers that Jesus always spoke to the wider crowds in parables but explained everything to his disciples: "With many such parables he spoke the word to them, as they were able to hear it; he did not speak to them without a parable, but privately to his own disciples he explained everything" (4:33–34). Even though Jesus has turned inward, his public ministry remains and the masses are welcome to peer through the parables, draw near to Jesus, and become insiders.

CHAPTER 4

Insiders to Outsiders, Outsiders to Insiders (Mark 4:35–8:21)

Jesus has turned inward: only those closest to him—disciples and those with him, around him, in his very presence—will receive ever deeper revelation as they encounter him directly. Yet Jesus's public activities of healing and exorcising continue, and will even expand. On one hand, those who resist and reject Jesus—namely, scribes and Pharisees—are effectively done. On the other hand, the masses are still invited to hear Jesus in parables, and if they will, they can press in to Jesus and make themselves insiders. And, on a third hand, Jesus will open up his ministry now to pagans in his voyage to the Gentile territory of the Decapolis southeast of the sea of Galilee, commissioning the Gerasene demoniac whom he exorcises, "Go home to your friends, and tell them how much the Lord has done for you, and how he has had mercy on you" (Mark 5:19).

Among his fellow Jews, however, Jesus will continue to feel rejection, especially at his hometown of Nazareth (6:1–6). We see the pattern so common to the New Testament: On the human level, Jewish rejection of the Jew Jesus leads to Gentile inclusion. And yet, on the divine level, Gentile inclusion was always part of the divine plan. The original promises to Abraham in Genesis 12:1–3 involved all the families of the earth being blessed in him (not just Israelite or Jewish families!), and prophecies like those of Isaiah promised hope for

Gentiles: Those in darkness in "Galilee of the nations" will see a great light (Isa 9:1–2 in the LXX; see Matt 4:14–16), and the Spirit-filled Servant will bring righteousness to the nations, in whose name they will hope (Isa 42:1, 4 in the LXX; see Matt 12:18–21).

Mark 4:35–41: Twelfth Sunday in Ordinary Time / Saturday of Week 3

Jesus now crosses the sea, with no pause on land, to launch a mission in the region of the Decapolis, pagan territory southeast of the Sea of Galilee. In his tale of this crossing of the sea, Mark presents the first of three boat scenes in which the disciples appear ever more thick and hard of heart. This first boat scene comes immediately after Mark has set up the insider–outsider division, and so the story begins breaking down that division immediately. The theme of discipleship failure begins precisely here (though hinted at in the mention of Judas's betrayal in Mark 3:19); from now on, the spiritual distance (represented often by physical distance) between Jesus and the disciples will increase until they all fall away.

Our technology of accurate cartography, modern watercraft, sonar, scuba gear, and deep-sea submarines has tamed the waters and disenchanted some of their mystery. For ancient people, however, the waters were dangerous and mysterious. People swam, but not very deep. God tames the waters in Genesis 1 in the unfolding process of creation, and it was the waters that all but destroyed the human race in the great Flood in Noah's day when God rewound creation, letting the waters once more take over before rebooting creation (see Gen 9, which repeats some language from Gen 1, such as the command to be fruitful and multiply). God holds back the waters of the Red Sea at the exodus and, again, the waters of the river Jordan as the Israelites enter the land. The seas were mysterious and even hostile or evil, home to Leviathan (see Ps 104:26 and especially Isa 27:1: The LORD "will slay the dragon that is in the sea") and any number of monsters and demons (see Dan 7:3).

Jesus and the disciples set out at evening, furthering the sense of mystery and danger. A great storm arises, threatening to swamp the boat and send all the seamen to the depths of terrifying doom. And so, the disciples panic while Jesus sleeps: "Teacher, do you not care if we perish?" (4:38). The situation is ironic: The seasoned fishermen who could be expected to have endured storms before panic, while Jesus the "landlubber"[1] sleeps in what's likely the driest spot in the craft. The disciples fail to trust in Jesus, while Jesus is trusting not only in their seamanship but also in the God who controls the waters.[2]

Jesus's rebuke of the wind produces a "great calm" (*galēnē megalē*, 4:39), just as the tempest was a "great storm" (*lailaps megalē*, 4:37). Further, Jesus "rebukes" (*epitimaō*) the storm, just as he "rebuked" the demons in 1:25 and 3:12. In Mark's world, everything chaotic is rooted in the satanic oppression of the cosmos: disease and death, demon possession, and even the seas. And like his restoration of the wilderness to Eden after besting Satan in the Temptation Narrative (1:13), here Jesus stills the storm to the point of perfect "peace" (4:39b).

---

[1] The use of this word for discussing these boat scenes in Mark is borrowed from Morna D. Hooker, *The Gospel According to St. Mark*, Black's New Testament Commentaries (London: Continuum, 2001), 139. According to the Oxford English Dictionary, a "lubber" is a clumsy or stupid person. *American Heritage Dictionary* (4th ed.) and *Merriam Webster Collegiate Dictionary* (11th ed.) trace the term back to the Middle English *lobur*, a "lazy lout."

[2] See Job 9:8, as well as Pss 3:5; 4:8[9]; 46:1 and 3a; 65:5; 107:23–32, esp. vv. 28–29. Some Old Testament texts ask the Lord God to awake and give aid; see Pss 35:23; 44:23–26; 59:4; and Isa 51:9. See D. E. Nineham, *Saint Mark*, The Pelican New Testament Commentaries (New York: Penguin Books, 1963), 146–47.

Jesus then accuses the disciples of having fear instead of faith: "Why are you afraid? Have you no faith?" (4:40). Here is introduced another major Markan theme, the opposition of fear and faith. The direct pairing is found twice in the Gospel, in the sandwich of the hemorrhaging woman and the raising of Jairus's daughter (see 5:33–34, 36), while "fear" is found throughout with the implication that faith is lacking (see 5:15, 6:50, 9:23, 9:32, 10:32, 11:32, and 16:8).

Faith, on the other hand, is what Jesus calls people to have in his initial announcement of the kingdom in Mark 1:15: "Repent and *believe* the gospel." Faith then achieves understanding, healing, miracles, and exorcism (see 2:5, 5:34, 9:24–27, 10:52, and 11:22–24). Faith involves the persistent seeking of Jesus, and is prior to all else; it can move mountains (11:22–24). It does not come from seeing, however. Those witnessing Christ's crucifixion are disappointed because they give priority to sight: "Let the Christ, the King of Israel, come down now from the cross that we may see and believe" (15:32).

Fear, in Mark's Gospel, is bad—it is the opposite of faith. But, like the division between insiders and outsiders, the division between faith and fear is not fixed. The hemorrhaging woman is afraid (5:33) but Jesus commends her for her faith (5:34), which he declares is what healed her. The father of the demon-possessed boy has imperfect faith—"I believe; help my unbelief!" (9:24b)—and yet Jesus exorcises the boy (9:25). So too for the disciples. While they surrender to fear here instead of exercising faith, they will still engage in mission successfully (6:7–13) and stick with Jesus almost to the end.

And yet, this first boat scene reveals their precarious spiritual position. Mark states that "they feared a great fear" (a literal translation of *ephobēthēsan phobon megan*, 4:41a). Given the negative portrayal of the disciples in Mark's Gospel, this is not religious reverence or awe. Further, their question regarding Jesus's identity—"Who then is this, that even wind and sea obey him?" (4:41b)—indicates ignorance. The disciples were among those who, in 4:10–32, had received insider information, even the mystery of the kingdom of God, and the invitation to go ever deeper into the depths of Jesus Christ.

Here, then, in the passage in which Mark's theme of discipleship failure flowers, the disciples display ignorance of Christ, ignorance that will peak when discipleship failure peaks with Peter's final words in the Gospel: "I do not know this man of whom you speak" (14:71). The disciples could have exercised faith in the midst of the storm, but they surrendered to fear and started down a bad path, a road leading far from the way of discipleship.

One final comment: Is this passage an allegory about Jesus saving the Church (represented by the boat) from its sundry storms? Some modern scholars have thought so,[3] but I think it unlikely that Mark has here composed an allegory along those lines. The characteristic literary marks of the genre of allegory are lacking. On the other hand, readers engaging in allegoresis (the allegorical reading of texts not necessarily composed as allegories) and, thus, the Church's broader interpretive tradition regarding this passage are not unjustified, and they may be justified on Mark's own terms. For Mark has invited readers as insiders in the material immediately prior to go ever deeper into the mystery of Christ and find meaning in Mark's mysteries beyond the boundaries of his Gospel.

Mark 5:1–20: Monday of Week 4

Jesus now crosses the sea to the eastern side, pagan territory. He leaves secrecy behind, and it suggests that Mark is dealing

---

[3] See Ernest Best, *Mark: The Gospel as Story* (Edinburgh, UK: T&T Clark International, 1988), 61, and Nineham, *Saint Mark*, 147.

with three categories of people: the Jewish leadership who, by their own accusations of blasphemy and murderous conspiracies, have relegated themselves to the status of outsiders; the broader crowds, who can yet make themselves insiders if they use their ears to hear; and now pagans, who get the full measure of the gospel from the demoniac, once exorcised.

Jesus here shows a striking disregard for Jewish purity law. He disembarks in an area near tombs, even though coming near a graveyard gave one corpse impurity. Further, the scene is spooky: the tombs and caves in this area would have been regarded as haunted by specters and demons. And no sooner does Jesus step on land than a demoniac greets him. All attempts at binding the man with chains have failed; readers remembering Jesus's Parable of the Strong Man in Mark 3:27 wonder here whether Jesus will be able to bind the satanic demon, given its strength.

The demoniac sees Jesus, runs up to him, and kneels before him (5:6a). Is it a demonic challenge, an attempt to defend Satan's turf, or a desperate human cry for help? Perhaps both. The demoniac is approaching Jesus as an insider would, even though he's possessed; Mark is suggesting there's enough in him to recognize in Jesus hope for his deliverance. But the demon speaks and—with no small measure of irony, given that he (they, actually) has been torturing the man—begs Jesus not to torture him (5:6b). He knows who Jesus is: Son of the Most High God, which also indicates Jesus is in pagan territory, as that title would be employed by or with reference to Gentiles.[4]

---

4   See Num 24:16; Deut 32:8; Isa 14:14; and Dan 3:26. Luke employs the phrase in his works, appropriate given their Roman setting; see Luke 1:32, 35, 75; and Acts 7:48 and 16:17.

Jesus asks for the demon's name. In our culture of casual familiarity, names are next to nothing. We engage in giving nicknames, entertainers use stage names, we come up with creative social media handles, and some people file for name changes in court. Parents get creative in naming children with appellations that have no real precedent in sacred or secular tradition. Students even expect to be on a first-name basis with their professors. Like everything else in liquid modernity, names have become plastic as culture becomes casual.

But, in the ancient world, names mattered. They had a direct relationship to the things and people they named. And (with certain exceptions) names were given, not chosen. Consider of course the great name changes in Sacred Scripture: at the most significant moments of their roles in salvation history, Abram becomes Abraham, Sarai becomes Sarah, Jacob becomes Israel, and Simon becomes Peter.

And there is power in names. According to the legend, Romulus never named what we call the eternal city "Rome." Rather, he gave it a secret name that he told no one lest, knowing the name, the city's enemies triumph against her. We just call it "Rome" after the first syllable of Romulus's name.

And so too with demons: names matter, and if the exorcist gets the name of the demon (or the demon gets the name of the exorcist), he has power over his opponent in the exorcism. That's why Jesus adjures demons to silence when they declare his divine identity, and also why he demands the demon's name in this passage.

And the demon's name is Legion, for they are many (5:9), riddling the man's mind like a corpse crawling with cockroaches. Readers cannot miss Mark's allusion to Rome. Indeed, the Tenth Legion, *Legio X Fretensis*, was stationed in Syro-Palestine from the very earliest years of the first century AD, if not earlier, and prior to that, it might have been stationed in Judea well before the time of Jesus. And one of its symbols was none other than a species of swine, the wild boar.[5]

The demons enter the pigs, and the pigs rush into the waters, meeting their demise and returning the demons to the depths of hell under the sea. The scene reminds the reader of the drowning of the Egyptian army in the Red Sea, and so we have here the theme of Mark's New Exodus. And, given the demons' name of Legion and the boar as symbol of the nearest Roman legion, the scene suggests Jesus will one day triumph over the earthly oppressors as well, not only the demonic oppressors behind them.

The herdsmen report the drama, and crowds return to find the demoniac now sitting, at peace, clothed, and sane (5:15a). He is restored, and it's likely significant that the anonymous young man who apostatizes in 14:51–52 is also described as "sitting" on the right side and "clothed" in a white robe (16:5): he too will have been restored by the coming grace of the Cross and power of the Resurrection. The demoniac's healing is a miraculous sign of the Resurrection.

All of Jesus's miracles, whether nature miracles, healings, or exorcisms, are *signs*. If the point were pure earthly mercy, Jesus could have set up a tent here and there and run every injured, sick, or demon-possessed person through and healed them. Or he could have set up a supermarket that (thinking of the feedings of the five thousand and four thousand) he could have kept perpetually stocked. But Jesus's wonders aren't ends in themselves in the moment; they're signs pointing to the reality of the Resurrection at the End, when Satan will be finally defeated, death destroyed, and all sicknesses healed and hunger banished.

---

[5] See Ched Myers, *Binding the Strongman: A Political Reading of Mark's Story of Jesus*, 2nd ed. (Maryknoll, NY: Orbis, 2008), 190–193.

The people respond poorly because, instead of exercising faith, they are "afraid" (5:15b). And so, instead of drawing close to Jesus, they beg him to leave. Unlike them, the man, now sane, begs to come with Jesus "that he might be with him" (5:18b), just as the disciples were called to "be with him" (3:14). But here Jesus refuses and instead commissions him as a missionary: "Go home to your friends, and tell them how much the Lord has done for you, and how he has had mercy on you" (5:19). And he does so, "proclaim[ing] in the Decapolis how much Jesus had done for him," with the result that "all men marveled" (5:20).

Only here does Jesus tell someone healed to proclaim what's happened to them, and it's in Gentile territory, foreshadowing the Church's mission to the Gentiles. In Mark's world, the Jewish leadership has disqualified itself, while Jewish crowds get parables, but now, here, Gentiles receive the full-throated message. And in Mark's world, this missionary's efforts bear fruit. Jesus will return to the Decapolis in Mark 7:31–37, where and when he will be received with urgency, with a deaf man brought to him straightaway for healing. The Gentile crowd will respond positively: "He has done all things well. He even makes the deaf hear and the mute speak" (7:37).

One final note: Mark's chief concern is really Christology, the identity and mission of Jesus. For Mark, Jesus is God incarnate, even though he makes the reader work for it by presenting Jesus as such through the suggestive mechanism of allusion to the Old Testament or literary design. Here, through parallelism, Mark strongly implies that Jesus Christ is the Lord, the *kurios*, of the Old Testament: "Go . . . tell them how much *the Lord* [*ho kurios*] has done for you" [5:19]; the man "proclaimed in the Decapolis how much *Jesus* had done for him" (5:20). The Gentiles, then, aren't simply to come to believe in Jesus as healer, but to lay down their gods and recognize in Jesus the Lord God Almighty of Israel, and also of them.

Mark 5:21–43: Thirteenth Sunday in Ordinary Time (5:21–43 or 5:21–24, 35b–43) / Tuesday of Week 4 (5:21–43)

In Mark 5:21–43, we encounter what many regard as Mark's best sandwich. Mark ties the two stories of sick women together tightly and constructs a narrative progression so that one cannot be understood rightly without the other. Therefore the entirety of the passage should be read as the Gospel for the day.

In the A section of the sandwich, Jesus returns to Jewish territory, having launched a mission in the pagan Decapolis. He remains popular with the crowds, and again he's crushed as soon as he disembarks (5:21). A synagogue ruler, Jairus, falls at Jesus's feet and begs him to heal his little daughter, who is at death's door (5:22). As those of faith in Mark's Gospel so often do, he approaches Jesus prostrate in the desperation of faith (as will the hemorrhaging woman), believing that Jesus can heal his daughter so that she might live (5:23).

But it's a situation of dying girl, interrupted, as in the B section, the hemorrhaging woman emerges from convalescence, fights her way through the crowd, and touches Jesus's garments. Mark describes her as desperate: bleeding for twelve years, reduced to poverty by enriching feckless physicians, and getting sicker.

Her disease means exclusion. On one hand, she's really sick and probably doesn't have a lot of company, especially given that she's bleeding from a particular orifice. Whether in her day or our day, few wish to visit the sick; it's gloomy and depressing, and few really know how to comfort the suffering in compassion. That's why it's a work of mercy. On the other hand, it's not just that her hemorrhage is a messy matter of hygiene. She's also ritually unclean, suffering from menstrual impurity, and in ancient Judaism ritual impurity is contagious. The Mishnah and the Babylonian Talmud each dedicate a tractate to the issue of *Niddah*.

Her actions, therefore, are dramatic. We can envision her emerging from her convalescence, coming out of some dwelling, out of the darkness into the light, still oozing blood, and then fighting her way through the throng, and giving everyone she comes near menstrual impurity, making no friends in the process. That's faith, in Mark's Gospel: persistence in seeking Jesus in spite of impossible odds. And her faith is rewarded: she simply touches his garments, and shazam, she's healed: "Immediately" (there's that word again) "the hemorrhage ceased; and she felt in her body that she was healed of her disease" (5:29).

Mark is weird, even bizarre sometimes. Here, an honest reading of the passage suggests Jesus honestly doesn't know who touched him. Note how he's not the active agent of her healing: "Jesus, perceiving in himself that power had gone forth from him . . ." (5:30a). The power flows from Jesus without his direct willing. And so, he asks an honest question: "Who touched my garments?" (5:30b).[6] The hapless disci-

---

[6] The question of Jesus's knowledge has proved vexing in the history of Christological reflection. The *Catechism of the Catholic Church* allows for what the Gospels suggest at various points: that Jesus, in his earthly ministry, did not possess full and perfect knowledge of everything at all times: "This human soul that the Son of God assumed is endowed with a true human knowledge. As such, this knowledge could not in itself be unlimited: it was exercised in the historical conditions of his existence in space and time. This is why the Son of God could, when he became man, 'increase in wisdom and in stature, and in favor with God and man' [Luke 2:52], and would even have to inquire for himself about what one in the human condition can learn only from experience. This corresponded to

ples think the question is absurd, given the throng, but Jesus insists now on encounter (5:31–32): it's not enough to settle for Jesus's power; one must meet Jesus himself. Jesus's works can't be cut off from his identity.

The woman keeps coming. She does so in fear and trembling, the same fear and trembling in which the women at the end of Mark's Gospel flee from the empty tomb in Mark's final instance of failure. So the no-longer-hemorrhaging-but-now-healed woman's fear is deep, as deep as fear is felt. Nevertheless, she persisted: like so many seeking healing in Mark's Gospel, like Jairus, she falls down before Jesus, and now confesses the "whole truth" (5:33). Here we see a repeated Markan theme: Faith need not be perfect in Mark's Gospel; it can be mixed with fear or doubt ("I believe; help my unbelief!" 9:24b) and remain effective. And Jesus's response is tender in its mercy: "Daughter, your faith has made you well; go in peace, and be healed of your disease" (5:34).

The A' section now interrupts with intensity just as the hemorrhaging woman interrupted Jesus: "While he was still speaking" his tender words to the woman, a group comes to inform all that Jairus's daughter has died. Theirs is a counsel of despair: "Why trouble the Teacher any further?" (5:35). But readers of Mark's Gospel know that Jesus's teaching authority is expressed in his power to heal and exorcise ("What is this? A new teaching with authority! He commands even the unclean spirits, and they obey him," 1:27). Right when Jesus is speaking words of benediction to the woman, calling her "daughter," the group informs Jairus his daughter is dead, and the reader is to imagine the two utterances of "daughter" occurring at the exact same time.

---

the reality of his voluntary emptying of himself, taking 'the form of a slave' [Phil 2:7]" (CCC §472).

The woman's interruption has cost the little girl her life: "While he was still speaking, there came from the ruler's house some who said, 'Your daughter is dead. Why trouble the Teacher any further?'" (5:35). The reader has just seen an incredible miracle: Jesus, quite apart from his own knowledge or will, has healed a desperate woman, bleeding for twelve years and impoverished from doctor's bills. But the little girl has died in the meantime. And so, in their despair the reader perceives an incipient challenge as Mark ups the ante: Jesus healed the bleeding "daughter," without even trying; but can he raise the dead daughter?

Jesus certainly thinks so. He ignores their despairing counsel of surrender to death and challenges Jairus to have faith in spite of these most impossible odds: "Do not fear, only believe" (5:36). And the story now narrows in secrecy: He brings only the inner triad of Peter, James, and John with him (5:37). Arriving at the house, they encounter the mourning one expects in the presence of a child's corpse. Yet Jesus tries to console them: "Why do you make a tumult and weep? The child is not dead but sleeping" (5:39).

Jesus here employs the common early Christian metaphor of sleep for death.[7] Of course, Jairus's daughter is truly dead, not simply "mostly dead," *Princess Bride*-style. But sleep functions as a Christian metaphor for death precisely because death is not the final end, just as we surrender to sleep every night but rise again every morning. The pattern of death and resurrection is woven into our very natures.

But the mourners think Jesus has made a pluperfect ass of

---

[7] See, for instance, 1 Cor15:51 ("Behold! I tell you a mystery. We shall not all sleep, but we shall all be changed") and Eph 5:14 ("Awake, O sleeper, and arise from the dead, and Christ shall give you light"), or in the Old Testament, Dan 12:2 ("And many of those who sleep in the dust of the earth shall awake, some to everlasting life, and some to shame and everlasting contempt").

himself, and so they mock him with derisive laughter (5:40a). (In their defense, were someone to say such things at a child's funeral at which I was present, he'd get more than mockery.) Jesus finds their lack of faith disturbing. And so, in dramatic fashion, Jesus shuts everyone outside save Peter, James, John, and the girl's parents (5:40b).

Insiders thus remain as the secret scene now narrows. Jesus brings Jairus and his wife, the girl's mother, and those "with" him—Peter, James, and John, the inner triad (see 5:37). As he did with Peter's mother-in-law, as good as dead with a fever (1:31), and will do with the apparently dead demon-possessed boy who was "like a corpse" (9:26–27), Jesus takes the girl's corpse by its dead hand (5:41a). Jesus reaches out to the dead to raise them, powerless in the rigor of death to reach out to Jesus.

He speaks Aramaic, the magical, mystical Semitic language early Christian healers and exorcists would employ; it's possible here Mark is showing them how it's done. *Tal'itha cu'mi*, Jesus pronounces, with great and immediate effect: "And immediately the girl got up and walked; for she was twelve years old" (4:41). The progression of this Markan sandwich is like a concert, or magic show, or strongman's act: each new feat is greater than the prior.

Mark translates Jesus's Aramaic with *egeirō* (as we have seen, a word for resurrection), and the little girl "rises," *anistēmi*. Like *egeirō*, *anistēmi* has a common, simple meaning: to get up or stand up. But, like *egeirō*, *anistēmi* also becomes a resurrection word: it's the word Jesus employs in his three Passion predictions when speaking of his Resurrection (8:31, 9:31, 10:34). The little girl is raised from the dead, resurrected.

And she's raised bodily; that's why Jesus tells them to give her something to eat. As every contemporary entertainment junkie knows, even zombies get hungry, so how much more a dead girl restored to real life! It is no specter or spirit here, but a corpse once more remade an animate corpus.

As so often, those witnessing are overcome with amazement, not necessarily a positive reaction, and Jesus adjures them to secrecy. If the reader wonders how such a thing could be kept quiet, it might be supposed that those who knew the girl had actually passed were few enough in number that they could keep the secret. But Mark's concern isn't even so much with such plausible realism as it is with readers willingly suspending disbelief in their encounter with Mark's iconographic stories. Jesus here is back in Jewish territory, working with someone who sought him out, and so Jairus is rewarded with his daughter's healing.

The two stories are tied tightly together, then. Both Jairus and the woman are desperate, coming to Jesus in the face of impossible odds, throwing themselves at his feet. The sandwiching of the stories involves deep dramatic effect, but Mark has done more. He has stitched the stories together. Each female is called "daughter." Each has ritual impurity: menstrual impurity in one case, corpse impurity in the other. The girl is twelve years old, and the woman had suffered twelve years. Might the same demon be at the root of the suffering of each? And might "twelve"—the number of the Apostles—suggest that the Church is the mediator of healing? And both women are restored to fullness of life by Jesus's power, which conquers here the power of death and its demonic source, the devil.

Mark 6:1–6: Fourteenth Sunday in Ordinary Time / Wednesday of Week 4

Jesus now returns to his hometown, and he will achieve nothing but his greatest failure. Again, Mark always situates stories in particular ways—by sequence, by juxtaposition, by sandwiching, by intercalation—for rhetorical effect, to shock, surprise, and teach the reader. Jesus has shown himself Almighty Lord of all in everything in the scenes leading up to Mark 6:1–6, and his rejection at Nazareth is all the more remarkable because, in Mark's world, demons are at the root of chaos, sickness, and death. In the first boat scene, Jesus has shown himself absolute master of the chaos of the cosmos, stilling the storm on the sea as Lord over nature. In the exorcism of the demoniac, Jesus has shown himself master of demons and Lord of nations. And in the healing of the hemorrhaging woman and raising of Jairus's daughter, the sandwich bringing the sequence to a crescendo, Jesus has shown himself Lord over sickness and even death.

And then he's powerless in Nazareth. Jesus and his disciples who are following him return there (6:1), and he teaches in the synagogue, and the response is one of incredulity. His hearers are querulous and resentful, as the offended and aggrieved often are (6:2b–3). Jesus, in their view, is putting on airs, getting too big for his britches, and forgetting where he came from. You can't go home again, it seems.

So Jesus delivers his famous words: "A prophet is not without honor, except in his own country, and among his own kin, and in his own house" (6:4). And note the result precisely in the words Mark employs: "And he *could do no mighty work there*, except that he laid his hands upon a few sick people and healed them" (6:5; emphasis added). And here, and only here, does Jesus himself "marvel" (*thaumazō*, 6:6a). In another moment of Markan irony, Jesus is the one who's now amazed and astounded because of the depths of their unbelief.

Mark's broader ironic point concerns faith: because of who Jesus is—Lord of all and Lord of everything, God Almighty come to earth—faith in him can even raise the dead. But some sort of faith in Jesus and his power has got to be there. And in Nazareth, it's all but absent. Nevertheless, even when people fail Jesus, he doesn't fail them. He did heal a few sick people (6:5b). And he continues his mission, as "he went about among the villages teaching" (6:6b).

Mark 6:7–13: Fifteenth Sunday in Ordinary Time / Thursday of Week 4

The Son of God goes forth to war in the following sections as Jesus, together with his disciples now, engages in another round of mission with greater energy and reach than before. The reader encounters more healings, exorcisms, and controversies. The structure of the section may not be a perfect chiasm, but its opening and closing passages are certainly meant to be read in tandem. In the opening scene of the section (6:7–13), the disciples, sent out by Jesus, experience success in mission: "And they cast out many demons, and anointed with oil many that were sick and healed them" (6:13). But, in the passage closing this section, the third boat scene, Jesus will upbraid the disciples using the severest language reserved for outsiders because they have understood neither the feedings of the five thousand and four thousand nor Jesus's words about the leaven of the Pharisees and Herod (8:14–21).

We now encounter another Markan sandwich of particularly profound import. In Mark 6:7–13, the A section, Jesus sends the disciples out two by two on his mission of preaching and teaching, healing, and exorcising. In 6:14–29, the B section, the death of John the Baptist at the hands of Herod Antipas is finally told. In 6:30 (and possibly as far as 6:44, which would include the feeding of the five thousand), the A' section, the Twelve return to Jesus and report everything they did and taught. We have here an iconic verbal triptych, in the center of which stands the martyrdom of Jesus's forerunner, John the Baptist, which stands in parallel with, and thus

157

foreshadows in many particulars, Jesus's own death. The point of this triptych, this sandwich, is that sacrificial death powers Christian mission, that the advance of the kingdom in Christ's holy war that is marked by the healings and exorcisms will be consummated by his victorious death.

The first item of the disciples' threefold calling was simply to "be with" Jesus, and then to preach and to exorcise (3:14). Having completed their apprenticeship, Jesus now begins to send them out. He does so "two by two," reminiscent of the legal requirements for valid testimony (see Deut 19:15), and, practically speaking, working in pairs allows for mutual support and permits the coverage of more territory. The reader here has a sense of expanding ministry, of Jesus, his message, and his mighty works going beyond what has gone before. And it is ultimately Jesus who is going with them, Jesus they are bringing with them: the Twelve as missionaries have derivative authority given by Jesus himself (6:7b).

The disciples travel light, at Jesus's command, bringing nothing but a staff and sandals and a single tunic (6:8–9). The staff is of course a symbol of authority (see Gen 49:10, Exod 4:20), but also a weapon, which is not without significance, given that Jesus and the Twelve are engaged in holy war against the satanic hordes. Leaving bag, bread, and money behind means they must count on divine provision and human hospitality: mission operates best out of a position of poverty and humility. Further, in this greater section in the Gospel, Mark demonstrates in the two major feeding stories that God does indeed provide (6:30–44 and 8:1–10).

By this point in the Gospel, readers have seen that rejection of Jesus has the consequence of relegation to outsider status. So too here: rejection of Jesus's disciples, the Twelve, who are to shake the dust off their feet as classic symbolic testimony against those who reject them (6:11), means rejecting

Jesus. Yet the passage records not opposition but success: the disciples preach repentance (6:12), like John the Baptist and Jesus before them (1:4, 15), as the kingdom advances and John and Jesus's ministries bear fruit in the disciples, and succeed in exorcising demons and healing the sick by anointing (6:13).

This episode is the disciples' first and last success in Mark's Gospel, however. From here on out, they will fail in multifold ways. They will try one more time in Mark's Gospel to perform an exorcism in the case of the demonized boy (9:14–29) but will fail: the boy's father informs Jesus, "I asked your disciples to cast it out, and they were not able" (9:18b).

But the story isn't there yet. Rather, the present passage is a moment of triumph and hope, reminding readers that there is great spiritual power available for those who abide in Jesus and evangelize in his name. Indeed, so much for secrecy, as the mighty deeds done by Jesus's disciples have risen even to the ears of Herod Antipas (6:14).

Mark 6:14–29: Friday Week of 4 / The Passion of St. John the Baptist (6:17–29)

The relating of John the Baptist's death is the B section of the sandwich, the main panel of this iconic triptych. The sandwich means mighty works wrought by the disciples in the previous passage are the fruit of fearless fidelity in proclamation, suffering, and death, exemplified by John, forerunner of Jesus.

A literary artist, Mark is about to mess with narrative time. This passage will finally relate what ultimately happened with John the Baptist after his arrest, mentioned way back in Mark 1:14. But it's set up here as a flashback: Herod (Antipas, son of Herod the Great and brother of Herod Philip, whose wife, Herodias, he stole, forsaking his own wife, a daughter of the Nabatean king Aretas IV) hears of the disciples' working of these signs and wonders and credits it to John the Baptist being raised from the dead (6:16). Why?

Following Herod's declaration, readers learn what happened to John the Baptist, as Mark now tells us in detail. In summary, in a moment of weakness, Herod had John summarily executed as an impromptu part of an evening's entertainment. But why does Mark tell the story now? To suggest that death brings life and, John being Jesus's forerunner, that, after Jesus's death and Resurrection, such healing signs and wonders will advance the kingdom of God throughout the world. The prior passage in Mark 6:7–13 thus foreshadows the successful mission of the Church (represented by the apostolic Twelve, its first bishops and priests), and in a way, Herod is ironically right: John the Baptist has been raised after a fashion in Jesus, for whom John served as prophetic forerunner. Jesus continues John's ministry of proclamation even while transcending it with healings and exorcisms and expanding it by doing so through his disciples, his Church.

The scene connects John's and Jesus's stories deliberately, foreshadowing what will happen to Jesus. Indeed, the responses to Jesus's inquiry at Caesarea Philippi about what people think about his identity ("Who do men say that I am?") in Mark 8:27–30 are first found here in 6:14–16. In both passages, people reportedly think Jesus is (1) John the Baptist raised again, (2) Elijah, or (3) one of the prophets (compare 6:14b–15 with 8:28). Next, Herod identifies Jesus with John the Baptist raised from the dead (6:16), while Peter will identify Jesus as the Christ (8:29b). Finally, the circumstances of John the Baptist's death are related (6:17–29), standing in parallel with Jesus's first Passion prediction (8:31).

Mark then informs readers that Herod imprisoned John at the behest of Herodias, Philip's lawful wife whom Herod stole, for condemning the marriage (6:18), which violates Levitical law (Lev 18:16 and especially 20:21). Herodias, *femme fatale*, wants John dead, while Herod does not (6:19-20). Herod "knows" John is "a righteous and holy man" (6:20), and yet, when push comes to shove, he chooses the expediency of summary execution over principle.

Pilate knows and does likewise. He tries to get Jesus released, as he knew "it was out of envy that the chief priests had delivered him up" (15:10), and yet, like Herod, also chooses the broad path of expediency: "Pilate, wishing to satisfy the crowd, released for them Barab'bas; and having scourged Jesus, he delivered him to be crucified" (15:15).

There's more. John dies alone, like Jesus in Mark's Gospel. And as in Jesus's crucifixion, all humanity is implicated as complicit in the crime. Pilate, the Roman, accedes to the desires of the chief priests and crowd that Jesus be crucified. Herod Antipas, a partial Jew ruling at Rome's behest, accedes to the women's demand that John be beheaded so as not to suffer embarrassment in front of "his courtiers and officers and the leading men of Galilee" (6:21)—precisely the "Herodians" who conspire with the Pharisees to murder Jesus in 3:6, the Pharisees against whose leaven Jesus will warn in 8:15, and who will try to trap Jesus in 12:13 with their question about paying taxes to Caesar. In both executions, Jews conspire with Gentiles, thus representing all humanity, to kill those sent to redeem humanity.

Herod's craven caving to the wicked whims of his wife reminds readers of another royal power couple, Ahab and Jezebel. Jezebel orchestrates Naboth's murder and incites Ahab to take possession of his vineyard (1 Kings 21:1-16), and Elijah is sent to condemn Ahab and Jezebel for their crime (1 Kings 21:17-26). John is, in Mark's world, Elijah come again,[8] and so Herod and Herodias are a new Ahab and Jezebel.

The sumptuous luxury of the banquet contrasts with John's austerity but finds parallels in Jesus's own festive feasting (see Mark 2:15–22), which prefigures the sacrificial meal of the Eucharist. Thus a macabre contrast is established between Herod's banquet and Jesus's Eucharistic banquet. John's head is produced on a platter as if it's the next course of the night's meal, perhaps best accompanied with some fava beans and a nice Chianti, while Jesus gives his own Body and Blood in his sacred sacrificial meal.

Finally, while John and Jesus suffer deaths of extreme indignity, they both enjoy dignified burials. "When [John's] disciples heard of it, they came and took his body, and laid it in a tomb" (6:29), just as Joseph of Arimathea laid Jesus's crucified body in a tomb (15:46).

Mark 6:30–44: Sixteenth Sunday in Ordinary Time / Saturday of Week 4 (6:30–34) / Tuesday after Epiphany [or January 8] (6:34–44)

We now encounter the A' section of the sandwich: "The apostles returned to Jesus, and told him all that they had done and taught" (6:30). The extent of this section of the sandwich is debated; many commentators extend it through 6:31, as Jesus and his disciples depart by boat in 6:32. And yet the verses flow logically into one another. In 6:33, it is related that "many saw them going" and arrived ahead of the boat; there's no clear spatial break. And so, as Jesus disembarks, he encounters a large crowd and has compassion on them and teaches them (6:34).

The lectionary breaks off here for the sixteenth Sunday in Ordinary Time and Saturday of week 4, but Mark contin-

---

[8]   See the discussion of Mark 1:6 above on pp. 83–87.

ues with the feeding of the five thousand (the reading for the Tuesday after Epiphany or January 8), organically tied to the preceding verses. The scene continues in Mark 6:35, but now it's much later in the day, and so the disciples encourage Jesus to dismiss the hungry crowds (6:36). Jesus responds by launching the feeding of the five thousand by telling the disciples to feed the crowds themselves (6:37), which Jesus then performs himself (6:38–44).

And so, preachers must decide whether to treat only the verses the lectionary provides, Mark 6:30–34, or (as is perfectly legitimate) to also discuss the feeding of the five thousand in their homily. My own judgment is that the third part of the sandwich, indeed, the third panel of this triptych, extends all the way through the feeding of the five thousand. As the feeding is profoundly Eucharistic, it would suggest that the ultimate culmination of the disciples' mission that began in Mark 6:7–13, was reported in 6:30, and continues into our present—and thus of all Christian mission—is the Eucharist, which is of course the "source and summit of Christian life."[9]

The disciples have returned to Jesus with reports of "all they had done and taught" (6:30). In the A section of the sandwich, Jesus had given them authority to exorcise (6:7), but then they actually perform exorcisms and healings (6:13). In this A' section, the disciples also report all they had *taught*. And so, again, Mark's Gospel shows that teaching isn't so much words, but deeds: what Jesus and his disciples teach by their exorcisms and healings is that Jesus himself has the ultimate power and authority (1:27) to advance the kingdom of God by those mighty works. The wondrous deeds display the content of the teaching.

The "wilderness," the "desert," the "desolate place," and

---

9   Second Vatican Council, Dogmatic Constitution on the Church, *Lumen Gentium* (November 21, 1964), §11 (quoted in *CCC* §1324).

the "lonely place," as here in Mark 3:31, are all *erēmos* in Greek, a major Markan motif. At the beginning, Mark provides the prophecy of one crying in the *erēmos* to prepare the way of the Lord (1:3), and John shows up in the *erēmos* baptizing. After Jesus is baptized there, the Spirit drives him deeper into the *erēmos*, where he spends forty days deadlocked in a contest with Satan (1:12), and he emerges victorious, having pacified it: "and he was with the wild beasts; and the angels ministered to him" (1:13).

Many commentators think what we have in that passage is Jesus in some way restoring Eden, having tamed the wild beasts, like Adam in Eden was present with the beasts (Gen 2:18–20). It would then be no accident that, after this initial pacification, the *erēmos* is a place of prayer and refuge for Jesus and the disciples. For instance, Jesus goes alone to the *erēmos* for deep prayer in Mark 1:35. And so, in our passage, Jesus calls the disciples to an *erēmos* for the sake of rest.

They can rest there because he's tamed it. It's been cleared of Satan. It's pacified. The word for "rest" here, *anapauō*, is the very word used in the Greek Old Testament for the Sabbath rest God commands in Deuteronomy's version of the Third Commandment (Deut 5:14; cf. Exod 23:12). Given how the exorcisms and healings point to the conditions of the eschaton, and given that the concept of Sabbath rest becomes a model for that perfect rest the saints achieve in heavenly eternity,[10] where Satan has been conquered and sickness and death are no more, the disciples here enter a sort of heavenly rest foreshadowing the eschaton.

And in the Old Testament, God himself is the giver of rest: "My presence will go with you, and I will give you rest" (Exod 33:14). Could Mark's text here suggest Jesus's divine identity?

---

[10] See Hebrews 4:1–13; see also St. Augustine, *Confessions* 13.

If so, it would be no accident that Jesus has "compassion" on the crowds, for compassion (Hebrew *hesed*) is a major, if not *the* major, attribute of God in the Old Testament.

Jesus may be God himself come in compassion to care for the crowds, who figured out where Jesus was going in the boat and beat him there. Again, in a sign of the success of the disciples' preaching of repentance (6:12), Jesus proves so popular that he and his disciples can't even eat (6:31; see 3:20), and the crowds following him form a "great throng" as Jesus lands (6:34).

The throng arouses Jesus's compassion because they are "like sheep without a shepherd" (6:34), a phrase found throughout the Old Testament when Israel's leadership has proven feckless and derelict (see Num 27:17, 1 Kings 22:17, Ezek 34:8, and Zech 10:2). In such passages and others, God himself promises to shepherd his people directly: "Behold, I, I myself will search for my sheep, and will seek them out. As a shepherd seeks out his flock when some of his sheep have been scattered abroad, so will I seek out my sheep; and I will rescue them" (Ezek 34:11–12a).

His compassion takes the form of teaching (6:34) as the passage begins to slip into the feeding of the five thousand. As so often, he here teaches by deed, showing the crowds that his person and power is the content of his teaching. Jesus will display that he himself is God come to shepherd and feed his people, fulfilling Ezekiel's prophecy:

> I will feed them on the mountains of Israel. . . . I will feed them with good pasture. . . . There they shall lie down in good grazing land. . . . I myself will be the shepherd of my sheep, and I will make them lie down, says the LORD GOD. (Ezek 34:13b–15)

Ezekiel's prophecies are paramount for understanding the feeding of the five thousand, and the passage presents a Jesus and Eucharist every bit as divine and sacramental as St. John does in his famous sixth chapter.

In fact, with this feeding, we enter a section of Mark's Gospel in which the theme of bread (*artos*, "bread" or "loaf") dominates, the "bread section" (6:33–8:26) beginning with the feeding of the five thousand and ending with Jesus upbraiding the seaborne disciples for misunderstanding his dire warning about the yeast of the Pharisees and Herod (8:14–21). In that story, Jesus accuses the disciples of having eyes that do not see and ears that do not hear (8:18), and it's no accident that the broader bread section (6:33–8:26) includes Jesus's healing of a deaf man (7:31–37, a story found only in Mark's Gospel) and transitions into the famous discipleship section (8:22–10:52) with the odd story of the two-stage healing of a blind man (8:22–26). Jesus is God himself come to feed his people, but the disciples grow spiritually thicker, and yet there's hope for them because he can unstop the ears of the deaf and open the eyes of the blind.

Indeed, the feeding of the five thousand stands in obvious parallel with the later feeding of the four thousand and its context (8:1–30). Mary Healy observes: "Twice Jesus miraculously feeds a multitude with a few loaves and fish, each time followed by a crossing of the lake, a conflict with Pharisees, a healing, and finally a confession of faith." Why would Mark do this? "It is as if Jesus had to repeat the sequence for its full significance to dawn on his disciples."[11] Too bad it doesn't.

How, then, does the feeding of the five thousand present us with a divine, Eucharistic Jesus? The feeding occurs in the

---

[11] Mary Healy, *The Gospel of Mark*, Catholic Commentary on Sacred Scripture (Grand Rapids, MI: Baker Academic, 2008), 124.

erēmos, where, in Exodus 16, God fed the Israelites manna from heaven, which later biblical tradition calls "grain from heaven" and the very "bread of the angels" (Ps 78:24–25), and indeed, "food of angels" (Wis 16:20–21).

In Mark 6:39, Jesus has the crowd "recline" (*anaklinō*), suggestive of a banquet, as Jews and others in the ancient world reclined to eat, and he arranges them in groups, as the Israelites were arranged in groups in the desert (Exod 18:21–25). They recline on the "green grass," which not only recalls the mention of good pasture of Ezekiel's prophecy but also emphasizes the eschatological nature of the Eucharist, an eternal springtime.

Jesus then employs the language of the Eucharistic ritual to bless the bread and fish. Mark's version of the institution of the Eucharist reads: "And as they were eating, he *took* bread, and *blessed*, and *broke* it, and *gave* it to them" (14:22; emphasis added). In the feeding of the five thousand, Mark writes: "And *taking* the five loaves and the two fish he looked up to heaven, and *blessed*, and *broke* the loaves, and *gave* them to the disciples to set before the people." Jesus then "divided the two fish among them all" (6:41; emphasis added).

Why five loaves and two fish? This miracle of loaves reminds readers of Elisha's smaller miracle in 2 Kings 4:42–44, in which twenty barley loaves fed a century of men. Perhaps it's no accident that John, Jesus's forerunner, comes as Elijah, Elisha's forerunner. But another complementary option is also operative: the five loaves are the Mosaic Torah, a longstanding interpretation in Christian tradition.[12]

---

[12] St. Anthony of Padua writes, "The five loaves represent the five books of Moses, in which we find five refreshments for the soul" (*Sermons for Sundays and Festivals*, vol. 1, trans. Paul Spilsbury (Padua, IT: Edizioni Messaggero Padova, 2007), 180–181.

What of the two fish? In Christian tradition, we find a stream that explains the number two as indicating that the Church fed by Jesus's Eucharist includes both Jews and Gentiles. Further, it's possible that the fish symbolize Jesus himself. The symbol of the fish for Jesus—the Greek ΙΧΘΥΣ (*ichthus*) being an acrostic meaning "Jesus Christ God's Son Savior," immortalized in our day on the back of many a homeschool van—is ancient, simply assumed by Clement of Alexandria (AD 150–215)[13] and Tertullian (ca. AD 155–225),[14] and found in Priscilla's catacombs associated with the feeding of the five thousand. It could be that the acrostic symbol of the fish for Jesus is apostolic, generated perhaps by this very miracle.

God provided manna to the Israelites as "food in abundance" (Ps 78:25); Jesus provides the crowds a superabundance, more than they can possibly consume, satisfying all, with twelve baskets left over (6:43). The leftovers (if you will) of the twelve baskets represent the abundance Jesus will continue to provide his Church, the new Israel led by the Twelve Apostles and their successors, in the Eucharist: Jesus will continue to feed his gathered people as Ezekiel's divine shepherd.

And Jesus will do so through the Church. Note also that he has the disciples distribute the bread and then gives the fish to all himself, the idea being that Jesus is with his Church feeding his people through it. The Church mediates Jesus and his gifts.

---

[13] Clement of Alexandria writes, "And let our seals be . . . a fish" (*Paedagogus* 3.11, in *ANF*, 2:285).

[14] Tertullian writes, "But we, little fishes, after the image of our ΙΧΘΥΣ Jesus Christ, are born in water, nor have we safety in any other way than by permanently abiding in water" (*On Baptism* 1, trans. S. Thelwall, in *ANF*, 3:669).

Finally, Mark mentions that the miracle met the needs of five thousand *men*—in Greek, *anēr*, "male."[15] Five thousand men would roughly be the number of soldiers in a Roman legion by the age of Augustus, and legions sometimes swelled larger. It's possible we're dealing here with an incipient rebellion, especially as a leader organizing sheep without a shepherd in the Old Testament context often involves consideration of war (see Nah 3:18 and 1 Kings 22:17, with attention to context), and especially as the violent anti-Roman zealot movement started in Galilee, founded by Judas the Galilean in AD 6.[16] It's small wonder that the Jewish and Roman leadership would be concerned about a messianic pretender from Galilee. But it's all the more ironic, then, that they would crucify that pretender, Jesus, instead of Barabbas, a true murderer and revolutionary (15:7).

Many commentators will point out that Jesus refuses to take up military leadership and instead feeds these incipient insurrectionists with his teaching and with bread. The tradition begins with St. John, who makes Jesus's rejection of military-political leadership clear in his coda to his telling of the feeding: "Perceiving then that they were about to come and take him by force to make him king, Jesus withdrew again to the hills by himself" (John 6:15). Yet, Jesus is no pacifist when it comes to his apocalyptic holy war against sin, death, hell, and the devil. The military resonances of God mustering his scattered people as their divine shepherd are here, as Jesus has cleared the *erēmos* of Satan and given his people a foreshadowing of the holy sacrifice of the Mass, with which his Church will wage spiritual war. And instead of mustering for

---

[15] Observe that St. Matthew emphasizes that the numbers fed were males by adding "besides women and children" as a coda at the end of his versions of the feedings of the five and four thousand (Matt 14:21 and 15:38).

[16] See Flavius Josephus, *Wars of the Jews* 2.118.

war to liberate the Jews from Roman domination, Jesus would have them muster for spiritual war to liberate all humanity from satanic domination.

Mark 6:45–52: Wednesday after Epiphany (or January 9)

Mark's second boat scene is crucial for understanding the Gospel's broader narrative, and especially its Christology, for the scene presents Jesus as fully divine while showing the fearful disciples as dull to that reality.

The scene is a theophany in which Jesus would display his divine nature to the disciples, as if to answer the question they posed in the first boat scene: "Who then is this, that even wind and sea obey him?" (4:41b). But the disciples, caving to fear rather than exercising faith, mistake him for a phantasm and miss the theophany. Jesus nevertheless encourages them and informs them of his identity ("It is I," 6:50), upon which the wind ceases. The disciples suffer extreme astonishment because they lack understanding about the loaves and have hard hearts.

The pattern is similar to that of chapter four. The Parable of the Sower therein ends on a note of abundance ("And other seeds fell into good soil and brought forth grain, growing up and increasing and yielding thirtyfold and sixtyfold and a hundredfold," Mark 4:8; see 4:20), but the disciples later display incomprehension in the boat on the sea. So too with the feeding of the five thousand, where, in the wake of abundance, the disciples show their incomprehension in the boat on the sea.

Allusions to the Old Testament reveal the scene is a theophany, a manifestation of God. First, walking on the sea may not be strange for Jesus, but Mark's remark that "he intended to pass them by" (*parelthein autous*) is at least for many modern readers. But here, we have the LXX of Job 9:8 and 11 in play. In those verses, Job declares God treads the waves of the sea as God passes him by (*parelthē me*), but Job neither sees nor perceives him, just as Jesus treads the waves of the sea in this boat scene but the disciples do not perceive him.

Second, beyond that most direct allusion, *parerchomai* is the same word God uses when promising Moses in Exodus 33:22 that he will "pass by" him to reveal his divine glory (see Exod 34:6 for the fulfillment). And third, when Jesus informs them "It is I" (6:50), he's taking the divine name on his lips. In Mark's Greek, Jesus utters *egō eimi*, which is the divine name given by God to Moses in Exodus 3:14. In light of the other theophanic motifs and allusions in the passage, we ought to hear the divine name in Jesus's utterance here. Scripture always operates on both literal and spiritual levels, and so here we hear not only the literal level of Jesus announcing he's not a phantasm but the Jesus they know, but also that Jesus is God, the Jesus they don't yet know.

Jesus's divine identity explains the remark that they missed the theophany because "they did not understand about the loaves" (6:52). What did they not understand? It is that, in the feeding of the five thousand, Jesus already revealed himself as the divine shepherd feeding his people. Had they perceived that, they would have perceived the theophany. They hadn't, so they didn't, and having hardened hearts (6:52), they're at risk of apostasy.

Mark 6:53–56: Monday of Week 5

The boat traverses the northern side of the lake,[17] Jesus now wishing to continue his evangelization of greater Galilee; he wants to bring his divine power to all. Jesus goes everywhere—the villages, the cities, the country (6:56). It's as if he's engaging in a sort of *praeparatio evangelica* of Galilee, laying the groundwork for mission based there after the Resurrection, when the women and the disciples and especially Peter are to return there, as instructed by the young man at the empty tomb (16:7).

And the people respond. They recognize Jesus (6:54), unlike the disciples in the prior boat scene, who mistook the divine Son of God for a ghost (6:49). And they recognize the divine power in him, bringing Jesus their sick on mats, much like the friends of the paralytic did in 2:4. It's implied they have real faith. Indeed, the scene is frenzied, as the people "ran about the whole neighborhood and began to bring sick people on their pallets to any place where they heard he was" (6:55). The people display extreme faith, while the disciples are conspicuous by the absence of any mention of them in the passage.

Here widens the chasm between insiders and outsiders, but again in an ironic way. In Mark 4, the crowds received only parables, not direct revelation like the disciples, because the disciples were those who chose to be insiders by being with Jesus. But, since the first boat scene, and especially in the second, the disciples have been showing themselves ever more to be outsiders, while now the crowd presses in on him in faith

---

[17] If we understand *pros Bēthsaidan* in Mark 6:45 to mean "opposite of" or "across from Bethsaida," Jesus has not changed course at seeming random when he and the disciples land at Genessaret in Mark 6:53, nor would we have any contradiction with Luke 9:10–12, which places the feeding near Bethsaida on the northeast side of the Sea of Galilee.

seeking healing. Much like the hemorrhaging woman in Mark 5, they make themselves insiders. And so, like the hemorrhaging woman, who believed merely touching his garments would suffice for her healing (5:28), the crowds too believe they need only have their sick touch the tassels of Jesus's clothing to be healed. That's faith.

Further, for Catholics, it's obvious that, in passages such as this, we have scriptural roots for sacraments and even relics. Material things can mediate divine power. And, when tangible things that have touched Jesus and saints bring healing, those healings aren't merely ends in themselves good for people in the here and now, but signs of the eschatological healing Jesus will one day bring to the cosmos.

The crowds have faith not in faith (as many Americans understand faith as the power of belief itself) but faith precisely in Jesus. And the tassels (*kraspedon*, "fringes" in some translations) of Jesus's garment are significant here. These are the four tassels that pious Jews like Jesus would wear at the corners of their garment in obedience to God's instructions in Numbers 15:38-41:

> Speak to the sons of Israel, and bid them to make tassels on the corners of their garments throughout their generations, and to put upon the tassel of each corner a cord of blue; and it shall be to you a tassel to look upon and remember all the commandments of the LORD, to do them, not to follow after your own heart and your own eyes, which you are inclined to go after wantonly. So you shall remember and do all my commandments, and be holy to your God. I am the LORD your God, who brought you out of the land of Egypt, to be your God: I am the LORD your God.

Mark presents Jesus here as a pious Jew who obeys the commandment of wearing tassels and whose wearing of tassels signifies his obedience to the commandments. In doing so, Mark sets up the following passage, in which Jesus will face off with the Pharisees and scribes in a dispute about the tradition of the elders (7:1–23). Jesus, not the Pharisees and scribes, is the embodiment of faithful Israel.

Mark 7:1–8, 14–15, 21–23: Twenty-Second Sunday in Ordinary Time / Tuesday of Week 5 (7:1–13)

Now the Pharisees and certain scribes from Jerusalem (like those who accused him of being possessed in Mark 3:22) arrive to confront Jesus, annoyed that some of his disciples don't follow the rules of ritual washing before eating. It's likely they witnessed or heard of the feeding of the five thousand, which wouldn't have involved any washing. (Both the feeding of the five thousand and this passage mention eating "breads"; see 6:41, 44 and 7:2, 5, respectively.) The rules for washing in the Mosaic Torah applied to priests alone, but a major component of the Pharisees' program involved extending priestly Temple sanctity and, thus, ritual purity to all Jews around the world,[18] and so they're annoyed with Jesus.

In the prior passage, Mark mentioned Jesus's "tassels" (*kraspedon*) to indicate Jesus obeyed the Mosaic Torah (see Num 15:38–41) and to suggest, by juxtaposition with this controversy passage, that Jesus, not the Pharisees and scribes, is faithful to God and his law. And so, Jesus quotes Isaiah against them after calling them hypocrites: "This people honors me

---

[18] See Jacob Neusner, *From Politics to Piety: The Emergence of Pharisaic Judaism*, repr. (Eugene, OR: Wipf and Stock, 2003), esp. 144–46 (for a succinct summary of this central thesis of Neusner's book).

with their lips, but their heart is far from me; in vain do they worship me, teaching as doctrines the precepts of men" (7:6–7), and declares that their adherence to human traditions means they've abandoned the clear command of God (7:8).

Why "hypocrites?" Many Americans misread Jesus's charges of hypocrisy in the Gospels, for Americans above all other peoples abhor hypocrisy. For Americans, hypocrisy is failing to walk the talk, to put one's money where one's mouth is. For Jesus, however, it's not quite that. The Pharisees were in fact righteous by the standards of the law; Paul could even write that when he was a Pharisee, he kept the law flawlessly (Phil 3:5b–6). But for Jesus, the problem is twofold: Their traditions contradicted the plain law of God (that's the import of the *corban* discussion in Mark 7:9–13), and their hearts weren't in line with their exterior piety. Their problem is formalism without deep interiority.

For a few hundred years, and especially in America, religion has been reduced to a matter of the heart, with the concomitant denigration of ritual, and that's involved a deep misreading of Jesus. But Jesus doesn't do this; he doesn't desire a purely interior religion of the heart that dispenses with exterior ritual and piety. Were that the case, he wouldn't have made a ritual sacrificial meal the centerpiece of his Church's existence, as he does in instituting the Eucharist as an ongoing ritual in Mark 14:22–25. Rather, Jesus desires that one's interior and exterior align and function in harmony.

And so he calls the people together for an emphatic message: "Hear me, all of you, and understand" (7:14). He declares that "there is nothing outside a man which by going into him can defile him; but the things which come out of a man are what defile him" (7:15). And although the lectionary elides the setting for what follows, in the house with his insiders the disciples, he explains: "For from within, out of the heart of man, come evil thoughts, fornication, theft, murder, adultery, coveting, wickedness, deceit, licentiousness, envy, slander, pride, foolishness. All these evil things come from within, and they defile a man" (7:21–23).

Instead of developing human traditions based on biblical law and binding them to those for whom they were never intended like the Pharisees and scribes, Jesus would have his followers focus on the conversion of the heart, precisely so that their outward lives line up with their pure hearts. But ritual can effect that: liturgy and sacraments work on the heart through the body and its senses. We aren't just hearts, but bodies too, and so Jesus establishes a faith, a religion, that involves the body. He gave his very body at the crucifixion, gives us his Body and Blood in the Eucharist, and will raise our bodies at the end of time.

Yet Jesus does do something radical: Mark states that, by his teaching in this controversy, Jesus "declared all foods clean" (7:19). That's nothing less than a declaration that the dietary laws of the written Old Testament given by God to Moses are now irrelevant.

Now irrelevant. We must understand salvation history here and Jesus's role in it, lest we make Jesus into a postmodern cynic, an antinomian who breaks rules and boundaries as a matter of general principle. After all, Jesus didn't read a lot of French and Bulgarian theory. That's not why he declares all foods clean, tossing much of Moses out the window while he wears his tassels. The reason is that the Mosaic law—indeed, the entire Old Testament—is fulfilled in him.

Christians must read the Old Testament through Jesus, and that means dividing the Old Testament law into three parts. First, Jesus fulfills sacrificial law. The sacrifices and their rituals point to Jesus's crucifixion and Eucharist. They're not abolished so much as fulfilled. Second, Jesus and the early

Church following his example both intensify the moral law and make it an interior matter, as in the Sermon on the Mount in Matthew 5, or his teaching on the indissolubility of marriage in Mark 10:1-12, or the conclusion the Church comes to regarding rules for Gentile Christians in Acts 15. Christian sexuality, in particular, holds to a higher standard than one finds in the Old Testament.

Third, at issue here are what we might call "ethnic" aspects of the law. Those laws pertaining to diet and dress, for instance, are simply done away with by Jesus for the Church. They served to keep Israel separate from the nations lest they become like the nations and fall into idolatry. But Jesus is the Savior of all, Jew and Gentile, and dietary laws given only to Israel under the old covenant to keep them separate would fracture the unity of Jew and Gentile in the Church. And so, with Jesus's advent and his founding of the universal Church, they pass away.

This analysis bears on reading the import of Jesus's relationship to the Pharisees (and scribes) today, for many find in their conflict a model: Jesus is the great lawbreaker, the one who transgresses any and all rules, while Pharisees are those who insist on rules and teaching in a rigid way. And so Catholics or other Christians who obey Church teaching and practice often endure "Pharisee" as an epithet. But Catholics aren't being Pharisaic or legalistic or rigid when they insist on holding to what Jesus himself teaches through Scripture and Tradition; rather, those who employ casuistry and consequentialism to evade what Jesus himself teaches the Church are closer to the spirit of the rigid, legalistic Pharisees, who use human concerns to "void the word of God" (Mark 7:13) as given to the Church by Jesus through Scripture and Tradition.

Further, many lay Catholics often feel uneasy when confronted with this passage, for it lends itself at first glance to a sort of naïve Protestant reading that would pit Scripture (and Jesus) against any and all traditions. But, if the passage is read rightly on its own terms, Jesus here condemns those human traditions that would violate the word of God, whether this word is found in the Old Testament, from Jesus himself, or in the Church he founded through which he speaks. For Catholics, Jesus fulfills and interprets the Old Testament and establishes the Church to which he gives Tradition. Jesus, Scripture, Tradition, and magisterium therefore form a seamless whole. As the Catechism teaches, following the Second Vatican Council:

> It is clear therefore that, in the supremely wise arrangement of God, sacred Tradition, Sacred Scripture and the Magisterium of the Church are so connected and associated that one of them cannot stand without the others. Working together, each in its own way, under the action of the one Holy Spirit, they all contribute effectively to the salvation of souls. (*CCC* §95, quoting *Dei Verbum* §10)

Mark 7:14–23: Wednesday of Week 5

See the treatment of Mark 7:1–23 above for the texts assigned for the twenty-second Sunday in Ordinary Time and Tuesday of week 5. The passage for today consists of Jesus's urgent admonition ("Hear me, all of you, and understand") to comprehend that the heart is prior, that defilement (contrary not only to Pharisaic interpretive tradition but also the Mosaic Torah) is not a matter of eating unclean food, but one of sin in the heart.

While the lectionary omits it for the Sunday reading, here the Markan text operates again with the distinction between insiders and outsiders. Jesus enters a house, explicitly leaving the people behind (7:17), and then his disciples pose a question "about the parable," as they did in 4:10 regarding the Parable of the Sower. Jesus's opening words to them are harsh: "Then are you also without understanding? Do you not see . . . ?" (7:18).

Here we see again the language of perception ("see") linked with understanding. In the next and final boat scene, Jesus will ask them if they in fact neither see nor hear nor understand. This passage, then, emphasizes the theme of the disciples' growing incomprehension. On that score, this passage makes for an interesting contrast with Mark 4:1–20. There it was presumed they would understand: there wasn't a hint of incomprehension until the first boat scene at the end of the chapter in 4:35–41.

Like the explanation of the Parable of the Sower in Mark 4:13–20, here Jesus privately expands upon his public words, giving a traditional vice list explaining what he meant by defilement.[19]

Mark 7:24–30: Thursday of Week 5

Jesus now deliberately travels roughly forty or fifty miles northwest, deep into Gentile territory. The text does not hint at any specific reason why Jesus would go to Gentile territory, but the juxtaposition with the prior story of conflict with the scribes and Pharisees fits the New Testament pattern of Jewish resistance to Jesus leading to Gentile inclusion.

Jesus is trying to keep his presence secret: "And he entered

---

[19] The New Testament contains twenty-three vice lists: Matt 15:19; Mark 7:21–22; Rom 1:29–31; 13:13; 1 Cor 5:10–11; 6:9–10; 2 Cor 6:9–10; 12:20–21; Gal 5:19–21; Eph 4:31; 5:3–5; Col 3:5, 8; 1 Tim 1:9–10; 2 Tim 3:2–5; Titus 3:3; Jas 3:15; 1 Pet 2:1; 4:3, 15; Rev 9:21; 21:8; 22:15.

a house, and would not have any one know it" (7:24). The text is emphatic: there's no hint here Jesus wishes people to find him. But secrecy cannot last: "Yet he could not be hidden" (7:24b). We see here the constant pattern in Mark's Gospel: Jesus desires to slip away, but people find him. The pattern tracks with Jesus's express statements in the parables chapter: "For there is nothing hid, except to be made manifest; nor is anything secret, except to come to light" (4:24). In Mark's Gospel, secrecy is seldom maintained and not meant to last past the Resurrection.

A woman with a demon-possessed daughter finds him "immediately" and prostrates herself before him (7:25). We think immediately of two other "daughters" Jesus has healed in tandem, the hemorrhaging woman whom Jesus calls "daughter" (5:34) and Jairus's dead daughter (5:42). Moreover, this woman's persistence matches the hemorrhaging woman's faithful persistence, and not by chance (nothing in Mark's Gospel is by chance). The hemorrhaging woman was Jewish, but this woman is a Gentile, a true pagan. Mark tells us she's a "Greek," a marker of her cultural and religious identity, and a Syrophoenician, a marker of her ethnic identity. She's a solid pagan.

That's something she'll have to overcome with Jesus. For he responds to her begging for her daughter's healing by implying she's a "dog" (7:27), using a common Jewish epithet for pagans. Even if *kunarion* means "little dog," it's still a dog (and sometimes little dogs are the most annoying of all!). Nevertheless, she persists. She, marked doubly pagan as a Greek and Syrophoenician, and a woman to boot, is the only person in the Gospel of Mark to call Jesus "Lord" (*kurios*).

Now, *kurios* can, of course, be a polite form of address, like "sir" in English, or a formal title for nobility, as in Downton Abbey English, like "Lord Grantham." It's like *Señor* in Spanish or *Herr* in German. Here we may have a situation akin to Jesus's use of *egō eimi* in Mark 6:50, where it can mean "it's me!" or it can be the very name of God from Exodus 3:14. Here too: Scripture functions on both literal and spiritual levels, and so Mark would have readers perceive a reference to Jesus's divine Lordship here.

That's radical: a pagan calls Jesus the LORD. And yet, the passage emphasizes what the larger New Testament emphasizes is the pattern both theologically and historically: the Gospel comes first to the Jew, then to the Greek (see Rom 1:16). Jesus's first response to her hints at this pattern: "Let the children *first* be fed, for it is not right to take the children's bread and throw it to the dogs" (7:27). And the woman grants the principle: "Yes, Lord; yet even the dogs under the table eat the children's crumbs" (7:28).

Jesus relents, and performs the only remote healing or exorcism in Mark's Gospel: "For this saying you may go your way; the demon has left your daughter" (7:29); returning home, she finds her daughter in bed, demon-free (7:30).

Did Jesus relent? Jesus's actions seem harsh at first glance, and so we have two options for understanding his behavior. First, most interpreters, desiring to preserve an inclusive and kind Jesus welcoming of all, assert that he intends to help her all along and that his hesitation is a ruse designed to tease faith out of her, a rhetorical stratagem to get her to push harder. The problem, and the second option, is that a natural reading of the text suggests Jesus was not interested in helping her. Jesus is hiding, not wanting to be found, but she discovers him, and his initial response involves an epithet. Further, Jesus is a Jewish male, a Torah-observant one (see Jesus's tassels in Mark 6:56), who wouldn't naturally associate with a pagan woman.

Yet the first option commends itself on the grounds of Mark's Gospel itself, and it's not simply the result of a well-intentioned desire to save Jesus from himself here. Jesus does use the word "first" in his initial response to her, as if the Gentiles might receive the gospel "second." Moreover, he's already traveled to Gentile territory in the Decapolis and launched a mission there (5:1–20). Furthermore, Jesus will remain in Gentile territory, journeying in a circuitous route north, then east, then south from Tyre to and through Sidon and finally down to the Decapolis again, and there he will feed four thousand in Gentile territory (8:1–10) in a miracle matching the prior feeding of the five thousand in Jewish territory (6:30–44). The Gospel comes first to the Jew, then to the Gentile.

Respecting the particularities of the text, it's best to say Jesus doesn't wish to heal her outright—he's hiding, even though he's in Gentile territory for some reason—but neither does he reject her outright because she's a pagan woman and he's not. Rather, the problem is timing. But he grants her request because of her persistent, desperate faith, which Mark presents as a model.

Finally, note here the theme of "bread," so prevalent in this broader section. Both Jesus and the woman mention bread, and the context is *exorcism*. Remember the feeding of the five thousand (6:30–44): there, the Eucharist is subtly tied to exorcism, for it takes place in the desert, the *erēmos*, which Jesus cleansed of satanic dominion in the Temptation (1:12–13). The Eucharist, again, is not merely natural or spiritual food, but a sacrificial meal that drives demons away, a weapon in the Church's spiritual war on sin, death, hell, and the devil.

Mark 7:31–37: Twenty-Third Sunday in Ordinary Time / Friday of Week 5

Jesus remains in Gentile territory. The route outlined in Mark 7:31 (from Tyre through Sidon and then, presumably, around the north and east side of the sea of Galilee and down south or southeast to the Decapolis) is weird and inefficient at first glance, so either we conclude Mark was sloppy or bad at geography or we find a deeper purpose. If the latter, the purpose of Jesus's route is to keep him in Gentile territory. That's fitting: Jesus is reacting to his heated exchange with the Pharisees and scribes over the tradition of the elders (7:1-23) by remaining among the Gentiles.

Unlike in his prior reception in the Decapolis, when the inhabitants begged him to leave their territory (5:17), now the people bring him a deaf and dumb man. Presumably the mission of the Gerasene no-longer-demoniac met with significant success (5:20).

This passage, unique to Mark's Gospel, is marked by the pattern of violated secrecy, like the cleansing of the leper in Mark 1:40-45. Jesus takes the man aside privately, away from the crowd (7:33), to deal with his impediments. The healing is told in great detail in a sequence of seven deliberate steps (7:33-34). As in the scene of the raising of Jairus's daughter (5:41), Mark records Jesus's Aramaic code: "'Eph'phatha,' that is, 'Be opened'" (7:34).

The miracle unlocks the man: "And his ears were opened, his tongue was released, and he spoke plainly" (7:35). In Mark's Gospel, again, human faculties symbolize spiritual faculties. This man can now hear, indicating he can be receptive to Jesus and his message, and he can also speak, indicating he can be a herald of the Gospel. And not only the man but also "they" speak, although Jesus had adjured "them" to silence (7:36), and they do so in direct proportion to Jesus's urging: "the more he charged them, the more zealously they proclaimed it" (7:36b), and the result is astonished praise of Jesus (7:37).

That the passage is unique to Mark is suggestive, for it

plays a major role in the theme of the disciples' incomprehension. Jesus will shortly upbraid the disciples for having ears that do not hear and eyes that do not see (8:14–21). If we couple this passage of the healing of a deaf and dumb man with the healing of the blind man in 8:22–26, we might see Mark suggesting that there's hope for those like the disciples who cannot or do not see, hear, and understand: they will be healed, and they will speak, and glory will resound to the name of Jesus Christ.

Who is Jesus Christ? He is the one who fulfills the prophecy of Isaiah 35:5–6a, the only passage in the Greek Old Testament in which the word for "dumb" or "speech impediment" (*mogilalos*) appears:

> Then the eyes of the blind shall be opened,
>   and the ears of the deaf unstopped;
> then shall the lame man leap like a hart,
>   and the tongue of the dumb sing for joy.

The allusion to Isaiah implies that Jesus is bringing the eschatological healing of the New Exodus as he liberates men—here, Gentiles—from bondage.

Mark 8:1–10: Saturday of Week 5

Jesus now performs a feeding very much like the feeding of the five thousand (see above on Mark 6:30–44 for the sixteenth Sunday in Ordinary Time / Saturday of week 4), but now in Gentile territory. Once again, Jesus and his dull disciples are in a deserted place with a large crowd growing hungry, and Jesus performs a miracle of superabundance involving loaves and fish with Eucharistic overtones (see "took . . . given thanks . . . broke . . . gave" in 8:6 and compare with 6:41 and 14:22) and involving the disciples in their distribution as a symbol of the Church's mediation of the sacraments.

The similarities between the two feedings are so obvious they raise the theme of the disciples' incomprehension to comic heights. The disciples ask Jesus, "How can one feed these men with bread here in the desert?" (8:4), as if they deserve a diagnosis of retrograde amnesia.

But we find particularities and differences as well. In this feeding, Jesus takes the initiative. He declares his compassion on the crowd, for they've been with him for three days and gone without food (8:2), and he fears that, if they're dismissed hungry, "they will faint on the way; and some of them have come a long way" (8:3).

For the first time in his Gospel, Mark employs a significant phrase in Jesus's words: "on the way" (*en tē hodō*). It appears five other times in the Gospel—8:27, 9:33, 9:34, 10:32, and 10:52—all in the discipleship section. "On the way" is the path of discipleship. When disciples and others in Mark's Gospel are "on the way" with Jesus, their literal walking "on the way" in the story is a spiritual figure for the path of discipleship for all Christians.

Gentiles, then, are also called to be Jesus's followers, joining him on the path of discipleship. Further, this first occurrence of the phrase appears near the end of the bread section but before the discipleship section, and its introduction here links the two and suggests that *discipleship draws its strength from the Eucharist.*

On a literal level, then, Jesus must feed their bellies so that they will not faint on the way. On a spiritual level, Jesus must feed our bodies and souls with the Eucharist so that we will not faint while following him on the path of discipleship. The Eucharist feeds discipleship.

What of the three days the crowd has been with Jesus,

hungry (8:2)? Mark hopes his readers have ears to hear what's here to be heard. The mention of three days naturally evokes the traditional time Jesus was dead before his Resurrection. They've gone without bread, much like the Church abandons the Mass for a time during the sacred triduum. It suggests that, once Jesus endures his Passion, the way will be opened for the Gentiles too.

So let's talk about numerology and play some games with gematria.[20] What of the numbers involved in the two mass feedings that foreshadow our feeding in the Mass?

Above, I posited that the number 5,000 suggested a legion of soldiers and that Mark was showing the true way to conquer the world was through the Church's Eucharistic warfare for the world, not Jewish warfare against Rome. But it's also possible, in keeping with the first feeding involving Jews, that 5,000 evokes the five books of Moses fulfilled and transcended by Jesus (hence the thousands), and that would fit with the possibility that the number 4,000 represents the universality of the Church, including Gentiles, for the number four is the number of points on a compass, representative of the whole world, and again the thousands appended to four suggest transcendence, a powerful mission that won't be stopped. Further, it's possible the numbers of men fed decline from 5,000 to 4,000 indicate that followers of Jesus are falling away as the discipleship section progresses.

---

[20] Gematria is the belief in the ancient Near East that numbers bear deep symbolic meaning. The most famous example is, of course, the number of the beast in Rev 13:18, where the beast is Nero Caesar, whose name in Greek reverse-engineered into the magical language of Hebrew equals 666. What's more, the Greek word for beast itself (*thērion*) reverse-engineered into Hebrew equals 666. St. John is not just writing in code: he's saying gematria *proves* Nero is the beast. (I'm disappointed because my favorite candidate is *L'Empereur Napoléon*, identified as the beast by Pierre Bezukhov in Tolstoy's *War and Peace*.)

What of the baskets? In the first feeding, the word for "basket" is *kophinos*, which seems to denote a smaller basket Jews would use, while in the second feeding, the word is *spuris*, a much larger basket in use in the Gentile world. And so, here, we have another suggestion that the two feedings represent the Church's salvation of both Jews and Gentiles.

What of the numbers? Twelve (Jewish) baskets at the first feeding certainly means the twelve tribes of Israel being satiated by the Eucharist, while the seven baskets of leftovers at the second feeding likely evokes the seven pagan nations dwelling in Canaan (Deut 7:1) and, thus, Gentiles. But, whereas the prior confrontation of Israelites and Gentiles under the old covenant meant hostility and conquest, in the new covenant their encounter in the Church is reconciliation and peace.

Mark 8:11–13: Monday of Week 6

Jesus has returned to Galilee, if the unknown Dalmanutha (Mark 8:10) is presumed to be on the western side of the Sea of Galilee. This will be his last encounter in Galilee. And it is, to put it lightly, testy. The Pharisees get in Jesus's face, disputing with him, demanding a sign, testing him.

They've achieved the sort of outsider status generally reserved for Satan. Had they simply followed Jesus at some sort of remove, they'd have witnessed the very sign they're asking for, the feeding of the four thousand. They missed it, as they weren't with him at all. Further, their approach to Jesus is a mockery of the many insiders who come to Jesus seeking healing; they too approach Jesus but in hate, not faith. And finally, let's remember that it's Satan who originally tested Jesus (*peirazō*, 1:13) as they test him here (*peirazō*, 8:11)

The demand for a sign is important. Unlike John's Gospel, in which the wonders Jesus performs are signs to be sought and understood and which can generate faith, Mark's Gospel rejects the seeking of signs.[21] Faith is prior: one must have eyes to see and ears to hear if one is to perceive the significance of the mystery of Jesus. Indeed, the whole of Mark 13 is Mark's exercise in dissuading readers from seeking signs of the End. What they think are signs of apocalypse do not indicate the End; the End will be obvious, when cosmic phenomena occur with Jesus's unmistakable coming. That chapter ends with the Parable of the Doorkeeper, which emphasizes that the time of the End is unknowable; even Jesus doesn't know it (13:32). Therefore, the Christian is to remain vigilant, on the watch 24/7/365, not because one can perceive the signs of the End, but precisely because no one can.

And so, the Pharisees' demand for a sign is exactly backwards. They're demanding a sign as justification to have faith, but in Mark's Gospel, only those whose prior persistent faith brings them into Jesus's presence see signs and wonders. In fact, it's true to Scripture and human experience that seeing signs and wonders seldom leads to lasting conversion. For instance, Numbers 14:11 bears elegant witness to the failure of signs to solidify faith and fidelity: "And the LORD said to Moses, 'How long will this people despise me? And how long will they not believe in me, in spite of all the signs which I have wrought among them?'" Or consider Luke 17:11–19, in which only one of ten lepers cleansed returns to give thanks.

Contemporary Christians often engage in a sort of wistful nostalgia, thinking that faith is so very hard in the modern world, living as we do after Darwin, after Auschwitz, but that, if only we could have been there with Jesus and have seen his

---

[21] The indispensable (and unfortunately all-too-obscure) monograph on the subject is Timothy Geddert, *Watchwords: Mark 13 in Markan Eschatology*, Journal for the Study of the New Testament Supplemental Series 26 (Sheffield, UK: Sheffield Academic Press, 1989).

mighty works, we could believe. But of course, that's not necessarily true: the Gospels themselves bear witness that many who saw Jesus's mighty works failed to come to confident faith. For some, faith didn't take. Others doubted. One betrayed him, and another denied him. And some believed so strongly in Jesus's wonderworking power they sought to kill him.

And so Jesus declares that no sign will be forthcoming, and he leaves them. The stage is set, then, for contrast with the disciples. Unlike the Pharisees, they have witnessed Jesus's miraculous feedings because they were with Jesus. Nevertheless, they will fail to perceive the significance of the bread in the third and final boat scene.

Mark 8:14–21: Tuesday of Week 6

We come to the third boat scene, which concludes the bread section in Mark's Gospel; bread will not find mention again until 14:22, at the institution of the Eucharist. The scene is the culmination of the disciples' incomprehension: they fail again to see beyond the visible to the invisible, beyond the mundane to the spiritual.

That's allegory talk, and if there's one thing every scholar knows, it's that the Synoptic Gospels have nothing to do with allegory. Most would deny allegory is appropriate for approaching even John's Gospel. Fortunately, the Church's tradition reads and understands better than modernist biblical scholarship, rooted in (and often stuck in) the nineteenth century.[22]

John's Gospel certainly operates on two levels, and characters therein often fail to "look up," thinking only of things

---

[22] See CCC §§109–19, and see Leroy Huizenga, "The Tradition of Christian Allegory Yesterday and Today," *Letter & Spirit* 8 (2013): 77–99.

visible. And so, the Jews, angry about Jesus's cleansing of the Temple, misunderstand his words about raising the Temple on the third day (John 2:13–22). Nicodemus misunderstands Jesus's words about being born again (John 3:1–15). Would-be followers of Jesus flee when they hear his words about eating his flesh and drinking his blood as a call to cannibalism (John 6:52–59). John's Jesus would have them look up to the eternal, the spiritual, for the true significance of his words.

That's allegory. Unfortunately, Jesus's interlocutors are trapped in the realm of the visible. They suffer the "miserable slavery of the soul" that St. Augustine wrote of in his *On Christian Doctrine*, wherein they "take signs for things" and are "unable to lift the eye of the mind above what is corporeal and created, that it may drink in eternal light."[23]

So too is the mistake modern scholars make with Mark's Gospel (and, in fairness, many Fathers and medievals opined that Matthew, Mark, and Luke told of the human, corporeal nature of Christ, whereas John told of his divine nature[24]). But Mark's Jesus, it seems, would also have his followers look through visible things to the invisible and see their spiritual significance. That's why Mark's Gospel does so much with perception, with Jesus calling to those with ears to hear, or (drawing on Is 6:9–10) those with eyes not seeing and ears not hearing.

One sees Mark's concern for this sort of spiritual understanding, this allegory, clearly in this third boat scene. The disciples had forgotten to bring bread (8:14), but Mark informs readers "they had only one loaf with them in the

---

[23] St. Augustine, *De doctrina christiana* 3.5.9, in *A Select Library of Nicene and Post-Nicene Fathers of the Christian Church*, 1st ser., 14 vols., ed. Philip Schaff, repr. (Peabody, MA: Hendrickson, 1994), 2:559.

[24] For instance, see St. Augustine, *De consensu evangelistarum* 1.4.7, and St. Thomas Aquinas, *Commentary on John* 1, lec. 67.

boat." Do you see it? Either Mark is saying they practically had no bread with them or he's saying something else. Given the Eucharistic nature of the prior feedings of the thousands, Mark is saying something else. They do have bread with them, Jesus, the one loaf "with them" as they are with Jesus (see 3:14!) in the boat.

And so, the scene is set. Jesus then warns them to "beware of the leaven of the Pharisees and the leaven of Herod" (3:15). But they're not looking up. Their minds are on visible, mundane things: "And they discussed it with one another, saying, 'We have no bread.'" Double failure. Their first here is the failure to see the spiritual significance of whatever Jesus is saying (stay tuned). Their second failure is that they seem to have forgotten that Jesus is now in the habit of generating unlimited earthly bread on demand, and their dullness is compounded by the fact that they already failed in this manner in the feeding of the four thousand, where they flat forgot Jesus fed the five thousand prior to that. If Jesus's words were only about physical bread, well, he has that covered.

So what about the leaven of the Pharisees and Herod? Mark's Gospel itself gives the clue. In Mark 3:6, it was the Pharisees and Herodians who conspired to murder Jesus. In 12:13, Mark will inform readers that the Pharisees and Herodians will try to trap Jesus by his own words in the matter of paying taxes to Caesar. And of course, it was the fickle Herod Antipas, likely with many if not all of these Herodians present, who had Jesus's forerunner, John the Baptist, summarily murdered at his macabre banquet.

So the Pharisees and Herodians hate Jesus and want him dead. That's the cancerous leaven that risks infecting the disciples. They have to decide whether they will accept Jesus as God's Eucharistic gift or fall further away to a place where they could come even to hate him to the level of the Pharisees and

Herodians. They're in a most precarious position precisely because they can't see or hear spiritually.

Jesus makes that point: He upbraids them using Isaiah's language of lack of perception: "Do you not yet perceive or understand? Are your hearts hardened? Having eyes do you not see, and having ears do you not hear?" (8:17b–18a). Indeed, he asks them if their hearts are hardened (8:18b), like Pharaoh of old, the exemplar one having a hardened heart, who murdered God's Hebrew people through a systematic program of slow genocide.

Their hearts have been hardened since the second boat scene: "for they did not understand about the loaves, but their hearts were hardened" (6:52). Both there and here, they don't get the significance of the loaves of the feedings, and thus they miss what Jesus is saying here.

So what don't they understand? That Jesus is the divine Eucharist for the entire world. He asks them finally if they do not remember (8:18b) and reminds them rhetorically about how many baskets were taken up at each feeding: twelve at the feeding of the five thousand and seven at the feeding of the four thousand, which we saw above were respective references to the Eucharistic mission of Jesus and his Church to Jews and to Gentiles, thus to the whole world.

The passage implies the remedy: seeing things as signs, seeing the bread as Jesus's Eucharist. And that involves memory, intentional remembering, contemplating what Jesus has done and who he is. For Catholics today, that means Eucharistic adoration.

And so, there is hope for would-be disciples whose senses fail, as St. Thomas Aquinas reminds us in the *Tantum Ergo*: "Præstet fides supplementum sensuum defectui"—"Faith for all defects supplying where the feeble senses fail." And of course, faith isn't only intellectual assent; it's persistence in seeking Jesus, as Mark has made plain. And Mark will sound an oblique, mysterious, allegorical note of hope for the dull disciples and us in Jesus's next healing.

CHAPTER 5

The Cost of Discipleship on the Way of the Cross (Mark 8:22–10:52)

We now enter the discipleship section, which is framed by the healing of two blind men (8:22–26 and 10:46–52). Mark is suggesting through these physical healings that Jesus will restore spiritual sight to those lacking understanding, even while the disciples continue to flail and fail while following Jesus on the way of discipleship to Jerusalem and the Cross.

Mark 8:22–26: Wednesday of Week 6

This healing of an anonymous blind man is a hinge, both closing the bread section (6:33–8:21) and opening the discipleship section (8:22–10:56). Its position may also make for a sandwich, with the disciples' lack of understanding in the third boat scene (8:14–21) and Peter's confession and rebuke (8:27–31) making up the A and A' sections, and this passage (8:22–26) as the B section.

Indeed, the passage provides perceptible parallels with the healing of the deaf mute in Mark 7:31–37: each occurs outside of Galilee; each is initiated by others; in each, Jesus leads the man away from others; each involves dominical saliva; each involves Jesus's touch; and each involves secrecy. And each story links to Jesus's question to the dull disciples in

8:18: "Having eyes do you not see, and having ears do you not hear?" Mark implies that Jesus will someday, somehow unstop the ears and open the eyes of dull disciples then and now.

The healing is weird. First, there's the matter of spit. Why might Jesus spit on the man's eyes? One clue is found in the Talmud, where R. Reuben opines that the ability of one's spit to heal indicates that man is truly the firstborn of his father, and rabbinic sources speak elsewhere of spittle as a healing salve.[1] Further, Greco-Roman sources testify to the healing power of spittle.[2] On the other hand, the Torah indicates spitting on someone is offensive in Leviticus 15:8, Numbers 12:14, and Deuteronomy 25:9. It's possible Jesus is getting in the face of the disease of blindness and the demon behind it.

Second, the healing happens in two stages, as if the first attempt didn't take. The man sees, but not clearly: "I see men; but they look like trees, walking" (8:24). And so Jesus repeats the process, this time with success. Observe the language in 8:25: the man "looked intently" and then his sight "was restored" so that "he saw everything clearly." It's a pattern for those who would see: look intently at Jesus in persistent faith. Sight begets sight in intentional cooperation with Jesus, and then one will understand deeply and truly.

---

[1] In the Babylonian Talmud, see b. Bat. 126b, where the context concerns how to determine a true firstborn son for the purposes of inheritance, and b. Šabb 108b, where the discussion concerns whether one may use saliva to heal on the sabbath. See also y. Šabb. 14:14. Using later rabbinic sources for understanding the New Testament is fraught with difficulties, given the possibilities of anachronism, and yet, many of the traditions in rabbinic literature are much more ancient than the date of their written recording and prove illuminating for many otherwise obscure details in the New Testament.

[2] Celsus, De medicina 5.28, 18b; Galen, On the Natural Faculties 3.7; Pliny, Natural History 28.7 and 28.4, 22. Tacitus (Histories 4.81) and Suetonius (Vespasian 7.2) record a story in which the emperor Vespasian healed a blind man with spit.

The disciples aren't doing that at present, however, but the passage presents hope for them. For, in the very next story, Peter's confession and rebuke, Peter will get it half right, just like the man at first receives half sight. He's progressed enough from his dull state in the final boat scene in Mark 8:14–21 to come to confess Jesus as the Christ, but he refuses to accept just what Jesus says his messianic mission means. But the healing of this blind man in the middle of this sandwich suggests Peter, too, will see everything clearly one day. But, like Jesus adjures the no-longer-blind man to secrecy (8:26), so too does the restoration of Peter's spiritual sight remain a secret unknown outside the confines of Mark's Gospel.

Mark 8:27–35: Twenty-Fourth Sunday in Ordinary Time / Thursday of Week 6

We come to the thematic heart of Mark's Gospel: Peter's confession at Caesarea Philippi, Jesus's Passion prediction, and Jesus's teaching on cruciform discipleship. Jesus teaches that he, the Christ, must suffer, die, and be raised on the third day, and that those who would be his disciples must likewise take up their own crosses and follow him.

Jesus heads way north to Caesarea Philippi—in the present day Golan Heights, and in the ancient world, a repository of pagan gods like Ba'al and Pan, with a reputation among Jews and probably Jedi as a wretched hive of scum and villainy. No good Jew would visit this place. It is here that Peter makes his declaration that Jesus is the Christ. The location suggests that Jesus's mission isn't simply to the world: he will be the destroyer of the gods, the one who brings pagans to faith in Israel's God, his Father, through him, thus fulfilling the prophetic visions that the Gentiles would one day come to worship the Lord God.[3]

The answers the disciples give to Jesus's question, "Who do men say that I am?" (8:27b), are the same as those given in 6:14 concerning the identity of Jesus in the context of John the Baptist's execution. Readers are thus thinking of the links between John's and Jesus's deaths when Peter responds to Jesus's question with his famous confession, "You are the Christ" (8:29b). That is, Mark is already suggesting that the content of Christ contains crucifixion.

But Peter won't have it. Now Jesus adjures the disciples to secrecy, likely for an obvious reason: while different conceptions of the Christ are found in ancient Judaism, the dominant one was that the Christ would be a conquering hero who would liberate the Jews from Roman domination, much like the original Christ, David, who was anointed to be king (*christos* in Greek means "anointed one"), conquered and pacified the land and established a kingdom.

And Jesus then begins to correct their implicit and, ultimately, errant understanding of Christhood. Jesus immediately issues his first Passion prediction: speaking of himself as the "Son of man," the heavenly conqueror from Daniel 7, he says that he must "suffer many things and be rejected by the elders and the chief priests and the scribes, and be killed, and after three days rise again" (8:31).

By speaking of himself as the Danielic "Son of man," Jesus is assuring the disciples that he will, in fact, conquer and reign, but eschatologically, at the end of time. Mark's Gospel is about spiritual holy war, not earthly holy war. But Peter seems trapped in the wretched slavery of the spirit, looking down

---

[3] See, for instance, Isa 56:6–7, which Jesus will quote in part in the cleansing of the Temple (Mark 11:17).

at earthly signs rather than heavenly realities, and so he can't accept Jesus's words. Although Jesus gives his Passion prediction "plainly," Peter "began to rebuke him" (8:32), and right at the moment, Jesus "began to teach them" about the necessity of his suffering and death (8:31).

Let's have some sympathy for Peter. Jesus is presenting a picture of Christhood that no Jew had ever countenanced. One text from ancient Judaism, 4 Ezra 7:29–30,[4] has the Christ dying of natural causes after a reign of four hundred years, but the date of that passage is likely as late as AD 100. Further, no Old Testament prophecy pointed to a dying Christ: Jews didn't see the Isaianic Servant Songs (such as Is 52:13–53:12) as messianic prophecies (though early Christians, with the benefit of the hindsight of faith, could go back to the Servant Songs and other prophecies of the Old Testament and find hints there).

But Jesus is Jesus, Lord, Christ, Son of man, God on Mark's earth, and so Peter gets to be wrong. (If you want the low-hanging fruit from this passage, here's some: don't rebuke Jesus. Ever.) And so, Jesus turns and rebukes Peter, and calls him "Satan" (8:33), certainly the only step lower one can go after developing a hard heart (see 6:52 and 8:17b).

Peter here is captured by what theologians call a *theologia gloriae*, a theology of glory, which I have discussed more fully in the part I of the book. Theologies of glory are happy-clappy enthusiastic exercises in health and wealth that avoid suffering at all costs. American Christianity is shot through with a the-

---

[4] 4 Ezra 7:29–30: "For my son the Messiah shall be revealed with those who are with him, and those who remain shall rejoice four hundred years. And after these years my son the Messiah shall die, and all who draw human breath" (trans. Bruce M. Metzger in *The Old Testament Pseudepigrapha*, vol. 1, *Apocalyptic Literature and Testaments*, ed. James H. Charlesworth, Anchor Bible Reference Library [New York: Doubleday, 1983], 537).

ology of glory, given our national will-to-power, pragmatism, and high-achiever, do-it-yourself attitudes. What Jesus teaches and lives and dies is the *theologia crucis*, the theology of the cross, which is necessary for Jesus (8:31: Jesus "must [Greek: *dei*] suffer many things") and for would-be disciples: "let him deny himself and take up his cross and follow me" (8:34).

And that's the only way. In the paradoxical economy of salvation, the price of salvation is one's life, one's soul (*psuchē*): "For whoever would save his life will lose it; and whoever loses his life for my sake and the gospel's will save it" (8:35). Jesus drives the point home in 8:36–38 (not part of these lectionary readings, but read on Friday of week 6): whatever we achieve or accumulate on earth, death ends it. There's no ultimate profit in gaining the whole world and losing one's soul, and Jesus will one day come in judgment.

And so, as Lutheran martyr Dietrich Bonhoeffer put it, "When Christ calls a man, he bids him come and die."[5] That's a tough calling, and Jesus issues it broadly: "And he called to him the multitude with his disciples, and said to them, 'If any man would come after me, let him deny himself and take up his cross and follow me'" (Mark 8:34). It's no accident he's at Caesarea Philippi; he calls the multitude of these pagans, representative not only of all humanity but also of humanity at its idolatrous and sinful darkest. All need the Cross, for only the Cross can save all.

Jesus calls them to "follow" him, and those who respond will follow him "on the way," a key word and a key phrase Mark employs in the discipleship section for which this passage sets the tone. First, "on the way" (*en tē hodō*) is, on a literal level, the road to Jerusalem, where Jesus will be crucified. Figuratively, it's a phrase signifying the way of discipleship. Second,

---

[5] Dietrich Bonhoeffer, *The Cost of Discipleship*, trans. R. H. Fuller (New York: Touchstone, 1995), 89.

to "follow" (*akoloutheō*) Jesus on that way to Jerusalem symbolizes discipleship. And so, in the discipleship section, the disciples and others follow Jesus on the way to Jerusalem, where not only he will be crucified, *but also they with him.* Christians make a metaphor of Jesus's words here too quickly (following, I suppose, Luke's lead, whose version of Jesus's call reads, "let him take up his cross *daily*," Luke 9:23). But in Mark's story, the crosses to which Jesus calls those who would follow him are literal Roman gibbets. He's calling them to a real crucifixion. And everyone knew what crucifixion entailed. Spartacus's slave revolt ended with six thousand slaves crucified up and down the *Via Appia* that ran in and out of Rome. At a banquet for some favored guests and concubines in 88 BC, the Jewish king Alexander Jannaeus once crucified eight hundred Pharisees who had crossed him, while the throats of their wives and children were slit before their eyes.[6] Josephus records that, during the siege of Jerusalem, the Romans crucified hundreds of captured Jews outside the city to terrify those inside.[7]

And so, in the world of Mark's story, Jesus is calling all people, as well as the disciples, to a most literal crucifixion, and they knew what it meant. It's a wonder they began to follow at all. By the end, of course, many will have made it even to Jerusalem, but none will follow all the way to the cross. Peter will almost achieve the cross, following Jesus *this close,*

---

[6] Flavius Josephus, *Antiquities of the Jews* 13.380.

[7] Flavius Josephus, *Wars of the Jews* 5.450–451: "Titus indeed commiserated their fate, five hundred or sometimes more being captured daily. . . . But his main reason for not stopping the crucifixions was the hope that the spectacle might perhaps induce the Jews to surrender, for fear that continued resistance would involve them in a similar fate. The soldiers out of rage and hatred amused themselves by nailing their prisoners in different postures; and so great was their number, that space could not be found for the crosses nor crosses for the bodies" (trans. H. St. J. Thackeray, in Loeb Classical Library 120 [Cambridge, MA: Harvard University Press, 1928]).

even to the courtyard of Caiaphas's house, but "at a distance" (14:54), and then will fail, denying Jesus thrice.

And yet, the passage's juxtaposition in the sandwich with the two-stage healing of the blind man suggests there's hope for Peter and all who fail to carry their cross all the way to crucifixion. Just as Peter had it half right in his confession of Jesus as the Christ, the blind man first received half sight. Jesus is the one, however, who can restore full sight so that we might see everything clearly (8:25), take up our cross, and follow Jesus to Jerusalem and salvation.

Mark 8:34–9:1: Friday of Week 6

In the passage the lectionary provides today, we find Jesus closing his great teaching on the cross (the immediately preceding section on 8:27–35) with an eschatological warning. It operates with a binary opposition between this "adulterous and sinful generation," epitomized by Caesarea Philippi, and the "glory" of the kingdom of heaven that Jesus will bring at the last day (8:38). That kingdom is ultimately what's real, and its coming is ineluctable, inexorable, unavoidable, and so it makes no sense to hoard and preserve what one can in this passing life. For life is short, and eternity is long.

Jesus also employs the rhetoric of shame: "For whoever is ashamed of me and of my words in this adulterous and sinful generation, of him will the Son of man also be ashamed, when he comes in the glory of his Father with the holy angels" (8:39). In the ancient world, and in most societies even today, human relationships operate along honor-shame lines. Society rewards certain deeds with honor, and others with shame. Moreover, clients can shame or honor their patrons, and patrons return the favor, sometimes cutting off clients who shame them totally and finally. Further, shame can be so severe the only way to restore one's honor is death, usually by suicide, even if one is innocent of any wrongdoing.[8]

Jesus's words here operate within this honor–shame system. Jesus will return shame for shame, cutting off those who reject him and his Cross eternally, like dishonorable, shameful clients. And yet, the paradox, the irony, here, is that it's precisely through the suffering of the most shameful death possible, crucifixion, that Jesus will conquer sin, death, hell, and the devil, liberate those in bondage to those powers, saving them, and find himself exalted to honor. Put another way, Jesus commits a sort of willing suicide in carrying his Cross to his death so that we don't have to, even though the shame of our sins merits our destruction.

Paradoxically, then, the shameful way of the Cross is the only way to honor, to the "glory" with which Jesus will return (8:38), and the only way for his followers to achieve glory. The ancient pagan world sees shame and glorious honor as opposites exclusive of each other, but the Christian way sees the shame of the Cross as the precise and singular way to glory and honor.

For that reason, Christianity effected a sea change in those cultures it transformed. The paradigm shifted from honor–shame to sin–grace, precisely because shameful deeds became understood as sins against the ultimate patron, God, who, instead of acting like a Roman *paterfamilias* would act in eliminating shameful clients, acted like the Father that Jesus proclaimed and forgave sins, thus breaking the honor-shame system from within. God offers us a way out besides ostracization and suicide.

---

[8] The prime example is the case of the Roman noblewoman Lucretia, whose rape at the hands of Sextus Tarquin, lout son of the last Roman king Tarquinius Superbus, shamed her to the point that she committed suicide to restore her honor (see Livy, *History of Rome* 1.57–58).

The risk, of course, is antinomianism, that the possibility of release from the shame of sin can involve indulgence in cheap grace. That's why the Christian tradition from Jesus on has always insisted that forgiveness involves intentional amendment of life: "Go and do not sin again" (John 6:11).

In any event, it's no accident that, as Western societies become ever less Christian, shame culture is making a vengeful comeback, where failure to hold the right *bien-pensant* opinions on crucial cultural questions means running the risk of being run right out of civil society, where virtue signaling achieves cheap and easy honor *sans* virtue, and where suicide rates are rising as fast as we can shame people.

The disciples will fail, as we know; Jesus will die alone. And yet the Gospel of Mark, here too, as it does so often, breaks down one of the dichotomies it establishes. Although all fall away, too ashamed to suffer the shame of crucifixion, the Gospel promises a chance to try again, inviting us to return to Galilee ("He goes ahead of you to Galilee" in Mark 16:7 brings readers back to 1:14–15) to once more hear Jesus's call and begin to follow him anew.

But Mark, as always, operates with intensity, and so Jesus closes his speech with words of immediacy: "Truly, I say to you, there are some standing here who will not taste death before they see the kingdom of God come with power" (9:1). Jesus's closing is a warning to the effect of "take up your cross now, right now," similar to how the portrayal of the call of Jesus to the two pairs of brothers in 1:16–20 illustrates that the presence of the kingdom in Jesus demands decisive response. And yet, it's ironic, paradoxical, as it suggests that the kingdom will come so quickly some will avoid the rigors of the cross.

Mark 9:2–13: Second Sunday of Lent (9:2–10) / The Transfiguration of the Lord (9:2–10) / Saturday of Week 6 (9:2–13)

The Transfiguration in Mark's Gospel is many things. It fulfills and explains Jesus's cryptic words in Mark 9:1, it reveals Jesus as the summation of the Old Testament, and it encourages the three witnesses with a vision of glory while yet reminding them of the Cross.

Many doubters have pointed to Mark 9:1 as a reason to reject Christian faith, for, read on its face, it seems Jesus was simply wrong. The last real public atheist, Bertrand Russell, adverted to it in his *Why I Am Not a Christian* as a major reason he wasn't a believer.[9] But did Jesus expect the coming of the kingdom within the lifetime of his disciples? Is that really what Mark means by Jesus's words here?[10]

Mark's narrative structure provides the answer. The Transfiguration of Jesus Christ is a proleptic, before-the-fact disclosure of the Resurrection glory of the kingdom. Mark makes the link clear by informing readers that the Transfiguration happened only six days after Jesus's words (9:2a).

The Transfiguration is a moment of revelation so secret only the inner triad of Peter, James, and John witness it. Jesus leads them deliberately "up a high mountain apart by themselves" (9:2). Mountains are natural locations for supernatural revelation, given that, in the ancient conception of the universe, the dwelling of God is up in the heavens above the

---

[9] Bertrand Russell, *Why I Am Not a Christian: And Other Essays on Religion and Related Subjects*, Routledge Classics (London: Routledge, 2004), 13.

[10] It's ironic that many of the same people who would make this claim would also date the Gospel of Mark relatively late. But, if the Gospel was written late, why would the author include these words of Jesus, which, if they mean Jesus expected an imminent kingdom, would seem ever less likely to be true as time marched on?

earth, and so Jesus leads them up a high mountain, like Moses receiving the Torah at Sinai.

The three disciples witness his metamorphosis (*metamorphoō*) as he becomes whiter than we can imagine. Mark trips over himself in describing the indescribable, writing that Jesus's garments "became glistening, intensely white, as no fuller on earth could bleach them" (9:3). He has to use analogical language to describe the Resurrection reality of Jesus's Transfiguration here, for it transcends any human experience while remaining intelligible. It's a display of the kingdom glory of which Jesus spoke in 8:38. It is the kingdom come with power.

Moses, the great lawgiver, and Elijah, the great prophet, now appear in Mark 9:4 to indicate that Jesus is the fulfillment of both the law and the prophets. Further, Jews believed both were assumed into heaven,[11] and both had met with God on Sinai/Horeb (Exod 19–20; 1 Kings 19:9–18).

The vision overwhelms the disciples; they are terrified (*ekphobos*, 9:6), never a good sign in Mark's Gospel. And so, Peter speaks when he should be silent: "Master, it is well that we are here; let us make three booths, one for you and one for Moses and one for Eli'jah" (9:5).

Now we approach the heart of Mark's concerns. Peter's desire to make three booths indicates both (1) that he yet doesn't get Jesus's identity as one superior to even Moses and Elijah and, more importantly, (2) that he's enraptured, overcome with a theology of glory. "Booths" is significant here; it likely evokes the Festival of Tabernacles or Booths, which was the second and final Jewish harvest festival later in the fall.

The first harvest festival was Pentecost, with which Chris-

---

[11] With regard to Elijah, see 2 Kings 2:1–12 and 1 Macc 2:58. For Moses, see: b. Yoma 4a in the Babylonian Talmud; Pesiqta Rabbati 20:4; Josephus, *Antiquities* 4.325–26; and the *Testament of Moses*.

tians are much more familiar. It's no accident the Holy Spirit descends at Pentecost, for it's the birthday of the Church when the Holy Spirit arrives to empower her for mission, for a great harvest of souls.[12] Pentecost begins the great harvest. Booths or Tabernacles, then, takes on an eschatological character: it would be the end of the season of harvest. And so, when Peter wishes to make booths, it suggests that Peter, enraptured as he is by Jesus's eschatological glory, believes they've arrived— and managed to duck the cross after all.

But then comes the cloud of the divine presence and the heavenly voice. God the Father shows up to correct Peter, saying, "This is my beloved Son; listen to him" (9:7b). As at the Baptism, the heavenly voice here alludes to Isaac, the original sacrifice, and so the voice now reminds Peter, as it initially informed Jesus at the Baptism, that Jesus is to be a sacrifice. That's his mission. Further, the Father makes sure Peter doesn't miss the point; he tells Peter to "listen to him." The last words Jesus spoke before this scene concerned the necessity of the cross for Jesus and for his disciples.

And so, the voice is reminding Peter and the disciples that the only way to the glory they seek is through the way of the cross. They've been given encouragement for their way of the cross with this vision of Transfiguration glory; the cross isn't the end. And yet, they must remember there are no shortcuts. The way to glory runs the way of the cross.

And the scene folds up: they see only Jesus, and descending the mountain, Jesus charges them to keep the vision secret until after the Resurrection (9:8–9). Glory will come, but now is the time to live and proclaim the cross, lest a theology of glory run rampant and risk salvation. And yet, even here,

---

[12] Jesus himself used the language of harvest for mission: "The harvest is plentiful, but the laborers are few; pray therefore the Lord of the harvest to send out laborers into his harvest" (Matt 9:37–38).

they lack understanding: although Jesus had spoken to them "plainly" (8:32a) about his Passion and Resurrection, and although they had just witnessed it in proleptic display, they question "what the rising from the dead meant" (9:10).

In their defense, no Jew was expecting a resurrection of one person in time. Most Jews believed in the general resurrection of the dead at the end of time. A crucified and risen Christ is a singularity for which they were unprepared, but it is precisely that singular complex of events that will bring the eschaton into their own time, and they should have trusted Jesus's words.

Mark 9:14–29: Monday of Week 7

We now come to one of the most vivid scenes depicted by Mark, the most vivid writer among the evangelists, the healing of a despairing father's demon-possessed boy. The last exorcism in Mark's Gospel, it follows on the heels of the Transfiguration in the same way Mark's Temptation Narrative followed on the heels of the Baptism of Jesus. The story answers Peter, James, and John's confusion regarding "what the rising from the dead meant" (9:10) as they descend the Mount of Transfiguration.

Jesus and the three disciples encounter a scene of disarray: scribes, the other disciples, and the crowds contending with each other in the wake of a failed exorcism. Jesus takes charge, asking the scribes what the argument is about (9:16). The father of the boy emerges from the crowd to explain to Jesus in detail that his son suffers from possession and that the disciples were unable to exorcise the demon (9:17–18). Jesus then exclaims, "O faithless generation, how long am I to be with you? How long am I to bear with you?" (9:19).

We might think that this is directed toward the disciples, but nowhere else in Mark's Gospel are the disciples in view when Jesus uses the word "generation" (*genea*; see 8:12, 8:38, and 13:30). Rather, the crowd's lack of faith is sapping the power Jesus delegated to his disciples in 6:7–13, where they embarked on a successful mission of exorcism and healing apart from Jesus's direct presence. Indeed, the father from the crowd later declares his unbelief (9:24), and Jesus will cast out the demon before the crowd arrives (9:25), indicating that their lack of faith has made them outsiders and, thus, unworthy to witness the miracle of exorcism. And when the disciples later ask why they couldn't cast out the demon, Jesus does not upbraid them for lack of faith, but explains prayer and fasting are necessary (9:29). The disciples cannot exorcise here because of the crowd's lack of faith, just as Jesus could do no mighty works in Nazareth because of the people's lack of faith (6:1–6). And so, readings that suggest that the problem is that the disciples' failure to exorcise the boy involves the absence of Jesus come to grief.

The boy is brought to Jesus, and the demon shakes him as the boy displays classic signs of epilepsy (9:20). Jesus interrogates the father about the boy's condition, which the father says has been longstanding (9:21) and has caused mortal danger by fire and water on many occasions (9:22a).

The exchange between the father and Jesus at this point is simply poignant. The father, like so many in Mark's Gospel, is at a point of despair but yet hoping against hope in the presence of Jesus: "But if you can do anything, have pity on us and help us" (9:22b). Jesus's response is one of both incredulity and encouragement: "If you can! All things are possible to him who believes" (9:23). The father's following words are some of the most moving and encouraging in all of Scripture: "Immediately the father of the child cried out and said, 'I believe; help my unbelief!'" (9:24).

We see here again that, in Mark's Gospel, faith need not

be pure or perfect, but can be mixed. Like the hemorrhaging woman, whose faith was mixed with fear (5:33–34), the father here has faith enough to call upon Jesus, the object of faith. And so, Jesus performs the exorcism in response to the father's mixed faith (9:25–26a).

But exorcism is rough and tumble. The boy convulses horribly and then appears to be dead: "the boy was like a corpse; so that most of them said, 'He is dead'" (9:26b). But Jesus then performs a deed betokening eschatological resurrection: "But Jesus took him by the hand and lifted him up, and he arose" (9:27).

In this exorcism, we see the pattern of death and resurrection concordant with the Markan theology of the cross. Faith in Jesus does not place one on the straight path to glory. Rather, glory comes after the cross. In this scene of exorcism, it seems at first as if the father's faith in Jesus has led to the boy's demise. One might imagine the boy lying there still for some moments, precipitating the crowd's belief that he was dead (9:26b). Then, and only then, does Jesus raise him up.

This pattern of apparent death and raising as foreshadowing the eschatological resurrection fits two other scenes in Mark's Gospel. The first would be early in the Gospel, when Jesus "takes" Peter's feverish mother-in-law "by the hand" and "raises" (*egeirō*) her (1:31). The second is the raising of Jairus's daughter in 5:41: Jesus "takes" the corpse of Jairus's daughter "by the hand" and commands it to "arise" (*egeirō*). So too here: Jesus "takes" the corpselike boy "by the hand" and "raises" (*egeirō*) him too.

In Mark 9:28–29, the scene shifts to a private discussion with the disciples in which they, as insiders, get further information. They ask why they failed to drive out the demon, and Jesus reveals that the issue is not a lack of faith on their part, but rather a matter of technique: "This kind cannot be driven out by anything but prayer and fasting" (9:29). Perhaps the disciples hadn't been fasting or hadn't encountered this kind of demon before—it's a demon that made the boy specifically "dumb" (9:17).

Something else is operating here as well: authoritative prayer. Perhaps Jesus means to teach that prayer involves commanding demons directly, just as he will curse the fig tree as a form of prayer (11:14, 20) and will suggest to the disciples that telling a mountain to cast itself into the sea is a form of faithful prayer (11:23–24).

Mark 9:30–37: Twenty-Fifth Sunday in Ordinary Time / Tuesday of Week 7

The heavenly voice of the Father has reminded the three disciples closest to Jesus—Peter, James, and John—that, though the way of the Lord ends in glory, the way runs to and through the cross. "Listen to him" (9:7b) directs them to Jesus's prior words about the necessity of the cross. And yet, in this passage, the disciples will remain uncomprehending about the cross and ensnared in a theology of glory, even after Jesus delivers his second Passion prediction.

Jesus and his disciples pass through Galilee, but he keeps their presence secret (9:30). Two reasons suggest themselves. First, Jesus began turning inward in Galilee in chapters 3 and 4, having precipitated a murderous conspiracy there (3:6), after which he ever more goes to the Gentiles of the Decapolis, and even Caesarea Philippi. Second, Jesus has now shifted his emphasis to his journey to crucifixion, to Jerusalem. In 8:31, we're told that Jesus "began to teach them" that he must suffer and die, implying that he was shifting from his ministry of healing and exorcism to his final mission, the Passion. Now is not the time for distraction; he is on his determined way to Jerusalem, resolute.

Jesus is teaching his disciples, then, on the way to Jerusalem, about his Passion, and so he gives the second Passion prediction (9:31). It's terser than the first one, briefer, to the point. The verbs are suggestive: Jesus is delivered into the hands of those who will kill him, which is passive, but then, "after three days he will rise," which is active. Jesus surrenders himself to his necessary fate, but after the Resurrection, he will reign as Lord. The disciples, however, are marked by incomprehension and fear. They do not understand the saying and are afraid to ask him (9:32). And so the scene is set for what happens next, making for a most jarring juxtaposition.

They arrive in Capernaum, and alone in the house, Jesus asks the disciples a question. Earlier in the Gospel of Mark, the disciples would ask Jesus about things privately (see Mark 4:10–12), but now, the tables are turned. He asks them what they were talking about "on the way" (9:33). They're supposed to be on the way of discipleship, following Jesus to his Cross and theirs, the epitome of shame, but in spite of Jesus's invitation to speak, they maintain silence, for "on the way" (Mark repeats the phrase) "they had discussed with one another who was the greatest" (9:34).

The disciples do so right after the second Passion prediction, while they're "on the way," showing themselves perfectly obtuse. They suffer from the fever of the theology of glory, deaf to the words of the cross. Further, in discussing which among them was the greatest, they emulate Herod's sycophants, the first men of Galilee (6:21). And so, Jesus responds with a lesson in humility, a major theme in the discipleship section. He teaches them that the way to be "first" (*prōtos*, 9:35) is not to seek the honor of clientship to a patron like Herod Antipas, as the "first" (*prōtos*) men of Galilee were doing (6:21), but to be last and servant of all (9:35).

This paradox parallels the pattern of the cross: as the only way to glory is crucifixion, so the only way to rule is to serve. Jesus will make this message much more manifest in the case of the third Passion prediction 10:32–34, after which follows more obtuse concern for glory (10:35–45). The parallels between the two juxtaposed pairs of passages are perfect, with Mark and his Jesus expanding in the second on the themes adumbrated here, as Jesus will explicitly mention Gentile rulers and his own death.

Jesus then gives the first children's sermon, in the sense that he brings a child into the matter as an object lesson (9:36–37). Now, some say that, until relatively recently, children were held of little account, that childhood is a modern invention.[13] It is true that children are an economic asset in agrarian societies, where they begin working on the farm as soon as they were able, and it is true until very recently that many children died all too young. But it is not true that children were loved any less or thought unimportant. Funerary monuments, diaries, and other artifacts of history before the nineteenth century record many parents grieving their dead children, among them Martin Luther[14] and William

---

[13] Philippe Ariès published *L'Enfant et la vie familiale sous l'Ancien Régime* in 1960, which appeared shortly thereafter in English as *Centuries of Childhood: A Social History of the Family* (New York: Random House, 1962). The book has proven seminal, influencing most thought about the historical development of childhood since, especially Edward Shorter's influential *The Making of the Modern Family* (New York: Basic Books, 1977). Ariès argued that childhood did not exist before the sixteenth century, emerging as a concept only in the seventeenth century thanks to radical social changes in medicine, industry, and schooling. Recent scholarship has raised serious, even severe, questions about Ariès's thesis and its influence.

[14] See James M. Kittelson, *Luther the Reformer: The Story of the Man and His Career*, 2nd ed. (Minneapolis, MN: Fortress, 2016), 237, for a brief account of the death of Luther's daughter, Magdalena, aged thirteen years.

Shakespeare,[15] living well before the supposed invention of childhood and its Victorian sentimentalizing. Indeed, the Bible speaks often of children as a blessing, and for more than simple economic reasons.[16]

That said, for Jesus, children are emblematic of humble receptivity, the precise opposite of the prideful attitude of incomprehension the dense disciples are displaying. The child is the ideal picture of the disciple, and once the disciples would achieve a child's attitude of humble receptivity, then they would be effective apostles, welcomed by those who, in receiving them, receive not only Jesus but the Father as well.

Mark 9:38–50: Twenty-Sixth Sunday in Ordinary Time (9:38–43, 45, 47–48) / Wednesday of Week 7 (9:38–40) / Thursday of Week 7 (9:41–50)

This passage continues the theme of the contrast between the pride of the theology of glory and the judgment that comes with the theology of the cross.

In Mark 9:38, John (who, with his brother James, will shortly insist on sitting on Jesus's right hand in glory, in 10:35–37) seeks to maintain a prideful prestige of position for the Twelve against any and all outsiders. It's as if, having been chastised for seeking rank as the greatest among the Twelve

---

[15] Consider Shakespeare's lines from *King John*, act III, scene IV, composed not long after Shakespeare's only son, Hamnet, died in 1596 at all of eleven years old: "Grief fills the room up of my empty child / Lies in his bed, walks up and down with me / Puts on his pretty looks, repeats his words / Remembers me of all his gracious parts / Stuffs out his vacant garments with his form."

[16] See, of course, Rachel and Leah's desire for children in Gen 29–20; Israel's concern and lament for his sons, thought lost, in Gen 37:3, 42:36, and 43:14. See also Pss 37:26, 103:13, 113:9, 128:3, and especially 127:3–5.

(9:33–35), John still wants the Twelve to maintain rank for the apostolic college over all others. For he reports that they forbade a successful exorcist not of their number—"he was not following *us*"—from casting out demons (9:38).[17]

John sees the band in league with Jesus, presumably, but in light of his prideful failure in arguing about who among the Apostles was the greatest (9:34), acts and speaks with the greatest presumption. And his failure is compounded all the more, as our passage here follows immediately and logically from the story of the healing of the possessed boy in 9:14–29: the disciples shut down a successful exorcist acting in Jesus's name when they have just shown themselves incapable of performing exorcisms (9:18b: "I asked your disciples to cast it out, and they were not able"). Perhaps we may imagine jealousy motivated John's actions.

Jesus corrects him, for using the mighty name of Jesus means one will likely remain on Jesus's side, and at this point in the story (and going forward in the age of the Church), Jesus, as well as the disciples, can use all the friends he, and they, can get. John's use of "us" is also pretentious, a sign of John's concern for status and prestige, but Jesus reminds them that such men will be of use to the Twelve and the wider Church: "For he that is not against us is for us" (9:40).

It is often overlooked in Mark's Gospel that Jesus turns outward to gather more insiders even after he's turned inward to insiders. Jesus and the apostolic band make up a unit, but the kingdom powered by his name is to extend through them to others, and so Jesus informs them that "whoever gives you

---

[17] Emphasis added. If one asks why this anonymous exorcist was successful while the seven sons of Sceva got their lunch handed to them by a demon (Acts 19:11–20), the short answer is that this exorcist is presumably acting in faith in Jesus's sacred name, while the sons of Sceva were treating it as an automatic magical incantation. Jesus is a person, not a formula, and power flows from him.

a cup of water to drink because you bear the name of Christ, will by no means lose his reward" (9:41).

In Mark 9:41, Jesus promises reward for the proper treatment of his missionaries in their ministry of teaching, healing, and exorcising. But punishment is also possible; Jesus's holy war to liberate the cosmos is not like hobbyists' reenactment of historical battles, but a real war with real casualties. And so, in 9:42, Jesus promises punishment for the converse, the improper treatment of disciples: "Whoever causes one of these little ones who believe in me to sin"—more literally, "to be scandalized," scandal meaning to cause one to lose faith in Jesus—"it would be better for him if a great millstone were hung round his neck and he were thrown into the sea."

John and the rest of the Twelve, in forbidding the anonymous exorcist (a "little one" like the proverbial humble, receptive "child" of Mark 9:37) to continue his work, may have scandalized him, and so they are now the immediate target of the terrifying threat. Now, many Christian ecclesial bodies believe as a matter of confession that Christians are saved once and for all and, thus, that any threats in the Bible must be directed at unbelievers. But other Christians, such as Catholics and traditional Wesleyans and Pentecostals, read passages such as this and many others[18] more honestly, seeing in them the possibility that disciples of Jesus may not make it.

And the warning is dire. A "great millstone" (9:42) required beasts of burden to turn its mill, and being cast into the sea isn't simply drowning. That's horrifying enough today, but again, in the ancient world, the sea was mysterious and frightening.[19] Indeed, in ages before deep sea diving and submarines, we can imagine the ancients might have thought that

---

[18] Consider the Gospel of Matthew in particular, especially 7:21–27 and 18:23–35, and Paul, especially Gal 6:7–8.

[19] See above on the first boat scene in Mark 4:35–41 on pp. 142–45.

the sea was the gate to the underworld—Revelation 20:13 links the sea, death, and Hades. And so, being cast into the sea with a giant millstone wasn't simply drowning, but final damnation.

Jesus then engages in hyperbole, teaching that it's better to surrender one's body parts and "enter life" (9:43, 45) and "enter the Kingdom of God" (9:47) than to enter *geena*, Gehenna, Hell. Jesus here is presenting the doctrine of the "two ways," as he does in Matthew 7:13–14 (the "narrow gate" passage) and 7:24–27 (known as the Parable of the Wise and Foolish Builders) and as found in the *Didache*.[20]

Gehenna is the Valley of the Sons of Hinnom, a location of child sacrifice under Ahaz and Manasseh (see 2 Kings 16:3 and 21:6), a practice finally stopped under king Josiah (2 Kings 23:10). It becomes a common Jewish and Christian symbol for eschatological punishment, and Jesus's description of it as a place "where their worm does not die, and the fire is not quenched" (9:48) is taken from Isaiah 66:24, in which the prophet's vision involves those who have been finally saved at the end of time viewing the corpses of those who had rebelled against the LORD.

Jesus's final words in Mark 9:49–50 are a catchword concatenation whose logical flow is present but not obvious: "For every one will be salted with fire. Salt is good; but if the salt has lost its saltiness, how will you season it? Have salt in yourselves, and be at peace with one another."

The salt of fire here could be the persecution that will come the disciples' way,[21] but in its context, it makes more

---

[20] "There are two ways, one of life and one of death, and there is a great difference between the two ways" (*Didache* 1:1, in *ANF*, 7:377).

[21] If Mark is written during or after Nero's persecutions, Jesus's words would have a special resonance, as Tacitus records Nero burned Christians on crosses to illuminate his garden parties (*Annals* 15.44).

sense to see here the trial by fire that is the judgment everyone will face (see 1 Cor 3:10–17), and in line with that understanding, it also makes sense to see a subtle allusion to the whole burnt offering sacrifices of the Old Testament, which required salt (Lev 2:13) and involved the total reduction of the victim to ashes. Christians are thus to offer themselves (in Paul's words) as "living sacrifices" (Rom 12:1) so that they remain on the way of life, the way of the kingdom.

Salt cannot really lose its savor. Jesus speaks wildly here, using something foundational for human existence to make the point that Christian disciples are foundational for the human race: if Christians fall away, the world is spoilt, lost. And so, the disciples are to remain salty for the world's sake and, instead of seeking the prestige of position among themselves or over and against the wider world, be at peace with each other (9:50).

In Mark's Gospel, then, the "Gospel of the Way," Jesus teaches there are two ways: the way of the Lord—which is the way of life, the way of the kingdom—and the way of Gehenna. That Jesus threatens the disciples in this way indicates again their precarious spiritual position.

Mark 10:2–16: Twenty-Seventh Sunday in Ordinary Time (10:2–16 or 10:2–12) / Friday of Week 7 (10:1–12) / Saturday of Week 7 (10:13–16)

In the preceding material, Jesus has taught the Twelve— celibates, the first clergy—about the radical demands of discipleship as he traveled by stealth through Galilee. In the following material, Jesus will teach the crowds—representative of the laity—about the radical demands of discipleship as it applies to common matters of life, such as marriage, children, and possessions, as he travels through Judea on his final approach to Jerusalem.

The Pharisees take another shot at him, testing him on the question of divorce, asking him whether a man can divorce his wife (10:2). They phrase the question here in absolute terms, as if Jesus's views on the absolute indissolubility of marriage were already widely known. Moses had permitted divorce (Deut 24:1–4), and Jews of Jesus's day and later had a spectrum of opinions regarding what conditions were legitimate grounds for divorce. Rabbi Hillel thought men could divorce their wives for almost any reason, including bad cooking, while Rabbi Shammai permitted it only in the case of adultery. Rabbi Akiva, whose crucifixion by the Romans at the end of the Bar Kochba rebellion will delight many a woman once they learn his opinion, taught that a man could divorce his wife simply if he found a prettier prospect.[22]

Moses's permission was designed under sin to make the best of bad situations, in which providing a woman with a certificate of divorce freed her to marry again lest she wind up in the streets or in the grave. Moses's mechanism of divorce provided a means for women to move on. But it's under sin, in Deuteronomy, in a second giving of the law. And that's the key for understanding how Jesus can leapfrog back over it to the original intention of creation in Genesis 1–2.

In the Torah, the Israelites fail repeatedly, engaging in idolatry and rebellion. God and Moses each are tempted at times to give up on them. The ultimate act of rebellion is found in Numbers 15, when the congregation rejects the report of the twelve spies and God swears that none of that generation will enter the land (Num 15:20–23). The prophet Ezekiel, likely referring to this episode, refers to the LORD giving the Israel-

---

22 In the Mishnah, see m. Git. 9:10.

ites "statutes that were not good and ordinances by which they could not have life" (Ezek 20:25). Those are likely the statutes and ordinances of Deuteronomy in particular.[23] Ezekiel mentioned the law of Sinai in 20:11, but here (20:25), he is referring to the second giving of the law, Deuteronomy.

Deuteronomy is thus a lesser law for a sinful, recalcitrant people. Unlike the Sinaitic law, which was a positive law whose two tables taught the people how to love God and neighbor, Deuteronomy is a negative law of restraint designed to keep the people from falling headlong into total sin. It's no accident that, when Paul is most negative about the law, he's usually dealing with Deuteronomy.[24] And so, Jesus can rightly say, "For your hardness of heart he wrote you this commandment" (10:5).

Jesus, then, goes straight back to creation, quoting Genesis 1:27b and 2:24 in Mark 10:6 and 7–8b. He draws the moral for them: "So they are no longer two but one flesh" (10:8b), and since God himself joins man and woman in marriage, no one may separate them (10:9).

That's absolutely radical, in the ancient world and today. How can Jesus leapfrog back past not only Deuteronomy 24 but even Genesis 3? Why can he cancel Moses and speak as if the Fall is irrelevant? For the reason that he is Jesus, the divine Son of God and authoritative interpreter of the Torah, not Moses, and unlike Moses, he can not only save but also sanctify his people. He does not simply teach difficult things as a matter of dominical law but also empowers his people to do what he commands through their union with him in Cross and Eucharist.

---

[23] See Scott W. Hahn and John S. Bergsma, "What Laws Were 'Not Good'? A Canonical Approach to the Theological Problem of Ezekiel 20:25–26," *Journal of Biblical Literature* 123 (2004): 201–18.

[24] See especially Gal 3:10–14.

And so, seeing the participatory, Eucharistic nature of Jesus in Mark's Gospel is absolutely crucial, lest we be left with a legalism we find impossible to live with. The bread section precedes the discipleship section for a reason: grace comes before law. Once fed with Jesus himself, we have the grace to fulfill his commands, for he himself is in us, enabling us to live his own crucified and resurrected life.

Now, as so often in Mark's Gospel, the disciples are inside with Jesus and ask him for further clarification. We find the pattern here as in Mark 4, for Jesus has returned to addressing crowds, as he was doing in Mark 4. Insiders receive deeper knowledge, and so Jesus explains to them the import of his teaching that marriage is indissoluble. He explains that divorce and remarriage means adultery, which works logically when one assumes the indissolubility of marriage involved in Genesis 1 and 2. Man may break the bond, but the bond is not broken.

Actually, man *or* woman, or man and woman *together*, can "break" it and it still not be broken. The form of Jesus's teaching here is egalitarian, assuming conditions under which both men and women may divorce. Some have said this indicates the Gentile, and specifically Roman, setting of Mark's Gospel, since, under Roman law, women could initiate divorce, whereas they supposedly couldn't under Jewish law.[25] Be that

---

[25] See Josephus, *Antiquities* 15.259, but the picture in Jewish law is not nearly so clear-cut. One example comes from Mark's Gospel itself: Herodias divorces Philip to marry Herod Antipas (Mark 6:17; see Josephus, *Ant.* 18.110). Rabbinic literature includes grounds for Jewish women seeking divorce, which courts could then enforce against men, using a beating if necessary to achieve the man's consent (see m. Ketub. 5:6; 7:2-5, 9; m. Ned. 11:12; b. Ketub. 77a; m. Gịt. 9:8, and m. ʿArak. 5:6; this last speaks of "writs of divorce for women"). Philo of Alexandria assumes women can divorce husbands in his treatment of Deut 24:1-4 (*On the Special Laws* 3.30). Other ancient documentary evidence reveals Jewish women initiating divorce well before and after the time of Jesus; see James R. Edwards,

as it may, a better literary and canonical reading of the passage sees Jesus here giving his teaching in a way that parallels the mention of both sexes, male and female, man and woman, in the relevant verses of Genesis 1 and 2, and Mark might have made Jesus's teaching here egalitarian as a way of slamming Herodias, responsible for John the Baptist's murder (6:14–29).

I write as the debate regarding Pope Francis's *Amoris Laetitia* is raging, and my view is that this beautiful document can be rightly and fairly read as a pastoral exhortation in continuity with John Paul II's *Familiaris Consortio* and the broader Catholic Tradition on marriage, which is my own Ordinary's understanding of the document. Francis has issued a clarion call to better attend to the pastoral care of marriage so that it might be a joy and not a burden, and Mark's recipe for joy is ready embrace of the cross.

For those who fail in marriage, however, Mark's Gospel is also a source of hope. Mark's Jesus teaches, "all sins will be forgiven the sons of men" (3:28), and as we will see ever more clearly as we approach its final chapters, Mark's Gospel is a Gospel for failures, like Peter and the disciples, who are ever invited to return to Galilee (16:7) and to follow Jesus on the way of discipleship, embracing the cross of their salvation again and again.

The lectionary makes the following verses concerning Jesus's reception of children optional, but if one follows the flow of Mark's Gospel, they flow naturally from Jesus's teaching on marriage, as one would expect.

Mark's Gospel is a Gospel of the Church and written for the Church, its ultimate context. In Mark 10, Jesus addresses

---

The Gospel According to Mark, Pillar New Testament Commentary (Grand Rapids, MI: Eerdmans, 2001), 304, and David Instone-Brewer, "Jewish Women Divorcing Their Husbands in Early Judaism: The Background of Papyrus Şe'elim 13," *Harvard Theological Review* 92 (1999): 349–57.

the crowds (10:1), representative of laypeople, marriage, children, and possessions in that order, and the order is suggestive. Laymen and laywomen who marry according to Jesus's teaching (10:2–12) ought to have and welcome children as Jesus himself welcomed them (10:13–16), and economic life (10:17–31) comes last, presumably because it is to be oriented around marriage and family and serve them. This contrasts with the sad state of modern life, in which many put economic concerns of career first, reject children, and engage in serial monogamy.

Many who had borne children bring them to Jesus for his blessing touch, but the disciples, of course, rebuke them (10:13), perhaps wishing to keep Jesus to themselves (as John does in 9:38), or perhaps seeing Jesus himself as so high and mighty that he shouldn't be bothered, an attitude Jesus will later reject with direct reference to himself in 10:45: Jesus came "not to be served but to serve, and to give his life as a ransom for many."

"Rebuke" is a strong word: in Mark's Gospel, demons are rebuked (1:25, 3:12, 9:25), and Peter has recently been rebuked as Satan (8:33). And Jesus's response is commensurately strong: He is "indignant" (9:14a), the sort of anger that arises not from personal slight, but the sort aroused by perception of deep injustice. And so, Jesus speaks his famous words: "Let the children come to me, do not hinder them; for to such belongs the kingdom of God" (9:14b).

And we're back to children as a model of discipleship. Their humble receptivity illustrates the way one receives blessing from Jesus. And it's the only way: "Truly, I say to you, whoever does not receive the kingdom of God like a child shall not enter it" (9:15).

Mark 10:17–30: Twenty-Eighth Sunday in Ordinary Time (10:17–30 or 10:17–27) / Monday of Week 8 (10:17–27) / Tuesday of Week 8 (10:28–31)

In this passage, the discipleship section turns again to the theme of eternal life (raised at its outset by Jesus in his call to the cross that he emphasizes again in his teaching to the disciples at the end of Mark 9): the rich man is called to recognize Jesus's identity and trust in God, not his wealth. But he cannot and will not and, so, exemplifies the opposite of childlike humility and receptivity in rejecting Jesus's call to the cross.

The man approaches Jesus like many would-be insiders, kneeling before him. He engages in honest flattery and asks about salvation: "Good Teacher, what must I do to inherit eternal life?" (10:17b). The flattery is honest, and Jesus does not really rebuke him but, in 10:21, looks upon him with love. Indeed, Jesus's response, "Why do you call me good? No one is good but God alone" (10:18), isn't a denial of Jesus's goodness or divinity, but rather a subtle call to the man to both recognize who Jesus really is (we've seen several places in Mark's Gospel where Jesus is suggestively identified as God come to earth, especially in the second boat scene, 6:45–52) and also to trust in him.

Indeed, one thinks here of C. S. Lewis's famous trilemma from *Mere Christianity*, in which, reading the Gospels rightly, he asserts that we can't simply pay lip service to Jesus as a good man and teacher, which is how the rich man addresses him. Given what the Gospels report, Jesus is either lunatic, liar, or Lord.[26] The rich man here is forced to confront the same options.

---

[26] C. S. Lewis, *Mere Christianity* (London: Collins, 1952), 53–54.

Jesus responds by naming some commandments (10:19). The commandments he lists come exclusively from the second table of the Law, which deals with love of neighbor, and Jesus here adds something summarized from Deuteronomy 24:14: "Do not defraud" (10:19). The man replies that he's kept what Jesus lists from his youth (10:20), which Jesus seems to accept. Although he is wealthy, the passage suggests the rich man has come by his wealth honestly and, as a good Jew, loved his neighbor.

But does he trust in God? And if so, can he—will he—make the next steps to trust in Jesus, who readers of Mark's Gospel know is God?

Now Jesus moves subtly to the matter of the first table of the law, which deals with love of God. It's not enough, in Jesus's view, to keep the second table. One must also love God, and in Mark's Gospel and in Christianity most broadly, that means encountering God in Jesus. The man lacks one thing, and it's not poverty as such. He lacks Jesus, who calls him to sell his possessions and give them to the poor so that he can follow Jesus on the way of the cross (10:21), unencumbered in body and heart. Jesus invites the rich man to follow him as he called the first disciples on the shores of Galilee (1:16, 18), as well as Levi (2:14), and they left their livelihoods behind, whether their fishing gear (1:16–20) or tax tables (2:14). That's how one has treasure in heaven and finds eternal life.

But the rich man won't: "At that saying his countenance fell, and he went away sorrowful; for he had great possessions" (10:22). Jesus had gazed at him intently (*emblepō*) in love, but apparently the man couldn't meet his divine gaze. He, like other failing disciples, does not have eyes to see, whereas those disciples who do follow Jesus have eyes to see, like the blind man in 8:22–26 who came to see everything clearly.

Key to the passage is the issue of trust; the man can't, or won't, relinquish his riches to follow Jesus and trust in God's providence, the God who through, with, and in Jesus can quickly feed a multitude with meager fish and loaves. And so Jesus will remind the disciples that it is hard "for those who *trust* in riches" (10:24) to enter the kingdom of God (emphasis added).

Trust, in Mark's Gospel, is the meaning of faith, and so it's oriented to the cross. And so the rich man's ultimate problem is failure to embrace the cross. Of such men, Léon Bloy wrote:

> Those among the rich who are not, in the rigorous sense, damned, can understand poverty, because they are poor themselves, after a fashion; they cannot understand destitution. Capable of giving alms, perhaps, but incapable of stripping themselves bare, they will be moved, to the sound of beautiful music, at Jesus's sufferings, but His Cross, the reality of His Cross, will horrify them. They want it all out of gold, bathed in light, costly and of little weight; pleasant to see hanging from a woman's beautiful throat.[27]

That's why Jesus says that it's hard for the rich to enter the kingdom (10:23).

The theology of the cross runs counter to the logic of the world, of course, but also counter to the logic of a major strain of the Old Testament, the Deuteronomistic theology, in which blessings are a sign of divine favor. That's why the disciples are amazed at Jesus's words (10:24a). Jesus doubles down, however, with his radical remark that it's easier for a camel to come through the eye of a needle than for a rich man to be

---

[27] Léon Bloy, *Pilgrim of the Absolute* (New York: Pantheon, 1947), 175–76.

saved (10:25), and the disciples now are "exceedingly astonished" and ask, "Then who can be saved?" (10:26).

It may be the disciples are yet thinking along the lines of the theology of blessing, which is in essence a theology of glory, where material rewards are a sign of divine favor. If so, they're certainly forgetful of Jesus's recent call to the cross (8:34–38), and they've had issues with forgetting before ("And do you not remember?" in 8:18). They fail here, enamored yet of the theology of glory that's part and parcel of the theology of blessing. But Jesus gazes at them as he gazed at the young man, reminding them that with God salvation is possible (10:27), for God can open eyes and unstop ears and soften hearts so that they, and we, might embrace the cross, trusting in the God revealed in Jesus.

Many in the West today are wealthy beyond the wildest dreams of kings and queens of old. As the legacy of the postwar economic boom continues, prosperity remains a problem for many Western Christians. And so, this passage is a special challenge. Some scholars, reading the Gospel as a reflection of the history of the situation of Mark's own community, have said Mark's emphasis on the cross is meant to be a comfort for those who suffer (or suffered) under Nero's brutal persecution. But the opposite is possible: perhaps Mark emphasizes the cross to the ultimate, unflinching, inescapable degree he does not to comfort the afflicted but to afflict the comfortable, to shock Christians unacquainted with suffering out of their complacency. So too can Mark function today.

Finally, at the close of the passage, we see the pattern we already encountered in the story of the Transfiguration: a scene of glory to encourage those on the way of the Cross. The cross is not the final word, not the destination, but the journey. The journey ends in Resurrection, in glory. Peter reminds Jesus the disciples have left everything to follow him (10:28). Jesus responds with a promise: all they have left will be restored, and above all, they will receive eternal life (10:29–30). But the only way to life is the way of death, the way of the cross. And so, many who appear to be first—the wealthy, those who seem to be favored—will be last, and the last—those who appear as the wretched of the earth—will be first, forever (10:31).

Mark 10:32–45: Twenty-Ninth Sunday in Ordinary Time (10:35–45 or 10:42–45) / Wednesday of Week 8 (10:32–45)

The discipleship section comes toward a close with the third Passion prediction, after which the disciples, far from acting like children, comport themselves as spoiled brats, again displaying colossal obtuseness as we once more see the contrast between the theology of the cross and the theology of glory.

The third Passion prediction (which the lectionary omits for the twenty-ninth Sunday in Ordinary time but includes for the weekday reading for the Wednesday of week 8) is the most vivid of the three, where many Markan catchwords and themes meet. The disciples are "on the way" (*en tē hodō*), the way of discipleship, going up to Jerusalem, where Jesus has already predicted his necessary death. "Up" is not without significance: geographically, Jerusalem is on Mount Zion, a small mountain, and pilgrims and travelers would make an arduous upward journey. Here the way of the cross begins to transform into the way of glory.

Jesus is leading (*proagō*) them, as if he's ahead and those who follow are some distance behind because they're "afraid" (10:32). The other two times *proagō* appears, in 14:28 and 16:7, Jesus and then the young man at the empty tomb indicate a final journey to Galilee, after the Resurrection. And so, here we see the cross–glory and death–resurrection patterns again: Jesus is leading the way to his and their crucifixion in Jerusalem, but he will also lead the way for them after his Resurrection.

His way is their way: they've been called to carry their own crosses (8:34), and here Jesus reminds them that "we" are going to Jerusalem, and gives them the most detailed Passion prediction of all. In the first Passion prediction, Jesus stated that the elders, chief priests, and scribes would reject him (8:31). In the second, Jesus stated that he would be handed over into the hands of men (9:31). Here, in the third, Jesus states that the chief priests and scribes will hand him over to the Gentiles (10:33). It's as if the first Passion prediction involved the Jews, the second Gentiles, and the third both: representative of the whole world, Jew and Gentile conspire together to kill the Christ, to kill God.

The vivid details of this third Passion prediction provided in Mark 10:33–34 also predict the precise events of the Passion according to St. Mark. He is handed over (14:41) to the chief priests and scribes (14:53), who will condemn him to death (14:64) and deliver him to the Gentiles (15:1), who then will mock him (15:29–30), spit on him (14:65; 15:19), flog him (15:15), and kill him (15:37). But Jesus will rise, as he predicts (16:1–8).

Jesus proves himself a worthy prophet in Mark's Gospel; his prophecies come true. Beyond the above, he predicts his betrayal (14:17–21) and the apostasy of Peter and all the disciples (14:26–31). Mark does more than simply show that Jesus is a reliable prophet, however; dominical prophecy serves irony. Immediately after Jesus's prediction about his being condemned to death comes true (14:64), those spitting on and beating Jesus dare him to "Prophesy!" (14:65). Well, he just did.

And, of course, there is juxtaposition: the disciples are afraid, but they're not too fearful to engage in a bit of glory seeking as we return to play another round of "who is the greatest?" James and John, part of the inner triad, among the first disciples called, come to Jesus like mischievous children wanting a "yes" before letting their parents know what they want. Addressing Jesus as a mere "teacher" (10:35), like the rich man who failed to follow Jesus, they state that what they want is glory, as if they didn't hear or just plain forgot the Passion prediction immediately prior. They wish to sit at Jesus's left and right in express "glory" (10:37), above the other Apostles. So much for heeding Jesus's command to them to "be at peace with each other" (9:50), as their furtive request makes the other disciples indignant when it's exposed (10:41).

Like the voice speaking to Peter at the Transfiguration, Jesus responds to their desire for glory with the word of the cross. The disciples don't know what they are asking because they've forgotten, if they ever knew, that the one and only way of glory is the way of the cross. Jesus asks them if they can undergo his baptism and drink his chalice (10:38), references to his coming suffering and death.[28] They don't know what they're asking, and when they reply, "We are able," they don't know what they're saying. But they're going to find out: Jesus informs them they will indeed receive Jesus's baptism and chalice (10:39), but their subsequent position in glory is not up even to Jesus (10:40).

"Baptism" and "chalice" (or in many translations "cup") in this passage are tensive symbols, suggestive, polyvalent. Catholic readers hear here the two chief sacraments of the

---

[28] In the Old Testament, the "cup" often refers to drinking the cup of divine wrath; see Pss 11:6; 16:5; 75:8; Isa 51:17–23; Jer 25:15–28; 49:12; Zech 12:2–3; Lam 4:21; and Hab 2:15–16.

faith. The passage presents the first instance in literature of "Baptism" linked to suffering.[29] In the world of Mark's story, it's natural to see Baptism as involving suffering, for Jesus received his call to sacrificial death precisely at his baptism when the heavenly voice (1:11) alluded to Isaac's sacrifice in Genesis 22. Jesus's baptismal vocation is suffering and death, and John and James and the others will be baptized with the same suffering, and the Sacrament of Baptism is baptism into Jesus's death (see Rom 6:1–4).

So too "chalice" or "cup." While, in the Old Testament, the "cup" is often negative, indicating judgment and wrath, it can also be positive and promissory (as in Ps 23:5, "my cup over-flows," and 116:13, the "cup of salvation"). And so too, the Eucharistic reference here connotes a positive paradox: Jesus will institute the Eucharist in Mark 14:22–25. The chalice of Jesus's suffering becoming the Eucharistic chalice of salvation as the way of cruciform death is also the way to life. John and James and the disciples drink there of Jesus's chalice (14:23, and so more prophecy is fulfilled), which is a chalice of both wrath and salvation.

Jesus declares that the Eucharistic chalice at that Passover meal is "my blood of the [new] covenant" (14:24; I believe "new" is original to Mark on the strength of the early manu-script support of Codex Alexandrinus, and its fit with Mark's emphasis on the newness of Jesus and the kingdom he brings). Like the blood of the aboriginal Passover lambs, which spared the Israelites from divine wrath and death at the time of the original exodus, Jesus's blood will spare the many for whom it is poured out from divine wrath and death as he inaugurates the New Exodus. And yet Jesus will drink it new as salvation mere days hence, after the Resurrection, when he drinks it

---

[29] See Edwards, *Mark*, 323.

new in the kingdom of God (14:25), after which it for us too becomes the chalice of salvation.

And so, the pattern obtains in the story and in the sacraments: suffering and cross precede salvation and glory, and Baptism and Eucharist connote and convey both.

The other ten disciples hear of James and John's request, and they're livid. Jesus then takes the occasion to level them, giving his famous teaching on humble service, perhaps the second heart of Mark's Gospel, after Jesus's teaching on the cross (8:34–38). In doing so, Jesus subtly recalls the theme of the earthly murderous powers like Herod Antipas and his Herodians: "You know that those who are supposed to rule over the Gentiles lord it over them, and their great men exercise authority over them" (10:42). But the Christian way is opposite: "But it shall not be so among you"; instead of ruling in a hierarchy of power, like Herod's, the way to greatness is the way of service, being a *diakonos* (10:43b), a table waiter, and being first, the greatest of the great, requires humiliation lower than that, slavery, being the slave (*doulos*) of all (10:44).

The pattern of cross and glory here is obvious in the subsumed paradoxical pattern of humiliation and exaltation, and so Jesus reminds them of his example: "For the Son of man also came not to be served but to serve, and to give his life as a ransom for many" (10:45).

In our age in which religion has been reduced to morality, exemplary readings of this passage abound, as if the main point was some sort of simple service to others. If we stop there, however, we lose the force of the cross; we lose grace, reducing religion to rules. In fact, the passage is relentlessly apocalyptic, the language of "ransom" raising the concept of *Christus Victor*. Christ will not simply serve by humbling himself to his humiliating death on his Cross; he will in fact hand himself over to the one who holds the power of death,

Mark 10:46–52

Satan, ransoming those whom Satan holds in bondage. Jesus makes himself slave to sin, death, hell, and the devil, and destroys them thereby.

Mark 10:46–52: Thirtieth Sunday in Ordinary Time / Thursday of Week 8

In closing the discipleship section, Mark presents Bartimaeus as the most powerful paradigm of discipleship on offer. The discipleship section opened with the healing of an anonymous blind man, and both healings begin the same way, with the phrase *kai erchontai eis* and then the place name, either Bethsaida or Jericho. Jesus has traveled from Galilee to Judea and restored the sight of the blind in each.

Further, this story is the last miracle in Mark's Gospel, and it's significant that Jesus here is identified as "the Nazarene" (*Nazarēnos*, 10:47), as he was in the story of his first miracle (1:24). It's more than a statement of Jesus's hometown origins, and it's more than a verbal tie linking stories opening and closing his healing ministry. It also suggests the presence of the divine power that flowed through Samson, identified as a *naziraios theou* (Judg 16:7 in the LXX), a Nazarite of God.[30]

Jesus and the disciples will begin their final ascent to Jerusalem, going two thirds of a mile in vertical elevation over a distance of roughly 150 stadia, or eighteen miles; the way of the cross is arduous. But, just as Jesus and the disciples depart, along with a great multitude coming with them, they encounter Bartimaeus, a blind beggar sitting "alongside the way" (*para tēn hodon*), soliciting alms from all those making the Passover pilgrimage (10:46).

---

[30] See ibid., 329.

233

Hearing that Jesus is approaching, he cries out to Jesus the Son of David for mercy (10:47). Only Bartimaeus among men and women calls Our Lord by his holy name of "Jesus" in Mark's Gospel; it's as if he knows Jesus's identity. But, whereas the demons who called Jesus either by name (5:7) or by some other appropriate appellation (1:24) sought to best him or at least escape with their demonic hide, Bartimaeus calls Jesus by name seeking mercy. "Son of David" means Messiah: most Jews believed the Christ would be a new David, the ultimate inheritor of the promises to David (see especially 2 Sam 7:13–14a) who, like David, would make war on the nations oppressing Israel, pacify the land, and establish a kingdom. For all the talk of the messianic secret in Mark's Gospel, Jesus here does nothing to reject the title, even as a multitude travels with him, and he will shortly enter Jerusalem displaying deliberate messianic symbolism.

As with the hemorrhaging woman, who had her illness and felt shame and had to fight her way through the crowd as an obstacle, the crowd here tells Bartimaeus more or less to shut up, drowning out his voice (10:48), which is all he has, since, being blind, he can't really fight his way through the throng to seize Jesus, unlike the woman. But like her, he persists, crying out all the more, "Son of David, have mercy on me!" And so Jesus stops and tells those in hearing to call Bartimaeus, and so they do: in obedience, they tell him, "Take heart; rise, he is calling you" (10:49).

"Take heart" (*pharseō*) is exactly what Jesus told the terrified disciples in the second boat scene (6:50), and here, Bartimaeus responds, unlike the disciples then. In Mark's Gospel, "rise" is always redolent of the Resurrection, to which all miracles ultimately point because it's that which powers all healings. Jesus is calling Bartimaeus to wholeness like he will one day call the faithful dead to wholeness.

And yet, Jesus asks Bartimaeus what he wants him to do for him (10:51a), just like he asked James and John what they wanted from him (10:36). Unlike the brothers, who, in their blindness, ignored the Passion prediction, Bartimaeus wants to see (10:51b). Indeed, having employed the very name of Jesus, he now calls Jesus *rabbouni*, which, in Jewish literature, is employed never in addressing human beings but only as a direct address of God.[31]

Using the same words with which he dismissed the healed hemorrhaging woman in Mark 5:34, "your faith has healed/ saved you" (*hē pistis sou sesōken se* with *hupage*), Jesus sends Bartimaeus on his way, no longer blind: "And immediately he received his sight and followed him on the way" (10:52). Mark expressly employs the language of discipleship here, "follow" and "on the way." Having sought sight and received it, Bartimaeus has now left the sidelines "alongside the way" (10:46) and joined Jesus "on the way" of discipleship, the way of the cross, the way of the Lord.

---

[31] See ibid., 331.

CHAPTER 6

O Jerusalem! (Mark 11:1–13:37)

We now come to Jerusalem, Jesus's goal. Although Mark presents the events in chapters 11–16 occurring over eight liturgical days,[1] from Palm Sunday to the Sunday of the Resurrection,[2] those chapters occupy over a third of Mark's Gospel and are organized not only thematically but

---

[1] Commentators note that it appears Jesus would have been to Jerusalem before, and perhaps would have already spent months there: Jesus seems to have allies in the city ready to assist him with animals (11:1–6) and Passover preparations (14:12–16); Jesus's entry into Jerusalem in Mark 11:8–10 suggests to many scholars the feast of Tabernacles, not Passover; the barren fig tree in Mark 11:12–14 suggests a season other than Passover; and Jesus's statement in Mark 14:49 that he taught in the Temple "day after day" (*kath' hēmeran*) without arrest suggests he spent more time in the Temple than Mark's narrative tells (though the Greek is better translated "by day," in contrast to night). Nevertheless, for Christians, the canonical form of the text is authoritative, and so we are interested in Mark's story rather than any reconstructed prehistory.

[2] Marcus rightly reconstructs Mark's Passion week as follows: the Triumphal Entry occurs on Palm Sunday (11:1–11); the cursing of the fig tree and Jesus's Temple action occurs on Monday (11:12–19); Jesus's debates with the authorities and his eschatological discourse occur on Tuesday (11:20–13:37); the plot to kill Jesus and his anointing at Bethany occur on Wednesday (14:1–11); the preparations for the Passover and the Lord's Supper, as well as the Gethsemane and arrest sequence and Jesus's trial before the high priest, occur on Thursday (14:12–72); Jesus's trial before Pilate and his crucifixion, death, and burial occur on Friday (15:1–47); nothing happens on Saturday; and the eighth day, Sunday, finds the tomb empty (16:1–8). See Joel Marcus, *Mark 8–16: A New Translation with Introduction and Commentary*, Anchor Yale Bible Commentaries 27a (New York: Doubleday, 2009), 768–69.

also liturgically. Chapters 11–13 concern the judgment and destruction of the Temple, as well as Jerusalem, while chapters 14–16 concern how Jesus and his Eucharist will become the new locus of the presence of God and new sacrifice going forward, as Jesus's Church continues Israel's work of redemption in the world.[3]

In broad outline, chapters 11–13 comprise a large Markan sandwich: Jesus will enact a prophecy of the Temple's destruction in chapter 11 by deed; he will teach truth in the midst of the corrupt Temple system in chapter 12; and he will expressly, but secretly to four of his disciples, condemn the Temple and city and commit them to destruction in chapter 13 by word. The small circle of disciples learns in secret what Jesus does and teaches publicly, as elsewhere in Mark's Gospel.

So too with chapters 14–16. In chapter 14, Jesus above all institutes the Eucharist, in chapter 15, he will give his life as a ransom for many in crucifixion, and in chapter 16, he will be raised from the dead. Jesus's cruciform death culminating in the centurion's sardonic, ironic confession of Jesus as the Son of God forms the middle panel of yet another Markan triptych. The crucifixion of the Son of God powers the Eucharist, which interprets the crucifixion, and it's the crucified Jesus who is risen, remaining a Eucharistic sacrifice forever.

---

[3] It is fair to say Jesus and Eucharist replace the Temple. But one must again remember that, when we are dealing with Jesus's life, the earliest Church, and the New Testament texts, we are dealing with debate and polemics intramural to Judaism, as Jesus was Jewish, as was the earliest Church, even after it began accepting Gentiles. Christianity moves from being a Jewish party within the parent body of Judaism to being a Jewish sect estranged from the parent body of Judaism to being a separate religion *sociologically*. But theologically, Christianity, especially Catholicism, remains Jewish, as recognized by modern Catholics like novelist and essayist Walker Percy, who often referred to the Catholic Church as a "Jewish sect," and like Pope Pius XI, who, on September 6, 1938, said to a group of Belgian pilgrims, "Spiritually, we are Semites."

Mark 11:1–10: Palm Sunday Procession of Palms (Option 1)

Just how triumphal is this entry? Matthew and Luke present Jesus's entry as a mesmerizing messianic event bringing the city to a fever pitch, but Mark's version is different: it's muted, suggestive, understated, fitting for a Gospel of secrecy. It's not certain whether the crowds hailing Jesus's arrival as the Son of David (11:9–10) are the crowds Jesus brought with him from Jericho (see 10:46 and compare "they" in 11:1) or the crowds already in and of Jerusalem. Nor is it certain that the inhabitants of and pilgrims to Jerusalem fail to receive him in the Temple (11:11), as if the triumphal entry flopped.

Given Markan secrecy, the precise language of Mark's text, and the phenomena of Markan juxtaposition and sandwiches, the following interpretation seems most likely: Jesus deliberately enters the city as the Christ, but subtly, so that those with eyes to see (like Bartimaeus, who addressed Jesus as "son of David," and thus as Christ in Mark 10:47–48) could perceive what he was about. Those hailing his entry with shouts of "hosanna" are those who followed him from Jericho with Bartimaeus, not the residents of and pilgrims to Jerusalem.

Jerusalem is doomed already, even before his arrival. The scribes from Jerusalem had declared Jesus to be possessed by Beelzebul (3:22) and challenged him on his disciples' failure to keep the tradition of the elders (7:1–5). And so, in 11:1, Jesus goes to Bethphage, which in Aramaic means "house of unripe figs." The very name indicates the Temple's destruction, for Mark will next present a sandwich consisting of Jesus cursing a fig tree for lacking figs and his Temple action symbolizing its destruction (11:11–26). The withered fig tree represents the spiritual desiccation of Jerusalem and its Temple, which the mention of Bethphage in 11:1 suggests. Jerusalem and the

O Jerusalem! (Mark 11:1–13:37)

Temple stand condemned before Jesus enacts and prophesies their destruction.

When Jesus arrives alone at the Temple and looks around with his divine gaze (11:11), then, it's not surprising that there's no crowd. Mark wouldn't have the disciples and followers Jesus has brought from Jericho accompany him, for the Temple is already done. But the lack of any reception on the part of the inhabitants of and pilgrims to Jerusalem indicates Jerusalem's utter and ultimate rejection of Jesus. The crowds of Jerusalem do not *turn* on him days later and cry for his crucifixion in Pilate's courtyard; Jerusalem has already rejected him. Further, Mark has Jesus go deliberately to the Temple in the evening (*opsias ēdē ousēs tēs ōras*, 11:11), after its services have ended, to indicate the cessation of its relevance and replacement by the Eucharist, which Jesus institutes precisely in the evening (*opsias genomenēs*, 14:17).

Jesus does enter Jerusalem deliberately as the eschatological Christ and even as God, the LORD. He goes to the Mount of Olives (11:1), which, in Zechariah 14:1–9, is where the LORD will plant his very feet to begin the End, dividing the Mount of Olives itself in half so that his people might flee (as Mark will have Jesus instruct his disciples to flee when Jerusalem is one day besieged, 13:14). The Mount of Olives is also where David retreated after Israel rejected him (2 Sam 15:30–31),[4] certainly significant for Mark's story: Jerusalem and the Israelites reject Jesus the Son of David as they once rejected David. Mark thus emphasizes the split between Jesus and Jerusalem as the crowd coming with Jesus from Jericho hails Jesus as the one who now brings "the kingdom of our father David" as Jesus's would-be army (11:10).

Jesus has two anonymous disciples commandeer a *pōlos*, a

---

[4] See Marcus, *Mark 8–16*, 772.

240

colt or young donkey (11:2), in the name of the Lord (*kurios*, 11:3), suggesting his divine identity and the power of the divine name and showing that Jesus's prophecies come true by the force of his very words (as in 14:12–16, in which Jesus similarly sends two disciples to commandeer a room to celebrate the Passover and institute the Eucharist). Mark shows Jesus's prophecies being fulfilled in the world of his story for the rhetorical purpose of encouraging his readers to believe his prophecies yet unfulfilled in the story, such as the destruction of the Temple and Jerusalem and his promise to come again.

The colt Jesus rides is unbroken, never ridden, a royal sacred animal (Num 19:2 and Deut 21:3), which is what Zechariah prophesied the Messiah would ride (Zech 9:9). Thus is fulfilled Jacob's prophecy in Genesis 49:10–11 that the scepter would not depart from Judah: Jesus the Judahite, the representative Jew, bears forth the mission of Israel. And he does so by his sacrifice and Eucharist, for Jacob prophesied: "He has washed his garments in wine and his vesture in the blood of grapes" (Gen 49:11b).

Further Old Testament passages resonate with the theme of royalty and inform Mark's story of Jesus's subtle messianic entry. In 1 Kings 1:38 and 44, Solomon, David's son, rides a mule on his way to his accession to the throne. In 2 Kings 9:13, cloaks are spread under Jehu the king, as the crowd does for Jesus (11:7). In the era of the Hasmonean dynasty, Simon the Maccabean king entered Jerusalem in triumph leading the people, who waved palms, having saved them from Trypho and cleansed the citadel from its pollutions (1 Macc 13:49–53). And the chants of the crowd accompanying Jesus are taken from Psalm 118:25–26, which addressed God and became hymns for the occasion of royal victories.

The reader seeing Jesus enter Jerusalem as the divine king might next expect his enthronement or the cleansing of the

Temple of any pollutions, or both. As Jerusalem has already rejected Jesus, though, so God has rejected Jerusalem, and so Jesus's next move is to enact prophetic announcements of its Temple's destruction.

Mark 11:11–26: Friday of Week 8

We encounter now not a threefold sandwich but a fourfold intercalation, the A sections in Mark 11:11 and 15–19 concerning the Temple's destruction and the B sections in 11:12–14 and 20–26 concerning a fruitless, withered fig tree symbolic of the Temple. We also see the contrast between Jesus's more oblique and suggestive teaching in public and his direct and revelatory teaching in private to his disciples. In the Temple action, Jesus teaches by suggestive action and allusion that the Temple will be destroyed. In his teaching to his disciples afterwards, he teaches expressly on faith, prayer, and forgiveness.

Jesus's entry in the Temple in Mark 11:11 seems anticlimactic, if one assumes Jesus received a ready reception into the city, for no one is there either to receive or to oppose him. Yet, there is no narrative dissonance if we assume (1) that the crowds hailing Jesus with hosannas came with him from Jericho, (2) that Jesus went to the Temple late in the evening (as the text states) when it was shut down for the day, and (3) that 11:11 begins an intercalation.

What we have in Mark 11:11 is the fulfillment of Malachi 3:1: the LORD is come to his Temple in Jesus. But the prophecy then asks, "But who can endure the day of his coming, and who can stand when he appears?" (Mal 3:2a). Not the Temple, which Jesus will, by his prophetic actions, soon declare is done.

In Mark 11:11, the A section, Jesus enters the Temple and looks around with his intense gaze (*periblepō*, which appears six times in Mark's Gospel, five times with reference to Jesus discerning the depths of a situation with his divine spirit: 3:5, 3:34, 5:32, 10:23, and 11:11; see also 9:8). He then retreats from the Temple and city, returning to the village of Bethany with his disciples, just as he will retreat with his disciples after his Temple action in 11:19.

In Mark 11:12-14, the B section, Jesus curses a fig tree that many commentators and skeptics have felt didn't deserve condemnation. Either Jesus is a mercurial, vituperative, rural hothead ignorant of agriculture, or something else is going on. We'll opt for something else, since the Catholic tradition teaches that perceived oddities in Scripture are a hint to look higher.

Jesus is "hungry" (11:12) and, seeing a fig tree, hopes to find something to eat, but it has nothing but leaves, "for it was not the season for figs" (11:13). He then curses it forever: "May no one ever eat fruit from you again" (11:14a). Why would Jesus do this when there shouldn't be figs anyway? Because the fig tree symbolizes the Temple. Because the Temple is now out of season, it will no longer satisfy spiritual hunger and will soon be razed, its sacrifices replaced by a meal that satisfies, the Eucharist.

In Mark 11:15-18, the A' section, Jesus enters the city and Temple with his disciples and commits his famous Temple action, historically called the "Cleansing of the Temple." Earlier generations of Enlightenment-influenced scholars who saw Christianity and Judaism as opposed often thought that the problem with the Temple was either sacrifice itself, because Jesus supposedly taught an ethical system and an interior religion of the heart, or, thanks to sentimentalism about St. Francis of Assisi, money changing and trade in the precincts of the Temple.

But the Temple's essence is sacrifice; that's what it's *for*. And the money changing and trade going on was necessary for its sacrifices. Pilgrims from far away needed good Jewish coinage to buy animals onsite, since you wouldn't drag your sacrificial lamb with you from Greece or Italy. Jesus isn't a reformer of the Temple, but its replacement. The problem is that the Jewish leadership, with its power center in Jerusalem and the Temple, has rejected Jesus. The city and Temple are already doomed by the time Jesus arrives.

Most people think prophets simply *speak* the words of the LORD. But they also *enact* prophecy. And so, when Jesus drives out animal merchants and money changers and kicks over tables, he's not throwing a petulant fit. He's enacting prophecy, like Hosea, whom the LORD called to demonstrate Israel's unfaithfulness by marrying Gomer the harlot and using her to father two sons and a daughter (Hos 1:1–9), or like Ezekiel, whom the LORD commanded to build a sandbox Jerusalem, next to which he was to lie for a long time to symbolize the city's siege (Ezek 4:1–17). So too Jesus: he's enacting a prophecy of the destruction of the Temple and the concomitant cessation of its sacrifices.[5]

This explains the import of Jesus's allusive quotations: "Is it not written, 'My house shall be called a house of prayer for all the nations'? But you have made it a den of robbers" (11:17). The first quotation is from Isaiah 56:7, and the context is foreigners from among the nations bringing their sacrifices(!) to the Temple on Mount Zion at the end of time.

---

[5] Indeed, *skeuos* in Mark 11:16, which the RSV tradition and the NAB render "anything," is often used of cultic vessels in the LXX, as well as in Josephus (*Antiquities* 18.85 and *Wars of the Jews* 1.39). It's also used within Jesus's Parable of the Strong Man in Mark 3:27, translated there as "goods" or "property": "But no one can enter a strong man's house and plunder his goods, unless he first binds the strong man; then indeed he may plunder his house." Given that *skeuos* appears in Mark only in these two passages, it may be that Mark has gone so far as to suggest that the Temple (by reference to its vessels) stands under Satan's domination.

The import is that the Jewish leadership should have gotten on board with Jesus's eschatological kingdom mission, and then the Gentiles would be praying and offering the sacrifices Isaiah prophesied.

But the leadership didn't, and so Jesus also alludes to Jeremiah's famous prophecy of the destruction of the first Temple in Jeremiah 7:1–15 with his words "den of robbers," taken from Jeremiah 7:11. These words have led some to think the problem with the Temple is trade itself or deceitful, unfair trade, but the full context reveals something else. The LORD, through Jeremiah, condemns the people's wickedness: they "steal, murder, commit adultery, swear falsely, burn incense to Ba'al, and go after other gods that [they] have not known" (Jer 7:9) and then have the temerity to retreat to the Temple and say "We are delivered" while continuing to commit "all these abominations" (7:10). The LORD then says:

> "Has this house, which is called by my name, become a
> den of robbers in your eyes?" (7:11)

The LORD compares the people of Jeremiah's day to "robbers," brigands, highwaymen, who would lie in wait and ambush travelers, kill them, take their possessions, and retreat to their hideaways in the hills—their caves, their dens. Such people preying on the innocent are the lowest of all criminals and merit exemplary and extreme punishment.

And the people of Jeremiah's day certainly received it, as the Babylonians came and razed Jerusalem, leveled the Temple, and deported the survivors en masse. It's a disaster beyond belief; and since the LORD God of Israel was thought to dwell in the Temple, it means either God doesn't exist, or the Babylonian deities are stronger, or God has abandoned the people for their sins. Most Jews opted to think the third.

In alluding to Jeremiah 7, then, Jesus is comparing the people of Jeremiah's day to the people of his own day, at least the Jewish leadership: they have made the house of the LORD, the Temple, a den of robbers. And thus, Jesus is predicting that the second Temple's fate will match the fate of the first Temple. For the Gentiles to be included in the people of God will now require a new Temple with a new sacrifice, Jesus with his Church and the Eucharist.

The chief priests and scribes hear (*akouō*) of it (11:18). But they leave Jesus alone at this point because the crowds are "astonished" (*ekplēssō*) at his teaching, just as the crowds were "astonished" (*ekplēssō*) at his teaching in 1:22 when Jesus "taught them as one who had authority, and not as the scribes." James Edwards writes: "The effect of this repetition is to convey that Jesus's authority supersedes that of the religious leaders in both the Temple and the synagogue. . . . The synagogue and the Temple were the two places in Judaism where the teaching of God was revealed and practiced. In the same two places the teaching of Jesus supersedes the Torah and Temple cult, holding the crowds in amazement."[6]

Mark's Gospel is liturgical, and it's not too much to see here Jesus fulfilling and passing on the fundamental twofold liturgical structure of Word and Sacrament. He is the ultimate teacher, interpreting and fulfilling the Torah as its ultimate referent, and he is the ultimate sacrifice, whose crucifixion and Eucharist fulfill Temple sacrifices. Both Word and Sacrament flow from Jesus, the one incarnate Word of God, and so Christians encounter Jesus in sermon and sacrifice, in ambo and altar.[7]

---

[6] James R. Edwards, *The Gospel According to Mark*, Pillar New Testament Commentary (Grand Rapids, MI: Eerdmans, 2001), 344–45.

[7] See pp. 10–11 above, on Pope Benedict XVI, *Verbum Domini*, §24.

Jesus and the disciples depart the city (11:19), just as Jesus departed earlier in 11:11, providing a parallel in the A–A' sections of this intercalation. And now, the next morning, bringing us to the B' section, Jesus and the disciples encounter the fig tree "withered away to its roots" (11:20). In 11:14, readers were informed that his disciples heard (*akouō*) Jesus curse the fig tree (just as the chief priests and scribes heard [*akouō*] of Jesus's Temple action in 11:18, Mark deftly linking Temple and fig tree), and now Peter exclaims, "Master, look! The fig tree which you cursed has withered" (11:21)! It's withered "to the roots," suggesting again that the Temple doesn't need reform, but destruction: it's now desiccated root, trunk, branch, and leaves, lacking the fruit to fill hungry hearts.

But Jesus's gospel can do so. In Mark 11:20–21, we find the Greek words *xērainō* (withered) and *rhiza* (roots), and we find them also in 4:6, in the Parable of the Sower, where Jesus talks about seed that falls on rocky, shallow soil, which springs up but, lacking roots, ultimately withers. Jesus's word, his Gospel, has failed to take root in the Jewish leadership, and so their Temple and city will suffer for it. But where Jesus's word of the Gospel finds good soil, it bears a crop thirty, sixty, even a hundredfold (4:8).

And so Jesus replies to Peter's exclamation with the typical Markan advice to "have faith in God" (11:22). He then declares that it's possible for those who have faith without doubt to command mountains to cast themselves into the sea, and it would happen (11:23). Note here that Jesus is now teaching by word what he already did by example of his deed: he had pronounced a curse upon the fig tree (11:14), and it happened (11:20).

This command is a form of radical prayer, which is why Mark's Jesus next shifts into express teaching on prayer: "Therefore I tell you, whatever you ask in prayer, believe that you receive it, and you will" (11:24). Normally, when one thinks of prayer, one thinks of speaking to God. But here we have an instance of Jesus teaching that prayer is also speaking commands to things under God's authority, in his name, in faith.[8]

Earlier in his Gospel, Mark gave an example. After Jesus exorcises the boy in Mark 9:14–29, he explains to his disciples, "This kind cannot be driven out by anything but prayer" (9:29). But Jesus didn't pray to his Father; he spoke a command to the demon. Elsewhere in Mark's Gospel he exercises authority in commanding deaf ears to open and blind eyes to see, paralytics to walk and lepers to be clean.

For Mark, that's radical, authoritative prayer: pure faith moves mountains. The other condition is forgiveness. Whenever one prays—and given how Mark shifts into forgiveness from prayer in this passage, especially when one is exercising the authoritative prayer of command—one must forgive others to receive God's forgiveness (11:25–26).

Now, talk of radical prayer in which one commands demons and disease to flee makes people nervous. In our day, it's the province of Pentecostalism, and Mark's Gospel, especially the present passage, is a favorite of faith healers. And yet, we have to take Mark seriously here, even if outlandish claims, on the one hand, or our own weakness and fear, on the other, lead us to seek an interpretive way out through the door to the shadowlands of domesticated faith.

Two true things are relevant here. First, Mark's Jesus prays radically and teaches his disciples to go and do likewise, to command mountains to upend themselves into the sea. Unless we wish to settle for a domesticated faith, we need to take that

---

[8] On "Authoritative Prayer," see Richard Foster, *Prayer: Finding the Heart's True Home* (New York: HarperOne, 2009), 229–42.

seriously. Second, Mark's Gospel centers on the cross, opposing its theology to a theology of glory, and so even Jesus had a prayer denied in his moment of greatest crisis. As C. S. Lewis wrote:

> There are, no doubt, passages in the New Testament which may seem at first sight to promise an invariable granting of our prayers. But that cannot be what they really mean. For in the very heart of the story we meet a glaring instance to the contrary. In Gethsemane the holiest of all petitioners prayed three times that a certain cup might pass from Him. It did not. After that the idea that prayer is recommended to us as a sort of infallible gimmick may be dismissed.[9]

And Gethsemane is the key: all seeming paradoxes are resolved in the cross. Only through embracing the cross, where we have perfect faith in God, though He slay us, and where we come to the point where we can forgive those who have hurt us, though they slay us, can we have achieved in us the spiritual perfection and power that permits us to command demons and disease to desist in our exercise of radical prayer.

Back, then, to Mark's story more directly. What mountain was it, finally, when Jesus speaks about "this mountain" in Mark 11:23? One possibility is that it was the more or less artificial mountain of the fortress known as the Herodion, which was constructed by Herod the Great and may have contained his tomb. Here, Jesus would be hinting at the symbolic overthrow of the Herodian dynasty that causes him and John the Baptist before him so much grief. Perhaps a better possi-

---

9 C. S. Lewis, *The World's Last Night and Other Essays* (New York: HarperOne, 2017), 3.

bility is that Jesus is referring to the Temple mount, as he will do in 13:3 when he is sitting opposite from it on the Mount of Olives. Just as Jesus had faith enough to command the fig tree to wither, he implies that he himself has faith enough to command the Temple's destruction.

Mark 11:27–33: Saturday of Week 8

We now begin a new subsection in Mark's Gospel concerning Jesus's authority (11:27–12:44), a major theme of Mark's Gospel (see 1:22 and 27, and 2:10), which he shares with his disciples (see 3:15, 6:7, 13:34). Jesus's authority is rooted both in it being God-given and in his own identity as divine, as Christ, as Son of God, as Son of man. Those who have faith in Jesus recognize his identity, at least in part, and those who reject him do not. The latter bring judgment on Jerusalem, the Temple, and themselves.

After Jesus judges Jerusalem and condemns the Temple, the priests, with the scribes and elders, push back on the question of Jesus's authority (11:27–33), and (in Mark's dramatic telling) Jesus will then hit them hammer and tongs in several episodes of conflict and teaching in the Temple itself in Mark 12.

Triads abound. Jesus enters the city now for the third time, with his disciples, and meets the three elements of the Jewish high council, the Sanhedrin: the chief priests, the scribes, and the elders, the same whom Jesus predicted would kill him in his first Passion prediction (8:31; Mark indicates that the chief priests and scribes wish to destroy him in 11:18 after his Temple action). We thus come full circle.

The chief priests, scribes, and elders challenge Jesus precisely on the question of his authority to do "these things" (*tauta*), asking him, "By what authority are you doing these things, or who gave you this authority to do them?" (11:28).

The two-part structure to their inquiry reflects the dual nature of Jesus's authority: his authority is both bestowed upon him by God and part of his very identity as (ultimately) God and the other appellations invested with inherent authority—Christ, Son of man, Son of God.

"These things" certainly refers to his action in the Temple and may also refer to the others things he's done to court controversy—like the healing of the paralytic, in which story *tauta* also appears (2:8). But it's intriguing that *tauta* also shows up in Mark 13 in sections that deal with Jesus's prediction of the destruction of the Temple (13:4, 8, 29, 30). The disciples express wonder at the magnificence of the Temple complex, and Jesus responds, "Do you see these great buildings? There will not be left here one stone upon another, that will not be thrown down" (13:2). The disciples then ask when "these things" (*tauta*) are to be accomplished (13:4). "These things" (*tauta*) in Mark 13 thus refers to the destruction of the Temple, and so, when Jesus's antagonists use the phrase in 11:28, it indicates that they themselves have picked up on the import of Jesus's action in the Temple and his allusion to Jeremiah 7.

Jesus responds with a question, and his invitation to his antagonists to "answer me" (11:30b) is an allusion to Micah 6:3, in which the LORD demands of Israel, "Answer me!" The broader context in Micah concerns Israel's rejection of LORD for the embrace of idols in spite of all the LORD has done for them. And of course irony abounds: here in Mark's Gospel, after they presumed to demand an answer, the custodians of the Temple are themselves required to answer the true LORD of the Temple who has now finally come to his Temple, fulfilling the prophecy of Micah 3:1.

Jesus's question concerns whether the baptism of John the Baptist comes from heaven or men (11:30), and it subtly involves the question of Jesus's authority, for he received his baptism from John and received the Holy Spirit directly. Accepting John's legitimacy means accepting Jesus's. The antagonists argue (*dialogizomai*) with one another, as Jesus has placed them on the horns of a dilemma. Six times prior in Mark's Gospel, *dialogizomai* has involved confusion about or rejection of Jesus's words (2:6, twice in 2:8, 8:16, 8:17, and 9:33), and so too here. But they cannot reject Jesus outright here and deny John's legitimacy, for "they were afraid of the people" (11:32), who all believed John to be a true prophet. And so they will condemn Jesus, as Pilate out of fear and expediency will condemn Jesus (15:15). Jesus's antagonists here duck the truth question and instead, in their ironic logic of power, simply chicken out.

Their cynical refusal to answer is ironic in that they are representative of the Sanhedrin who are effectively accusing Jesus of blasphemy, like the scribes did in Mark 2:7, and will condemn him of it again in 14:63. Blasphemy seems to have been a capital offense in Jesus's day (see m. Sanh. 11:1 in the Mishnah), as Mark's Gospel presumes (again, 14:63), and so, while they hold life and death power over Jesus, they refuse to answer him because they think he holds no ultimate power over them.

They do not respond to him, and so Jesus refuses to respond to them, fitting the pattern of Mark's insider–outsider motif. Instead of exercising the smallest mustard seed of faith, they are afraid. They haven't been with Jesus, they're not seeking him honestly, they refuse to engage, and so they are cut off from the revelation Jesus would offer them: his authority comes from God and from his own identity. And while they have challenged Jesus's authority but received no answer as self-made outsiders, Jesus will later declare to the disciples, yet insiders, that the whole world will one day know his authority (13:24–27).

But Jesus never cuts outsiders off completely. Throughout the Gospel of Mark, even after his turn inward, he gives the crowds teaching in words and deeds by which he reveals truth to them subtly, indirectly. And so, he will answer the question of the chief priests, scribes, and elders in the stories that follow, particularly in the parable immediately following, the Parable of the Wicked Tenants (12:1-12).

Mark 12:1-12: Monday of Week 9

The chief priests, scribes, and elders of the people had refused to answer Jesus's question about John's baptism, and Jesus refused to answer theirs about his authority in turn. But now, in the Parable of the Wicked Tenants, Jesus does provide a veiled answer.

It's veiled because they're outsiders, thanks to their fear (11:32, 12:12) and their rejection of Jesus. And, as outsiders receive parables (4:33-34), Jesus "began to speak to them in parables" (12:1a). Parables proclaim truth in a veiled, subtle way, but the import is there for those with ears to hear, for those who would go deeper.

Jesus's antagonists here perceive in some degree the import of the parable—"they perceived that he had told the parable against them" (12:12)—but the irony of it is that, instead of repenting, their limited insight leads them to desire to do exactly what the parable predicts: arrest him (12:12a) so that they might do away with him.

This parable is the only major parable told outside of chapter 4 and, in many ways, forms a fitting parabolic coda. The Parable of the Sower (4:1-9) taught that good soil bears good fruit—that, in spite of manifest and multifold failing and apostasy, Jesus's word sown will one day issue forth in a great harvest. The Parable of the Wicked Tenants here, then, shows that the Jewish leadership is not fruitful soil.

The parable echoes the song of the vineyard in Isaiah 5:1–7. The LORD has planted Israel as a vineyard (Isa 5:1–2, 7), "but it yielded wild grapes" (5:2b). The LORD calls the "inhabitants of Jerusalem and men of Judah" to judge between him and his vineyard (5:3–4) and declares that judgment is coming (5:5–6), for the LORD "looked for justice, but behold, bloodshed; for righteousness, but behold, a cry!" (5:7b).

Isaiah's song of the vineyard is more than a general background for the parable; it's prophetic, particularly suited for Mark's story, especially the version in the LXX. There, the song is described as a song "to *my* beloved a song of my beloved [*agapētos*] concerning my vineyard" (Isa 5:1a in the LXX; emphasis added). In Mark 12:6, the landowner's son is expressly called a "beloved" (*agapētos*) son, as Mark's God twice elsewhere describes Jesus as the "beloved" (*agapētos*) Son, at the baptism and at the Transfiguration (1:11, 9:7).

Further, the song calls out the "inhabitants of Jerusalem and men of Judah" specifically, the very people and region in Mark's Gospel causing Jesus the most trouble. And finally, the song closes with the LORD declaring that he finds "bloodshed" and "a cry" instead of justice and righteousness. A good reader, the model or ideal reader, would know Isaiah 5 is in the background and hear, or anticipate, or later come to realize, that Jesus would cry out his cry of dereliction (15:34) as he sheds his sacrificial blood on the Cross.

The point of the parable is obvious. In Mark's view, the Israel contemporary with Jesus is fruitless, just as was the Israel of Isaiah's day. The LORD had sent prophet after prophet to Israel, but they suffered and died at the hands of the people to whom they were sent, like Isaiah himself (according to tradition, sawed in half upside down) and Zechariah (stoned to death). Indeed, the parable's story is absurd, like many of

Jesus's parables. No human landowner would long tolerate such treatment of those sent to do his will, and so the parable is obviously about God's forbearance towards his recalcitrant people.

Most shocking is the landowner's decision to risk his beloved son. Here, authority and eschatology combine. The son comes with the landowner's full authority to claim his rights, just as Jesus comes as God's Son, bearing full divine authority (1:22). And he came bearing the kingdom of God (1:15), thus inaugurating the eschatological age, just as the beloved son of the parable comes "last" (*eschaton*, 12:6).

But the Jewish leadership, like their ciphers, the wicked tenants, reject the eschatological authority of the Son. In the parable, the tenants utter, "come, let us kill him" (*deute apokteinōmen auton*, 12:7), employing the exact words from the LXX that Joseph's brothers used in first suggesting murdering him in Genesis 37:20. Just as Joseph was to rule his brothers, the fathers of the twelve tribes of Israel, Jesus was to rule and lead Israel in its missionary endeavor to be a light to the nations. And just as Joseph's brothers sold him into that pagan slavery that reached its lowest point in an Egyptian dungeon, the Jewish leadership will hand Jesus over to pagans who will crucify him. Joseph rose, however, to become Lord of the known world, just like Jesus will rise again as Lord of the world.

It's important to note here, however, that the punishment meted out in Mark's parabolic vision isn't leveled against Israel as a whole, but against the *tenants*, and thus the Jewish leadership: "What will the owner [*kurios*, "Lord," suggesting both God and, perhaps, Jesus the Lord himself] of the vineyard do? He will come and destroy the tenants, and give the vineyard to others" (12:9). The "others" means the Church, consisting of Jews and Gentiles who believe in Jesus, who will carry Israel's mission of the world's redemption forward after the crucifixion and resulting destruction of the Temple.

Mark 12:13–17: Tuesday of Week 9

The next three stories involve challenges from the Pharisees, then the Sadducees, and then a scribe, three groups whose representatives would have sat on the Sanhedrin. The challenges come in breathless, rapid-fire succession, and in each story Jesus dominates, displaying his total authority. His interrogators address him as "teacher" (12:14, 19, 32), showing, at least in the first two instances, a lack of understanding of Jesus's true identity: Jesus is a teacher but also much more, and when he teaches, he does so more by deed than word, demonstrating his divine authority and identity. In the third instance, an exemplary scribe interacts seriously and respectfully with Jesus and calls him "teacher" in affirming his teaching about the greatest commandments, with Jesus in turn declaring that the scribe is not far from the kingdom of God.

The Pharisees and Herodians are the sort of strange bedfellows politics makes. Many envision the Pharisees as a pious, if rigorous, apolitical party within Judaism, but the witness of the Gospels shows that they were anything but, willing to make political alliances of convenience in a world that knew nothing of what we moderns call the separation of Church and State.[10]

The Pharisees and Herodians had conspired to destroy Jesus in Mark 3:6, and Jesus warns against the leaven of the

---

[10] See p. 201 above on Alexander Jannaeus's crucifixion of 800 Pharisees and execution of their families; these Pharisees had crossed Jannaeus politically. Further, if Acts 23:6–7 is to be believed, the Pharisees held significant seats on the Sanhedrin, which would indicate their deep involvement in politics.

Pharisees and Herod in 8:15. Here they try to trap him with a question about paying taxes to Caesar. Strange bedfellows indeed, for it's likely that most Pharisees loathed paying taxes to Rome, while the Herodians would have supported Rome as the price of their power and benefited from Roman taxation.

Jesus's antagonists here heap insincere flattery upon Jesus (12:14a), which is ironic, since the things they say about Jesus—that he is "true," that he "care[s] for no man," that he does not regard men's position but "truly teach[es] the way of God"—are perfectly, ultimately true but they themselves don't believe the words they utter about him. It's similar to the situation of the centurion at the crucifixion, who sarcastically speaks the truth he doesn't believe: that Jesus truly was the Son of God (15:39b).

They go for the jugular, asking Jesus a question crossing both religion and politics: "Is it lawful to pay taxes to Caesar, or not? Should we pay them, or should we not?" (12:14b–15a). Answering either way would get Jesus in trouble: he would be branded either a rebel *against* Rome or a collaborator *with* Rome.

Jesus knows their hypocrisy, and it's not just a matter of their insincere flattery. Their hypocrisy involves their having a coin they produce when he asks (12:15b–16a); they've already given their answer. The coin is a *kēnsos*, the word being a Greek transliteration of the Latin *census*. The tax it paid, referred to in this passage, was instituted in AD 6 and was the tax that precipitated Judas the Galilean's revolt and the subsequent Zealot movement that endured to Jesus's day.[11] Judas himself declared a theocratic Jewish republic with God alone as king. Given Galilee's reputation as a hotbed of sedition, Jesus isn't simply being put in an uncomfortable spot,

---

[11] See Edwards, *Mark*, 363.

but more or less asked if he himself is a Zealot—and of course Simon the Zealot is numbered among his Twelve Apostles.[12]

Jesus asks, "Whose likeness and inscription is this?" (12:16b). The census coin, a denarius, had Tiberius Caesar's image on one side, accompanied by the inscription *Tiberius Caesar Divi Augusti Filius Augustus*—"The Blessed Tiberius Caesar, Son of the Divine Augustus." The other side bore the inscription *Pontifex Maximus*, high priest among the Roman pontiffs. And so, the coin is full of idolatry, revealing the hypocrisy of Jesus's antagonists in their implied loyalty to Caesar, whose authority they recognize as absolute, even divine, either as Herodians or as Pharisees aligning themselves with Herodians. In the end, they're Caesar's men.

Jesus's famous response indicates he is the king's servant but God's man first: "Render to Caesar the things that are Caesar's, and to God the things that are God's" (12:17). Cryptic enough to keep the crowds from seeing him as a collaborator and commentators busy composing commentary, Jesus's declaration can be understood only in terms of his question to them, "whose likeness and inscription is this?" (12:16b). "Likeness" here is *eikōn*, the very word that the LXX of Genesis 1:26–27 employs for the divine image in which God made man. Things bearing images belong to those whose images they bear, so Jesus can have us surrender the coin to Caesar, but we must surrender ourselves to God. We remain the king's good servants, but God's first.

Here, Jesus's hearers and Mark's readers are faced with a choice about who God is, for Zealots would consider surren-

---

[12] See above on the Feeding of the five thousand on pp. 162–170. Further, it's intriguing that the disciple Simon is not identified in Mark as a Zealot as he is in Luke 6:15 and Acts 1:13 but as Simon the "Cananaean" (3:18). Mark's Gospel distances Jesus from mundane political revolution at every turn even while suggesting that Jesus is Lord of all the world, the one with true and ultimate authority who may lead the only legitimate revolution.

der to God to mean making ready for rebellion. But Mark and Mark's Jesus have a different picture of God: for them, surrendering to God means suffering violence from the state, as exemplified in the crucifixion, not inflicting violence upon the state. Rebellion against Rome would be yet another indulgence in the theology of glory, but the glory of Rome is overcome only by the glory of the Cross.

We belong to God first, made in his image. And so, the next story shifts from matters of state to matters of religion, to the question of the God who raises the dead.

Mark 12:18–27: Wednesday of Week 9

The Sadducees now rush in to engage Jesus. The Sadducees were a priestly party within Judaism like the Pharisees. Unlike the Pharisees, they were elites who controlled the levers of religious power in Jerusalem by dominating the Temple (though Pharisees were well-represented on the Sanhedrin; see Acts 23:6–7). And, also unlike the Pharisees, they denied any life after death and denied that any books beyond the Mosaic Torah were scriptural.

And so, they challenge Jesus on the question of the resurrection, alluding, it seems, to a Septuagintal book Catholics recognize as part of the canon, Tobit, using the practice of levirate marriage (see Gen 38:8–10 and Deut 25:5–6) as a rhetorical tool. They ask a question involving a hypothetical woman who married seven brothers serially, each dying leaving her childless, until she too died (12:19–23), reminiscent of the situation in Tobit 3:7–15.

They imagine that this obviously disproves the resurrection, for by this time in Judaism, almost everyone assumed and practiced monogamy and most Jews (but not the Sadducees, whose canon of the Torah had nothing direct to say about

eternal life[13]) assumed that eternal life stood in radical continuity with earthly life. For the Sadducees, eternal life would
mean polygamy in eternity, given the law of levirate marriage
and the real practice of serial marriage in a time when people
died early and often.

The Sadducees thus think the resurrection is an obvious
absurdity. Their question—"In the resurrection whose wife
will she be?" (12:23a)—can't be answered in their terms. So
Jesus declares their terms are wrong, for they "know neither
the scriptures nor the power of God" (12:24). Ouch.

Jesus begins with power and displays his authority; God
indeed has the power to raise the dead, but the Sadducees
suffer a failure of the imagination. Jesus, in his authority, does
not argue from any principles scriptural or natural but simply,
in his authority, declares discontinuity of earthly and eternal
life: "For when they rise from the dead, they neither marry nor
are given in marriage, but are like angels in heaven" (12:25).
Those who are raised are like angels in that they're eternal and
unmarried. But note that the phrase "neither marry nor are
given in marriage" implies that resurrection existence is sexed
as male or female, and thus embodied.

He then turns to Scripture, drawing on their shared Torah's
famous episode of the burning bush to school the Sadducees
on eschatology. God speaks to Moses in the present tense in
Exodus 3:6: "I am the God of Abraham, and the God of Isaac,
and the God of Jacob" (12:26). The patriarchs abide in God's
abode—"He is not God of the dead, but of the living"—and
the Sadducees are thus "quite wrong" (12:27).

Unlike the Pharisees, who were reduced to total amazement (12:17), the Sadducees here are reduced to total silence,

---

[13] In the Old Testament, the clearest passages bearing on the possibility of
resurrection are Isa 26:19, Ezek 37, and Dan 12:2.

as Mark records no reaction whatsoever. And so, the stage is thus set for an exemplary scribe to speak, filling the silence made by Jesus's drop-the-mic moment.

Mark 12:28–34: Thirtieth Sunday in Ordinary Time / Thursday of Week 9 / Friday of the Third Week of Lent

Jesus has bested the Pharisees, reducing them to amazement, and the Sadducees, reducing them to silence. The flow of the story now turns in Jesus's favor, as he encounters a scribe who approaches him with sympathy, who will affirm Jesus and, in turn, be affirmed by him as Jesus asserts his authority. Jesus will then be in a position to ask the most important question in Mark's Gospel: who is Jesus, really (12:38–40)?

The story of this exemplary scribe reveals divisions within Jewish officialdom, even the Sanhedrin, consisting of members of the parties of the Pharisees and Sadducees, and now a member of the office of the scribes.[14] The scribe's affirmation of Jesus's organizing the law around the dual love of God and neighbor affirms Jesus's continuity with Judaism and shows his total authority to be its true interpreter.

In Mark's Gospel, as we have seen on several occasions, sense perception (seeing and hearing) is allegorical for spiritual perception. Only those with eyes to see and ears to hear can perceive who Jesus is and what he's about. And in this scribe, Mark presents us with someone who hears and sees. The scribe comes up to Jesus, having "heard" Jesus and his antagonists disputing and "sees" that Jesus answered them well (12:28). He's thus been around Jesus, in his presence,

---

[14] Officeholders like scribes and elders could belong to the parties of the Pharisees or Sadducees or none, much like Catholic priests can be religious (Jesuits, Dominicans, Benedictines, etc.) or diocesan.

and again, in Mark's Gospel, proximity to Jesus is requisite for insight and understanding.

The question the scribe asks isn't simply which commandment is most important, but which commandment could function as the organizing principle to provide a coherent structure to the entire system of Mosaic law, something rabbis were always discussing and to which they were providing suggestions.

Jesus's answer is twofold. He first replies with the Shema from Deuteronomy 6:4–5, which begins with hearing (which is, of course, what the Hebrew *shema* means): "Hear [*akouō*], O Israel, the Lord our God, the Lord is one" (12:29). Mark's emphasis on the necessity of "hearing" is found then in Israel's fundamental confession of faith. The Shema continues by calling for love of the one God with one's heart, soul, and strength. But Mark's Jesus adds "mind" or "understanding" (*dianoia*) as well (12:30). The significance is twofold: first, the addition fits with Mark's concern for understanding (although the word he usually uses is *suniēmi*, as in 4:12, 6:52, 7:14, 8:17, and 8:21); and second, Jesus here displays his authority not simply to interpret the Torah but even to emend it.

Jesus then provides a second answer, this time from Leviticus 19:18—"You shall love your neighbor as yourself"—and declares, "there is no other commandment greater than these" (12:31). Jesus is the first Jew to link these two commandments in this way, and they form a unity even while love of God has priority.

Some further observations on Jesus's response here merit mention. First, we see here the profound continuity of Jesus's Christianity with his Judaism. Jesus affirms the Torah and its enduring validity by interpreting it and organizing it; he does not dismiss it. Indeed, Jesus here draws on the Torah to set up the fundamental constitution of Christianity. When St. Augustine will later do so much with love of God and neighbor as the essence of the Christian faith and the end of Scripture, he's simply channeling Jesus, who is himself channeling the Torah.

Second, Jesus is likely channeling the Ten Commandments in particular, the first table of which concerns love of God and the second table of which concerns love of neighbor. Thus, his twofold organizational principle reveals the intrinsic unity of the dual love of God and neighbor first revealed at Sinai.

Third, love of God has priority, for it is the truth of God that determines the truth of everything. The temptation to forget this truth, the temptation to idolatry, is ever present—as the old saying goes, God made us in his image and we returned the favor. And setting love of neighbor on some sort of par with love of God runs the risk of determining God and his will on human terms—in our image—thus reducing theology to anthropology, as so often happens in liberal Christianity, or separating love of God and love of neighbor.

The scribe affirms Jesus's response. Whereas the Pharisees flatter when they tell Jesus he teaches "truly" (*alētheia*, 12:14), here the scribe is sincere when he says Jesus has spoken "truly" (*alētheia*, 12:32). But then the scribe posits something Jesus didn't directly broach: dual love of God and neighbor "is much more than all whole burnt offerings and sacrifices" (12:33). Mark notes that Jesus regarded that as a wise answer (12:34a), but it makes difficulties for Catholics, who hold that Christianity remains sacrificial, that the Eucharist is in some sense a sacrifice.

In the world of the story, Jesus's affirmation of the scribe's coda fits Mark's anti-Temple polemic. Those who maintain the Temple system, the Jerusalem elite, give Jesus grief and will soon enjoy divine judgment. Indeed, in Mark's story, Jesus institutes a sacrificial ritual, so (as was the case with the so-called cleansing of the Temple) one can't read this passage as a rejection of sacrifice as such.

Further, the passage doesn't pit sacrifice and love against each other, but orders them. The scribe says precisely that love of God and neighbor is "much more" than whole burnt offerings and sacrifices. And in doing so, Mark's scribe points to a Catholic understanding of the sacrifice of the Eucharist. Burnt offerings, at least, were wholly consumed by the fire, not eaten by the people, while other sacrifices would be eaten either by the priests or by both priests and people.

In the case of the Eucharist, then, all the people (assuming the usual conditions) eat of Jesus's body. Unlike the Temple sacrifices, Jesus's Eucharist is much more about him offering himself for us and giving himself also to us, as we return the sacrifice of the Eucharist first given to us by God through Christ. Christ's sacrifice of himself for us is first given to us, and we return what has first been given.

Seeing the scribe's wise answer, Jesus declares that the scribe is "not far from the kingdom of God" (12:34b). The language of spatiality is present in "not far," for the scribe has been near Jesus, he's been given the insight to see what Jesus is about. And one suspects there's a double meaning here. Not only is the scribe not far from the kingdom because he affirms Jesus's organizing of the Torah, but he's also not far from the kingdom because he's in Jesus's very presence. Jesus is the locus of the kingdom. And, in Jesus's declaration to the scribe, we see Jesus display his authority. The scribe had approached Jesus sincerely but still came as one who would judge him. Jesus instead judges the scribe, and he does so with such authority that, after the encounter, "no one dared to ask him any question" (12:34c).

Thus concludes Mark's sequence of three stories about Jesus's authority. And the stories aren't simply random or grouped by topic. They follow a progression: the first, in which the Pharisees challenged Jesus on the question of paying taxes to Caesar, affirmed we belong to God, not Caesar; the second, in which the Sadducees challenged Jesus on the question of the resurrection, affirmed that the God to whom we belong raises the dead so that we might belong to him forever; and the third, in which the scribe affirms Jesus's Torah principle of the dual love of God and neighbor, teaches us about how to obey the God who raises us and thus to merit eternal life.

No more questions. Now it will be Jesus's turn to ask a question, having stormed the house of God and taken it.

Mark 12:35–37: Friday of Week 9

Jesus is yet in the Temple, the dwelling place of God, ground zero for Israel's very identity. The question he poses will subtly concern his very identity. Before, at Caesarea Philippi, Jesus instructed the disciples to keep his messianic identity secret (8:30). Now, in the Temple, Jesus will reveal hints about his identity. Again, Jesus doesn't totally turn inward after Mark 3. Rather, his insiders get full revelation, while outsiders get truth taught to them in an oblique, opaque manner. So too here. The crowds, who hear him gladly (12:37), are provided an opportunity to consider Jesus, to go deeper, to come closer, to become insiders.

Jesus poses a question: "How can the scribes say that the Christ is the son of David?" (12:35). "Son of David" had meant Messiah for decades before Jesus,[15] as Jews in the wake of the Babylonian captivity looked for an eschatologi-

---

[15] See Psalms of Solomon 17:21.

cal Davidic Christ to finally fulfill 2 Samuel 7:12–14a, which promised David an everlasting dynasty, with God as father and the Davidic regent his son.

Jesus here does not wish to deny that he is the son of David, the Christ. Instead, in quoting Psalm 110:1, he wishes to suggest that he is more than the Messiah.[16] Mark has already shown that Jesus is the LORD himself come to his Temple, and here Jesus invites his hearers—like the scribe in the prior passage, who is not far from the kingdom of God—to consider his identity ever deeper.

The Messiah might be David's son, but David himself, under the inspiration of the Holy Spirit, mentioned two Lords in Psalm 110. Originally the Psalm concerned royal enthronement: the LORD of Israel was he who guaranteed the success of the king, the lord of the Israelites. But Jesus's rhetoric seizes on David's use of *kurios*, lord, in the Psalm. "David himself calls him Lord; so how is he his son?" (12:37). Jesus here invites his hearers to consider the possibility that David's son, the Christ—Jesus—is more than Messiah. He's *kurios* as the LORD God of the Scriptures of Israel.

And so, Jesus gives his response to the repeated appellation of "teacher" in this section. The scribe had addressed Jesus as "teacher," but while that's true and necessary, it's not sufficient. It's inadequate, for Jesus is more than a teacher. He's God come to earth to invade and liberate the cosmos, as Mark has made plain elsewhere.[17] Jesus is not putting forth a predicament, as if one has to choose between the identity of David's Son as either Messiah or LORD. Rather, it's a genuine, if rhetorical, question with a real answer. How is the Christ

---

[16] Ps 110 is one of the most quoted Old Testament text in the New Testament, cited five times.

[17] Especially in the second boat scene (6:45–52), which affirms Jesus's divine identity beyond question. See pp. 170–71 above.

the son of David, given what David prophesied in Psalm 110? By being both Messiah and divine Lord.

What's quoted from the Psalm, as well as the wider background context of the Psalm, is also in play in this passage. First, Jesus quotes the line "till I put your enemies under your feet" (12:36b, quoting Ps 110:1). What's implied is that Jesus's enemies will be crushed, and at this point in the story, we know who they are. Second, Psalm 110:4 declares, "The LORD has sworn and will not change his mind, 'You are a priest for ever after the order of Melchiz'edek.'" While it's a matter of some controversy whether New Testament quotations are meant to actualize the wider background context of what is quoted from the Old Testament, it may be that this Markan passage points not only to Jesus's divine identity but also to his priestly identity. That would be fitting in the world of Mark's story, for Jesus has already declared that he will "give his life as a ransom for many" (10:45) and he will soon institute the Eucharist, the sacrificial meal interpreting and making present his sacrificial self as both victim and priest.

Mark 12:38–44: Thirty-Second Sunday in Ordinary Time (12:38–44 or 12:41–44) / Saturday Week of 9 (12:38–44)

We come now to the grand conclusion of Jesus's public controversy in the Temple. Mark sets the scribe and the widow in contrast, certainly, but they're representative of something greater. They represent the contrast between the Jerusalem authorities and the faithful. Indeed, the scribes display the diametric opposite of love of God and neighbor. In terms of St. Augustine's theological anthropology, they're turned in on themselves and turn everything and everyone else to themselves. The scribes represent those who self-aggrandize, who consume, who take, and never give. The widow, in contrast, represents the ideal disciple in giving everything she has to God, in two small coins, her whole living. As such, she represents Jesus, who also gives all he has to God, his very life (10:45).

Jesus, apparently addressing the crowds, tells them to "beware" (*blepō*) the scribes (12:38), just as he had told the disciples to "beware" (*blepō*) the leaven of the Pharisees and Herod (8:15), indicating just how dastardly the scribes are. Indeed, toward the beginning of Jesus's ministry, they had deemed him demonized (3:22).

What Jesus says about the scribes in Mark 12:38–40a, while polemical, fits the historical possibilities. Scribes were treated with serious veneration. They would be given seats of honor at the front of the synagogue, thus facing the people during worship. They would be greeted in marketplaces with great honor. Seating at meals was a matter of strict honor, with the most important guests to the front (compare Jesus's parable in Luke 14:7–11, advising his hearers to take the seats not of great honor, lest they be told to sit further back, but to take the seats further back so that they might be honored).

Jesus's line about devouring widows' houses deserves especial attention. Scribes were not paid, but rather subsisted on the generosity of others. Far from being beggars, however, they could be supported generously through arrangements that were more or less patron–client benefices. And, as widows had no right of inheritance, it's possible a situation would obtain where someone could support a scribe by impoverishing a widow for whom he would otherwise be responsible. In Jesus's view, scribes abused the system to the point of being as rapacious as highwaymen. Perhaps Jesus's allusion to Jeremiah 7:11 ("den of robbers") in Mark 11:17 has something to do with dirty financial dealings after all.

The Old Testament, of course, condemns the exploitation of widows and commands their care in emulation of God (see: Exod 22:22; Deut 10:18a, 24:14–21; Isa 10:1–2). Of special interest is Jeremiah 7:6, within the great prophecy of the first Temple's coming destruction, which mentions oppression of widows. Mark's anti-Temple polemic continues here. Just as the people of Jeremiah's day could have been spared had they not oppressed widows and others but would suffer destruction because of it, so too the people of Jesus's day will face the destruction of their Temple in great part because of their leaders' injustice, especially the impoverishing of widows. And all this covered by an ostentatious, fake piety. Jesus's final words are more forceful than most translations manage: they will receive a most severe judgment (12:40).

Mark then relates Jesus observing many putting money in the treasury (12:41). Receptacles shaped like rams' horns received the coinage and guided it to metal boxes. We can imagine the noisy clanging and clanking of many coins being poured in by the rich Mark mentions. Whether a given rich individual was sincere or hypocritical in his giving, it's a physical recipe for a public ostentation, much like the ostentation of the scribes making a show of florid prayers (12:40).

In contrast, Mark reports that a poor widow comes and puts in two *lepta*, the smallest Jewish coins in circulation (12:42), all she has to live on (12:44).[18] Perhaps a scribal beneficence had reduced her to absolute penury. And as she gives all, her piety is true. The scribes take all, but she gives all. She displays total love of God and neighbor, while the scribes display twisted love of self. She is the model of the disciple, for in Mark's Gospel, discipleship means surrendering

---

[18] Mark explains to his Roman readers that these two Jewish coins equal one Roman *quadrans*, the smallest Roman coin in circulation.

everything. The two pairs of brothers left everything behind to follow Jesus (1:16–20), and Levi left his livelihood (2:14). Peter reminds Jesus at one point, "Lo, we have left everything and followed you" (10:28). And Jesus calls those who would follow him as disciples to embrace the cross and surrender their very lives (8:34–38), which Jesus himself will do (10:45; 15:21–39). The widow gives her living; Jesus gives his life. The injustices done to her and to Jesus will mean the destruction of the Temple.

Mark 13:24–32: Thirty-Third Sunday in Ordinary Time

Mark 13 is a well-constructed intercalation in which Jesus teaches four of his disciples privately about the destruction of the Temple and his Second Coming at the end of the world. The disciples are enamored of the Temple complex's magnificent edifices, and Jesus, ever the apocalyptic killjoy, states: "Do you see these great buildings? There will not be left here one stone upon another, that will not be thrown down" (13:2). The A sections of the intercalation of Mark 13 (13:1–23 and 13:28–31) deal with the Temple's destruction, and the B sections (13:24–27 and 13:32–37) deal with the end of the world in the unknowable future. The lectionary provides the first B section, the second A section, and a verse from the second B section. Interpreting the Gospel for the day rightly will involve taking note of the intercalation from which the lectionary reading is extracted.

Mark 13:1–23, the A section, deals with the destruction of the Temple. An anonymous disciple marvels at the Temple, and Jesus pronounces its destruction explicitly (13:1–2). Four disciples, Peter, James, John, and Andrew, then ask him, "Tell us, when will this be, and what will be the sign when these things are all to be accomplished?" (13:4). Jesus refuses to answer the "when" question whatsoever; indeed, Mark 13 is more or less all about the impossibility of knowing the time of the End, and Mark disdains the seeking of signs in general. On the other hand, Jesus does discuss the destruction of the Temple in the chapter: "these things" (*tauta*) in 13:4 refers to Jesus's prediction of its destruction, and *tauta* is found again in 13:8, 29 and 30, which indicates that Jesus is there speaking of the destruction of the Temple, as "these things" marks also the second A section.

As most Jews of Jesus's day would regard the destruction of the Temple as a sign of the end of the world, Jesus endeavors to do two things in Mark 13. First, he tells the disciples not to seek signs of the End and that what they'd regard as indications of the imminent end are anything but. Second, Jesus thus separates the destruction of the Temple from the end of the world.

Jesus's first reaction to the four disciples' question is to refuse to answer the question. They ask "when?" and Jesus tells them to watch out (*blepō*) that they not be led astray, just as they were to watch out for the leaven of the Pharisees and Herod (8:15, *blepō*) and to watch out for the scribes (12:38, *blepō*). False Jesuses, wars, earthquakes and famines will all come, but "the end is not yet" (13:6–8).

In Mark 13:14–23, Jesus warns the disciples that, when they see the "desolating sacrilege"[19] set up, it's time for those in Judea to flee to the mountains and not to double back to

---

[19] Mark's phrase is taken from Dan 9:27 and 1 Macc 1:54. Josephus records that the Zealots trampled the sanctuary and made Phannias an unworthy high priest (*Wars* 4.151–58). Whether the abomination Mark's Jesus warns of is committed by a pagan (Roman) army or Jewish rebels is immaterial: either way, the destruction of the Temple and Jerusalem in AD 70 is in view.

grab anything. Flight will be hard for pregnant and nursing women, and it will be hard in winter.

Wait a moment. If it's the end of the world, which would presumably involve the entire world, why the mention of Judea alone? And if it's the end of the world, why run away? Where are you going to run to? Where are you going to hide? Jesus is talking about something else: the Roman siege of Jerusalem and the destruction of city and Temple in AD 70.

The "tribulation" (13:19) Jesus speaks of isn't the end of the world; it's the siege with which the Romans will invade Jerusalem forty years later. And the historical record of the siege and destruction of Jerusalem and its Temple surely merits Jesus's description of a great tribulation. The Romans at one point crucified five hundred captives a day to terrify the besieged inhabitants of the holy city. For their part, Josephus records even an instance of cannibalism among the Jews, which, for a people that doesn't even eat pork, is a sign of the severest desperation.[20]

Jesus, then, is preparing the disciples for flight, not fight. The defense of Jerusalem isn't their fight; Christians should flee instead of taking up arms against Rome, for the Temple's destruction is decreed, prophesied by Jesus in word and deed.

Jesus then begins to speak of the end of the world in Mark 13:24–27, the B section, with which the lectionary begins the week's Gospel. "Those days" (13:24) is set in contrast to "these things" pertaining to the destruction of the Temple. The End is distanced from the Temple's destruction by the far demonstrative pronoun, "those." And there will be no need to seek signs;

---

[20] Josephus, *Wars* 6.199–219. On the incident, see Honora H. Chapman, "A Myth for the World: Early Christian Reception of Infanticide and Cannibalism in Josephus, *Bellum Judaicum* 6.199–219," in *Society of Biblical Literature 2000 Seminar Papers* (Atlanta, GA: Society of Biblical Literature, 2000), 359–78.

the End will be obvious, as the sky will be filled with apoca-lyptic phenomena (13:24–25). Unlike false christs who have arisen before, Jesus the Son of man will return from heaven "in clouds with great power and glory" (13:26), something that fake christs would have a hard time faking. Then the angels will gather the elect from all over (13:27), not just Judea.

The point: the End will be obvious to all, so there's no need to seek signs and engage in apocalyptic speculation.

But the point of the next section, Mark 13:28–31, the second A section, is not so obvious to interpreters. Read a certain way, it sounds like the end of the world is in view. And yet there are plenty of signals that it's not, that Jesus here has returned to the theme of the Temple.

First, Jesus mentions the "fig tree" as an object lesson (13:28). In 11:11–25, the cursed fig tree was wrapped around Jesus's Temple action in an intercalation in which the desic-cated fig tree was a symbol of the Temple's destruction.

Second, "these things" (*tauta*) appears again in Mark 13:29, which, as above, refers to the events surrounding the destruction of the Temple. Thus, it's better to render the verse "you know that it is near." The Greek is *ginōskete hoti eggus estin*. There's no explicit pronoun for "he" or "it"; it's implied in the verb *estin*. As translation is interpretation, those who see the passage as concerning the end of the world translate "he," as if Christ's imminent Second Coming were in view. If the passage concerns the Temple's destruction, then "it" is a better translation.

Third, if this section concerns the destruction of the Temple, then Mark 13:30 ("Truly, I say to you, this generation will not pass away before all these things take place") is no cause for unease. Precisely one biblical generation passes from the time of Jesus to the destruction of the Temple. Indeed, the very fact that the verse was preserved and not altered or deleted by later scribes living well after the destruction of Jerusalem and the delayed return of the Lord reveals those scribes probably found it unproblematic; they too read it as if it concerned the destruction of the Temple. Otherwise they would have been tempted to change it.

Fourth, "heaven and earth" (13:31) is a Jewish circumlocution for the Temple, since the Temple was regarded as ground zero of the cosmos.[21] As the dwelling place of God, it was where heaven met earth. And so, when Jesus speaks of heaven and earth passing away, he's speaking of the Temple's destruction and comforts the disciples by reminding them that they'll have his words long after; they will never pass away.

Mark 13:32 begins the final section of the chapter, the second B section of the intercalation, which concerns the end of the world: "But of that day or that hour no one knows, not even the angels in heaven, nor the Son, but only the Father." *Nor the Son.* Jesus, the Son, expressly says not even he knows the time of the End ("that day or that hour"). And thus, Mark 13 (and Mark in general) can't be encouraging anyone to seek signs of the End.

That's a message many American Christians need to hear, for we're all too fascinated with apocalyptic speculation. When I was growing up (high school class of 1992), we went to war in Iraq for the first time. Many believed Saddam Hussein to be the Antichrist bringing the apocalypse. Then the war was suddenly over, and Hussein was eventually discovered and later hanged. But many American Christians remain undaunted, finding ever new Antichrists-*du-jour*.

---

[21] See Crispin H. T. Fletcher-Louis, "The Destruction of the Temple and the Relativization of the Old Covenant: Mark 13:31 and Matthew 5:18," in *Eschatology in Bible & Theology: Evangelical Essays at the Dawn of a New Millennium*, ed. K. Brower and M. Elliot (Downers Grove, IL: InterVarsity, 1997), 145–69.

While apocalypticism runs through Christian history, from the Chiliasts of the early Church to Joachim of Fiore in the twelfth century to Millerites in the nineteenth, it seems particularly American nowadays, given the Christian industrial-entertainment complex that feeds on and fuels wide sectors of American Christianity with offerings such as the best-selling *Left Behind* series. The search is always on for the next Antichrist.

Apocalyptic speculation flows from weak faith: some have deep difficulties believing in the Jesus of the past, so they look for certain signs of God working in the present. Or it's a psychological immanentizing of the eschaton rooted in the typical American allergy to suffering, where we want heaven *now*, without tribulation, cheerfully caught up to heaven, with the rest of humanity left to endure all sorts of satanic miseries on earth.

American Catholics are American, and so some are caught up in such speculation, though what the Church teaches in the *Catechism of the Catholic Church* is clear without any concern for speculative details. Toward the End, the Church must pass through a final trial in which the Antichrist offers seeming solutions to human problems at the price of apostasy (*CCC* §675). In fact, the *Catechism* teaches that this deception is found every time men attempt to found heaven on earth in their own power, particularly in instances of "secular messianism" (*CCC* §676); it is God, not any man or state, who will triumph in Christ over evil in the world at the end of time (*CCC* §677). That's it. No clever poring over Ezekiel, Daniel, Mark 13, and Revelation to decipher the identity of the Antichrist. Just a final purifying trial, the outcome of which is certain: God wins.

Apocalyptic speculation is not Catholic. It's not just the mistake of majoring in minors. Speculating about things that may or may not be signs of something is at the very least the bad stewardship of distraction. It's also akin to the sins of sloth, *acedia*, and *curiositas*. It might even be an incipient part of the Gnostic heresy, as we seek to join some sort of spiritual elite by discovering secret knowledge.

Catholics have knowledge already, revealed publicly. We can encounter God and Jesus working in the present. We have Jesus Christ, who gave us Scripture and Tradition. We know God and are called to love him ever more. Apocalyptic speculation doesn't serve that end. Think also about this: if we knew the time of the End, or if we knew that this or that world figure was a secret demon, or the Antichrist, or God's hidden agent, would we live differently? We shouldn't. Catholics ought to live as Catholics ought to live every day of our lives.

Apocalyptic curiosity is a bit like the lazy student who sloughs off his studies for the semester and then hopes to cram for the final a day ahead of time: indolence and lassitude reign in hopes that last-minute discipline will cover a multitude of ignorance. That usually goes poorly. It shouldn't take knowledge of the time of the End or finding in some figure the fulfillment of some obscure prophecy to motivate us to love God and neighbor, to cultivate the virtues of faith, hope, and love.

Catholics have been given signs, however. God has given the Church the signs of life that are the sacraments. Instead of trying to find God doing something in an obscure way in contemporary events, we find God revealed, publicly available in the sacraments. Those are the signs we seek.

If we could ever hope to interpret them rightly, the signs of apocalyptic speculation would at best reveal facts: the particulars of something happening in the divine plan. But the sacraments bring us Christ, and thus in the sacraments we encounter God himself. We can find God, today, in any sacraments available, especially in the Eucharist and, so, in adoration and the Mass.

Mark 13:32 is the introduction to the Parable of the Door-keeper, and Mark's story makes some crazy beautiful literary moves with it.

Mark 13:33–37: First Sunday of Advent

The lectionary gives a good apocalyptic text for the first Sunday of Advent. It's appropriate because Advent isn't simply prepa-ration for Christmas, but rather the season that looks forward also to the Second Coming of the Lord. In general, the texts for the early part of Advent concern John the Baptist or Jesus's apocalyptic teaching and those for the later part shift to the first coming of Jesus at Christmas.

The final section of Mark 13 tells Christians not to seek signs of the End but rather to be ready at all times for the coming of the Lord. Jesus tells his four disciples (and Mark his readers) that not even he, the Son, knows the time of the End, but only the Father (13:32). Given that fact, Jesus then tells the disciples to "Take heed" (literally, "watch," *blepō*) and "watch" (literally, "stay awake" or "keep vigil," *agrupneō*) pre-cisely because they "do not know when the time will come" (13:33). Again, as explained immediately above, Mark's Jesus warns his disciples against seeking signs of the End, instead adjuring them to be ready at all times.

To drive the point home, Jesus presents the very brief Parable of the Doorkeeper (13:34–36). A man goes on a journey and leaves his servants in charge, commanding the doorkeeper "to be on the watch" (*grēgoreō*, 13:34). The dis-ciples are again told to "watch" (*grēgoreō*) precisely because (Jesus tells them explicitly a second time for emphasis) they "do not know" the time when "the master of the house will come" (13:35a).

So far so good. Jesus says: since you don't know the time

of the End, keep watch and be vigilant all the time. But then something interesting follows: Jesus gives a four-watch schema during which the master might return—"in the evening, or at midnight, or at cockcrow, or in the morning" (13:35b)—during which Jesus warns the disciples that they had best not be found sleeping (13:36). And Mark's Jesus bends over backwards to remind the disciples and all (that is, Mark's readers) to remain vigilant: "And what I say to you I say to all: Watch" (13:37).

The four-watch schema Jesus gives isn't twenty-four hours. It's roughly a twelve-hour schema, from evening (the fall of the darkness) to the morning (the breaking of the dawn). That's a signal that something more is going on. Indeed, Jesus's final night will play out according to that very schema. Jesus will predict Judas's betrayal and Peter's denial and insti- tute the Eucharist at evening (14:17). Jesus will be betrayed and arrested in Gethsemane at midnight (the word isn't men- tioned in Mark 14, but the events fit the schema). Jesus will be denied by Peter at cockcrow (14:72). And Jesus will be deliv- ered to Pilate in the morning (15:1; see 15:25, where Mark relates Jesus is crucified at the "third hour").

Through the force of these literary maneuvers, Mark is engaging in his trademark intensity. He is reinforcing Jesus's message of vigilance, telling his readers to be ready all the time because "that day or that hour" (13:32) may come suddenly: in fact, it came for Jesus already that very night two thousand years ago. It's no accident that, at the time of his arrest, Jesus declares, "the hour has come" (14:41). Mark's doing the oppo- site of having his readers search for signs of the eschatological end in the future. With these literary maneuvers, Mark makes eschatology *personal*. Your hour might come very soon. Jesus's hour came that very night.[22]

---

[22] Preaching on Mark 13:32, St. Augustine made the day and hour of Jesus's words existential, personal: "The advice, Brethren, which ye have just

The Parable of the Doorkeeper has profound ties to Gethsemane (14:32–42). Peter, James, and John, three of the four disciples[23] who heard Mark 13 and the Parable of the Doorkeeper, fail to do in Gethsemane precisely that which Jesus warned them to do in 13:32–37. They fail to keep watch, and instead are caught sleeping when "the hour" comes.

At the end of Mark 13, Jesus had told the four disciples to "keep watch" (*grēgoreō*) three times (13:34, 35 and 37). In Gethsemane, Jesus will also command the three to "keep watch" (*grēgoreō*) with him in his agony (14:34). In 13:36, Jesus had warned the disciples not to be caught sleeping. In Gethsemane, Jesus catches the disciples sleeping three times (14:37, 40, 41), just as he warned them to "keep watch" three times at the end of chapter 13. Failing to heed Jesus's words in 13:32–37, Peter, James, and John fail to keep watch and are caught sleeping. They are wholly unready for "the hour" when it comes in Gethsemane.

The events Jesus spoke of in 13:32–37 were fulfilled not in the future, but nearly two thousand years ago. Mark's point,

---

heard Scripture give, when it tells us to watch for the last day, every one should think of as concerning his own last day; lest haply when ye judge or think the last day of the world to be far distant, ye slumber with respect to your own last day. . . . Let no one then search out for the last Day, when it is to be; but let us watch all by our good lives, lest the last day of any one of us find us unprepared, and such as any one shall depart hence on his last day, such he be found in the last day of the world. Nothing will then assist thee which thou shalt not have done here. His own works will succour, or his own works will overwhelm every one" (Sermon 47, in *Sermons on Selected Lessons of the New Testament*, trans. Richard Gell MacMullen, 2 vols. [Oxford, UK: John Henry Parker, 1854], 1:377).

23 There is no satisfactory answer to the question of why Andrew is excluded from the inner triad of Peter, James, and John at the Transfiguration or here in Gethsemane. Excluding him from Jesus's audience in Mark 13 or including him in Gethsemane would make the parallel perfect, for then the same disciples who heard Mark 13 would fail in Gethsemane. Mark is a master of surprise who has constructed a beautiful story, but his Gospel is simply rough around the edges.

made most dramatically, is that we shouldn't focus on the future when thinking of the End, but rather that we should be ready at all times, for our own hour may come much sooner than we think. A most fitting Markan word for Advent, as we prepare for the coming of the Lord.

CHAPTER 7

The Passion of the Christ
(Mark 14:1–15:47)

I n these final chapters, the wheel turning against Jesus turns full circle and crushes him, as he fulfills his cruciform mission. Events unfold as Jesus, in his supreme and sovereign authority, predicts them. He lays down his life in radical obedience to God's commission as his disciples deny, betray, and fall away. He dies a wretched death alone, cut off from both man and God, remaining faithful to the end.

Mark 14:1–15:47 or 15:1–39:
Palm Sunday Mass

In effect, Mark 14 sets up the events that will play out in Mark 15. Ideally, then, the longer option for the reading should be read in Mass. In Mark 14, Jesus displays his sovereign authority, especially in his prophecies of what will happen. The divine plan of Jesus's necessary death proceeds apace, even while the conspirators God is using bumble along.

In Mark 14:1–2, we encounter a conspiracy. Passover and Unleavened Bread (two festivals, technically, but often referred to together simply as "Passover") are approaching, and the chief priests and scribes hatch a plot to arrest and kill him "by stealth." Ironically, Jesus's antagonists now operate with secrecy while Jesus has been operating ever more openly in the Temple (11:15–19, 11:27–12:44). Jesus will remind them of that at his arrest: "Day after day I was with you in the temple teaching, and you did not seize me" (14:49a).

Mark has related that the conspirators have already feared the crowds (11:32, 12:12), and so, here they devise a plan to avoid a public incident when the city would be at a fever Passover pitch: they will take Jesus by stealth, but "Not during the feast, lest there be a tumult of the people" (14:2). Mark may be a master of surprise, but at this point, we're not surprised to encounter irony. For Jesus will be arrested during the feast of Passover, and his arrest will precipitate a near riot as the crowd screams for Jesus's crucifixion. And, although Jesus's antagonists feared the crowds and so desired to take him and kill him by stealth, Pilate satisfies the crowds (15:15) by handing him over to be crucified quite publicly. Irony abounds.

Back to Mark 14. The chapter focuses on three things: (1) Jesus's authority, by showing that he correctly predicts his betrayal and denial; (2) his sacrificial death in his institution of the Eucharist; and (3) his fidelity in contrast to his disciples' faithlessness.

Jesus will predict Judas's betrayal in Mark 14:17–21, which is fulfilled in 14:43–45, and he will predict Peter's denial, as well as the apostasy of all the disciples in 14:26–31. Peter says, "If I must die with you, I will not deny you," and Mark records that "all" the disciples "said the same" (14:31). All the disciples will forsake Jesus and flee (14:40), and Peter will finally deny Jesus and remember Jesus's prophecy with bitter tears (14:72).

Mark situates the institution of the Eucharist (14:22–25) between the predictions of Judas's betrayal and Peter's denial. We'll treat the passage in more detail immediately below, as it's assigned for Corpus Christi, the Solemnity of the Most Holy Body and Blood of Christ.

In the sweep of Mark's story, two things are noteworthy. First, the institution of the Eucharist in Mark's Gospel is explicitly a Passover meal (14:12, 14, 16), which Jesus adopts and adapts to become the Church's ritual unbloody sacrifice that will perdure after the crucifixion and destruction of the Temple as the Church continues Israel's mission in the world. Second, the institution of the Eucharist is sandwiched between Judas's betrayal and the prediction of Peter's denial in order to surround it with the deepest sins by Jesus's closest associates to suggest its propitiatory power. Further, this jarring contrast marks the beginning of the final breach between Jesus and his disciples, as he will end up abandoned, dying alone.

Jesus and the disciples depart to Gethsemane (14:32–42), and he calls the inner triad of Peter, James, and John away with him while he prays, telling them to "watch" (*grēgoreō*) while he prays in his sorrow in the face of his impending death (14:34). Jesus prays three times, and the three disciples fail three times.

1. Jesus prays in Mark 14:35–36 that "the hour" and "the chalice" might pass from him, yet he submits to the divine will. He finds the disciples sleeping a first time and adjures them to watch and pray (14:37), not so that they might avoid temptation in general but so that they will not fail in this time of eschatological, apocalyptic trial (14:37–38). We might paraphrase Jesus's words as follows: "Simon"—no longer Peter the rock, his failures reverting him to Simon— "are you asleep? Could you not keep vigil in this, my final hour? Watch and pray so that you do not fail in this hour of eschatological testing."

2. Jesus prays a second time, saying the same words (14:38), and returns to find the disciples sleeping

a second time (14:39–40a). Mark remarks: "Their eyes were very heavy; and they did not know what to answer him" (14:40b). It's not their normal eyesight that's failing, but rather their spiritual insight, as Mark so often uses natural perception as a figure for spiritual perception, and they lack understanding and thus are dumb, unable to speak.

3. Mark implies that Jesus departs to pray a third time, for he returns to find them sleeping a third time. And he declares: "Are you still sleeping and taking your rest? It is enough; the hour has come; the Son of man is betrayed into the hands of sinners" (14:41).

And so, in the Garden of Gethsemane, the inner triad of Peter, James, and John display spiritual incomprehension, and thus fail to keep watch and are found sleeping when "the hour" (13:32) comes for Jesus, even though he has charged them to watch and keep vigil, precisely because no one knows when "that day or that hour" (13:32) is coming.[1] Told by Jesus to keep watch (*grēgoreō*) three times in 13:32–37, the three disciples fail thrice in Gethsemane, found sleeping three times (14:37, 40, 41).

The three disciples who fail here in Gethsemane are the same three who witnessed the glory of the Transfiguration. And so, the theologies of glory and cross are in play in Gethsemane. Indeed, the heavy burden of their hunger for glory displayed throughout the discipleship section has cumbered their eyes. Led by Peter, the three wished to bear the weight of glory on the Mount of Transfiguration, but now, brought into

---

[1] See above on the Parable of the Doorkeeper (Mark 13:32–37) on pp. 270–80.

the valley of the shadow of the darkness of impending death in the Garden of Gethsemane, they cannot bear the weight of the cross as their eyes grow heavy.

Jesus rises to meet Judas's mob. "Rise, let us be going" (14:42) doesn't indicate a desire to flee. Rather, "rise" here is *egeirō*, suggestive of the Resurrection (see 1:31 and 5:41), as if Mark is suggesting the disciples are raised to life by Jesus's word even though they've been dead in their spiritual dullness. And "let us be going" is *agō*, a verb of encounter; *anachōreō* is a better word for withdrawal or retreat, which Mark employs in 3:7.

Like Gethsemane, in which Jesus wrestles with his impending doom, the arrest of Jesus (14:43–52) is marked by the cross. For Judas's crowd comes carrying swords and clubs, *meta machairōn kai xulōn* (14:43), which Jesus himself then mentions (14:48); Mark uses the phrase twice. Those words *machaira* and *xulon* are, respectively, the words for the knife and the wood of Abraham's sacrifice of Isaac in Genesis 22 in the LXX.[2] In Genesis 22, Abraham wields the sacrificial implements of the knife and wood to sacrifice his beloved son Isaac, while in Mark 14:43–52, God wields the crowd with swords and clubs to sacrifice his beloved Son Jesus.[3]

But Jesus, like the Isaac of Jewish tradition, is willing to go his way to sacrificial death. Instead of fleeing amidst the violence of the fracas that erupts (14:47), Jesus has faith, not fear, and so addresses the mob, which representatives of the Sanhedrin had sent by stealth because they had fear of the crowds, not faith: "Have you come out as against a robber, with swords

---

[2] *Machaira*, the knife to slay Isaac in Gen 22:6 and 10, and *xulon*, the wood of the burnt offering in Gen 22:3, 6, 7, 9.

[3] Perhaps translating the phrase as "knives and sticks" in Mark 14:43 and 38 would better reflect the Greek and reveal more clearly the parallels with Gen 22.

and clubs to capture me? Day after day I was with you in the temple teaching, and you did not seize me. But let the scriptures be fulfilled" (14:48–49). Now, ironically, it's Jesus's enemies who are attempting to operate in secret, seizing Jesus by night, while Jesus has been operating by day (a better translation of *kath' hēmeran* in 14:49a than "day after day") before their very sightless eyes in the Temple.

Jesus's antagonists fear the crowd, but the disciples fear the cross. And so Mark records: "And they all forsook him, and fled" (14:50), breaking their promise at the Last Supper, made along with Peter, to remain with Jesus even to death (14:31). And then we get the strangest detail: Mark relates that an anonymous "young man" (*neaniskos*) "followed" Jesus (thus he's a disciple) wearing only a linen garment (*sindōn*, 14:51), but when the mob seized him, he left the garment behind and ran away naked (15:42).

The only other time a "young man" (*neaniskos*) appears in Mark's Gospel is at the empty tomb (16:5). He announces the Resurrection to the women inside the empty tomb, making him the ultimate insider. He wears a white robe and sits on the right side. Like Peter and the others, he fails in chapter 14. But in chapter 16, he's been restored, and announces the restoration of Peter and all the disciples (16:7). More on that below.

One final disciple remains to fall: Peter. And Mark once again works his literary magic in depicting Peter's denial. Mark 14:53–72 contrasts Peter's denial of Jesus with Jesus's confession of his identity before the high priest in an intercalation:

14:53 (A): Jesus brought inside before the high priest
14:54 (B): Peter follows into the courtyard of the high priest but remains outside
14:55–65 (A'): Jesus questioned inside before high priest and confesses identity

14:66–72 (B'):   Peter questioned outside in courtyard before
                   servant girl and denies Jesus

On the page, Jesus's confession precedes Peter's denial.
But in the world of Mark's story, Jesus's and Peter's respective
trials occur at the exact same time.[4] In Mark 14:54, Peter is in
the middle of the "courtyard" of the high priest, and the story
returns to Peter in the "courtyard" in 14:66: "And as Peter
was below in the courtyard," where we last left him. There's
no indication that Peter's denial occurs after Jesus's confession. Rather, the Greek (*Kai ontos tou Petrou katō en tē aulē*, a
present genitive absolute) and the simple mention of Peter's
location in the courtyard in 14:66 mean the two trials are
simultaneous.

Mark is making an ironic and intense contrast. Jesus, being
interrogated by the high priest before a court of men with real
power, confesses his identity before them ("I am") and is condemned to death (14:62–64). Peter, being interrogated by a
mere slave girl before some bystanders, denies in the strongest
terms that he even knows Jesus (14:71) and thereby spares
himself from suffering and death.

Further, in fulfilling Jesus's prophecy that Peter would
indeed deny him (14:30), to which Mark draws our attention
in this passage (14:72: "Peter remembered how Jesus had said
to him . . ."), Peter's denials make the mockery and beating of
Jesus in 14:65 ("And some began to spit on him, and to cover
his face, and to strike him, saying to him, 'Prophesy!' And the
guards received him with blows") highly ironic. The fulfillment of Jesus's prediction in Peter's denial of Jesus testifies to

---

[4] For my full treatment of this intercalation, see Leroy A. Huizenga, "The
Confession of Jesus and the Curses of Peter: A Narrative-Christological
Approach to the Text-Critical Problem of Mark 14:62," *Novum Testamen-
tum* 53 (2011): 244–66.

the truthfulness of Jesus's confession, "I am," and encourages readers' confidence in Jesus's prophecy, "and you will see the Son of man sitting at the right hand of Power, and coming with the clouds of heaven" (14:62b).

Jesus's boldness contrasts with Peter's denial. Jesus is resolute, Peter craven. Jesus knows who he is and confesses it freely and fearlessly, while Peter denies emphatically that he even knows Jesus: "But he began to invoke a curse on himself and to swear, 'I do not know this man of whom you speak'" (14:71).

The simultaneous juxtaposition of Jesus's confession and Peter's denial is not restricted to this immediate passage; it's the climax of the diverging contrast between Jesus and the disciples (of whom Peter is chief) that has been building throughout the entire Gospel. Indeed, Peter (as Simon) is the first disciple called (1:16–18) and the last to desert. Although the disciples had all fled at the time of Jesus's arrest in Gethsemane (14:50–52), Peter has managed to follow Jesus "at a distance" into the courtyard of the high priest (14:54), raising hopes for readers that Peter might remain faithful, hopes that are dashed. Jesus's confession and Peter's denial are artfully counterposed to bring to dramatic heights the depths of Peter's failure and the irony in Peter's denial of Jesus at the precise instant Jesus is making the good confession, the culmination of all the failures of Peter and the disciples and the faithfulness and obedience of Jesus. Jesus remains faithful to the end.

Finally, this is not the first time Jesus has uttered the words "I am" (*egō eimi*). In Mark 6:50, in the context of the second boat scene, *egō eimi* evokes echoes of the divine name of the LXX of Exodus 3:14: Jesus takes the divine name on his lips in the theophany the disciples failed to perceive when he tried to present his divine identity to them. It is thus certainly possible—indeed, likely—that the high priest in the Markan story heard echoes of the Divine Name in Jesus's utterance of *egō eimi* and, thus, condemned him for blasphemy.[5] Jesus's antagonists have dared bring him into their direct presence, and so they get direct revelation of Jesus's deepest identity, which they reject.

We move to morning, to Jesus's trial before Pilate and his crucifixion. He's now charged before Pilate not with theological blasphemy but with political rebellion, as Pilate asks him, "are you the King of the Jews?" (15:2), the first time the phrase appears in Mark's Gospel. Jesus has confessed to being the Christ before the Sanhedrin's kangaroo court, when asked directly. (14:61–62). But how would the high priest know to ask that?

Jesus's belief that he's the Christ is likely one of the two things Judas betrays, since Judas was present at Peter's confession at Caesarea Philippi, where Jesus accepted Peter's appellation of him as Christ but charged them to tell no one about him (8:29–30), which command Judas has broken, getting Jesus crucified. The other thing Judas betrays is simply Jesus's location in Gethsemane; Jerusalem would swell with half a million pilgrims during Passover, making it hard to find someone under cover of darkness.

And since most Jews believed the Christ would make war on Israel's pagan enemies and establish a new everlasting kingdom like David's of old, Jesus's claim to Christhood involves the perception of kingship. But Jesus maintains silence in the face of further accusations, causing Pilate's amazement (15:3–5).

---

[5] See Sharon Dowd and Elizabeth Struthers Malbon, "The Significance of Jesus's Death in Mark: Narrative Context and Authorial Audience," *Journal of Biblical Literature* 125 (2006): 271–97, at 295; and E. Struthers Malbon, *Mark's Jesus: Characterization as Narrative Christology* (Waco, TX: Baylor University Press, 2009), 169–70.

Pilate tries to get Jesus released, offering the crowd Barabbas as an option instead. Barabbas is a truly violent man, guilty of committing murder in an insurrection (15:7). Further, his name in Aramaic means "son of the father." The stage is again set for irony: Jesus, the true Son of the Father, does not commit violence but suffers it, while Barabbas, a false son of the Father, is a violent rebel. Nevertheless, the crowd will cry for Jesus's crucifixion, and Pilate, craven like Herod in the matter of Herodias's designs on John the Baptist's head, will accede to their request. The bloodguilty rebel goes free while the innocent is condemned of incipient bloodguilty rebellion.

Jesus is handed over for crucifixion, and he endures ritual mocking at the hands of the guards (15:16–20). Mocking him as a mock king, they dress him with a purple cloak and crown of thorns and hail him "King of the Jews," kneeling before him and beating and spitting upon him. Irony again: Like the centurion at the crucifixion who speaks the truth of Jesus's divine Sonship he doesn't believe, the soldiers here rightly acclaim Jesus as king of the Jews even though they don't believe it.

For Mark, the Passion and crucifixion is a "parodic exaltation" of Jesus as king.[6] As with the title "Son of God," Mark is concerned that readers get Jesus's identity right, that no elevated title—Son of God, Christ, Son of man, Lord, King of the Jews—lead to a theology of glory. And so, Mark posits the theology of a royal Cross: "King" (*basileus*) appears here for the first time with reference to Jesus, in Mark 15:2, once the crucifixion is imminent, and "king" is then employed five more times with reference to Jesus in Mark 15. But Jesus's kingship is revealed only in the midst of the mockery, beatings, torture, and Cross he endures.

---

[6]   See Joel Marcus, "Crucifixion as Parodic Exaltation," *Journal of Biblical Literature* 125 (2006): 73–87.

Indeed, forms of execution that elevated the condemned above onlookers on a high gibbet, like crucifixion, were intended by authorities in power as a deliberate parodic mockery of the condemned's pretensions to greatness: "Crucifixion was intended to unmask, in a deliberately grotesque manner, the pretension and arrogance of those who had exalted themselves beyond their station."[7] Their attitude: "You think you're a king? Fine. Let us help exalt you." And so, Pilate unwittingly and ironically exalts Jesus as king. Pilate doesn't believe it, but Mark's faithful readers know it's the truth. Jesus's crucifixion is his exaltation; here the theologies of the cross and of glory coincide. Cross and glory are one.

Many Christians glory in the gore of crucifixion, as portrayed in medieval and renaissance art, as well as modern films like *The Passion of the Christ*. And crucifixion was gory, providing the condemned with an agonizing death like no other. The crucified might hang for days[8]—note that Pilate will be surprised Jesus dies so quickly (15:44)—suffering from hypovolemic shock and dying from exhaustion asphyxia.[9] And therefore much Christian teaching and preaching has traded in guilt, trying to motivate people to come to Jesus and do better for him in light of the most extreme pains he suffered.

But neither Mark, nor the other evangelists, nor Paul, nor other New Testament writers describe the physical horrors of crucifixion in the least. Mark simply states, "And they cruci-

---

[7] Marcus, "Crucifixion," 78.

[8] Josephus (*Life of Flavius Josephus* 76) records that, while on an expedition with Titus, he encountered some of his acquaintances hanging on crosses. He intervened, and they were removed from their crosses. Josephus records that two survived while a third died. The story implies they had been hanging for some time.

[9] See William D. Edwards, Wesley J. Gabel, and Floyd E. Hosmer, "On the Physical Death of Jesus Christ," *Journal of the American Medical Association* 255, no. 11 (1986): 1455–63.

fied him" (15:24a). Perhaps Mark didn't need to mention the horrors of crucifixion, as everyone knew what crucifixion was, since people were crucified all the time.

Further, Romans regarded crucifixion as so shameful it shouldn't be mentioned. That greatest of Roman republicans, the orator Cicero, wrote a hundred years before Jesus that one shouldn't even think about it: "The very word cross should be far removed not only from the body of a Roman citizen but from his mind, his eyes, his ears."[10] If we dare say so, Jesus suffered much less physically than many other victims of crucifixion in terms of duration: he's crucified for six hours, from the third Roman hour to the ninth.

Instead of focusing on the gore and physical suffering of Jesus's crucifixion, the New Testament plays up its shame. The homilist of Hebrews states that Jesus "endured the cross, despising the shame" (Heb 12:2). Mark, for his part, glories in the shame of Jesus's crucifixion, recording more mockery of Jesus, king of the Jews, on the part of all present (15:26–32): (1) the *titulus* hanging over his head mocks him as "King of the Jews" (15:26); (2) passersby mock him, taunting him to save himself (15:39–30); (3) the chief priests and scribes mock him because he can't save himself (15:31), taunting him to come down from the Cross so that they might "see and believe" (15:32a), an attitude diametrically opposite to how faith works in Mark's Gospel, whose Jesus promises revelation and healing to those who have faith; and finally, (4) even the two robbers crucified with him mock him (15:27, 32b).

Thus, even those crucified with Jesus take their stand against him, aligning themselves with those who mock them

---

[10] Marcus Tullius Cicero, *Pro Rabirio perduellionis reo* 5.16, in *Pro lege Manilia, Pro Caecina, Pro Cluentio, and Pro Rabirio perduellionis reo*, trans. H. Grose Hodge, Loeb Classical Library 198 (Cambridge, MA: Harvard University Press, 1927), 466–67.

too and who crucified them. Mark presents no Lukan penitent thief, no Johannine *pietà*. Why? Mark presents Jesus totally alone, cut off from everyone, from all humanity, to show that no one is faithful, save Jesus.

And so, Mark 15:21–32 shows Jesus is cut off from man. The next section, 15:33–37, shows Jesus then cut off from God. Darkness covers the land (15:33), and Jesus utters his cry of dereliction: *Eloi, Eloi, lama sabachthani* (15:34). And more irony: the bystanders hear *Eloi* as a cry for *Eli-jah*, Elijah (15:35); human misunderstanding of Jesus persists even in his death. And Elijah fails to come save Jesus; it appears to outsiders that Jesus is a failure. At the moment of his deepest need, the heavens are silent. Jesus utters a loud cry, no discernible words, and dies.

Many like to read the triumphant words of John's Jesus— "It is finished"—into this Markan cry. Perhaps that works on a canonical level, but in the world of Mark's story, it's wholly unjustified. Jesus's death in Mark's Gospel is not triumphant, but pathetic. But given the theology of the cross, the crucifixion is Jesus's ironic, glorious triumph.

That Jesus is so misunderstood indicates that physical suffering does matter in one respect. In the world of Mark's story, Jesus is really suffering as he's contorted by the Cross: readers are supposed to imagine that Jesus's breathing is so labored that he's barely able to utter words. Hence, it's easy for bystanders to mistake *Eloi* for *Eli-jah*. Which brings us to the nature of his death and the centurion's confession.

We must pay attention to Mark's precise language. At the moment of Jesus's death, Mark tells us as readers, "the curtain of the temple was torn in two, from top to bottom" (15:38). Readers have privileged information here. No one at Golgotha—including the centurion—could have seen through the walls of Jerusalem and through the walls of the Temple complex to the veil before the holy of holies. When Mark tells readers the veil was torn, he's telling us God has left the building. The veil is "torn" (*schizō*), just as the heavens were torn open (*schizō*) at Jesus's baptism (1:10). As the Holy Spirit tore through the cosmic breach in the heavens to possess Jesus, God the Father tears through the Temple veil, departing the sanctuary in recompense for the murder of his Son.[11]

The centurion sees and knows none of this. Mark emphasizes that he's focused squarely on his victim: "And when the centurion, *who stood facing him* . . ." Mark then writes, "saw that he thus breathed his last . . ." (15:39). The "thus" is crucial: the centurion saw Jesus die in a certain way, in a particular manner. And Mark has told us in what way, in what manner, Jesus died: hanging on the horrid Cross, mocked by men, cut off from God, misunderstood, uttering an unintelligible cry.

Only then does Mark relate that the centurion said, "Truly this man was the Son of God!" (15:39). The centurion's "confession" can only be ironic. He speaks the truth Mark would have readers believe but does not believe it himself. There's nothing Mark's centurion would have witnessed in Jesus's crucifixion to lead him to faith. The centurion is a model in one way: he "sees" the Cross and then utters an utterly formal confession of faith, but it's insincere. It's ironic.

Indeed, the centurion's ironic confession is the extreme example of Markan irony, as he's the one and only human in Mark's Gospel to call Jesus the Son of God. He speaks truth

---

[11] The earth's swallowing of the veil in the Jewish apocalyptic work 2 Baruch (6:7–9) and the shredding of the veil in the apocalyptic work known as the Lives of the Prophets (12:12) are associated with the departure of the divine glory; see Catherine Sider Hamilton, "'His Blood Be upon Us': Innocent Blood and the Death of Jesus in Matthew," *Catholic Biblical Quarterly* 70 (2008): 82–100, at 97. See also Josephus, who states on several occasions that God abandoned the Temple in light of sins and crimes during the Jewish war (*Wars of the Jews* 5.412, 6.300, and *Antiquities* 20.166).

he doesn't believe, saying sarcastically, "Truly this man was the Son of God!" (15:39). Unlike, say, Matthew's version, Mark's version of the crucifixion has nothing, not one thing, to lead the centurion to faith. Jesus dies horribly, alone, cut off from man (all mock him, even *both* robbers crucified with him, unlike Luke's version with the penitent thief) and cut off from God ("My God, my God, why have you forsaken me?"), and even then he was misunderstood, as the crowd thinks he's calling for Elijah. He screams and dies. Readers are told the curtain of the Temple was torn in two, but there's no way the centurion could see through the city walls and the Temple walls into the holy of holies to know that. And so the best read is that the centurion is sarcastic, mocking and deriding Jesus here as everyone else has at his crucifixion. But what horrible irony: the very one who killed the true Son of God speaks the very truth that could save him, but he doesn't believe it. The centurion may just be the prime example of discipleship failure, the most ironic disciple of all.[12]

The centurion's insincerity means irony: the centurion has committed the most sinful act in history, killing the divine Son of God as a nameless functionary of Roman power, probably bored with the whole affair. And yet, he's precisely the one who confesses the truth about him. Mark shows us here the depth of human sin. The centurion rejects ultimately and finally the one he speaks the truth about in killing him. The centurion is an ironic disciple, and his killing the Son of God is the prime example of discipleship failure.

---

[12] In *A Master of Surprise: Mark Interpreted* (Minneapolis, MN: Augsburg, 2002), Donald Juel writes: "I have come to believe that even 'Son of God' in 15.39 ought probably be read as a taunt ('Sure, this was God's Son'), in accord with the rest of the taunts in the account of Jesus's trial and death. The centurion plays a role assigned all Jesus's enemies: They speak the truth in mockery, thus providing for the reader ironic testimony to the truth" (74n7).

The Passion of the Christ (Mark 14:1–15:47)

This is the only place in Mark's Gospel that a human being calls Jesus the Son of God. Mark withholds "Son of God" on human lips until this very moment for narrative purposes: so that readers might understand that the Cross is an absolute necessity for Jesus the Son of God, that they can have Jesus as Son of God only if they receive him not as superstar, but as the crucified Son. Here we encounter the depths of Mark's theology of the cross, the total depravity of sin. The man who kills Jesus is the same man who speaks the totality of Jesus's identity as Son of God but doesn't mean it.

At this point, an ideal or model reader who doesn't know the end of Mark's story is reduced to utter despair. And so Mark, like a cat with a mouse, toys with his readers, teasing them into raising their hopes one last time as he introduces another character group: "There were also women looking on from afar" who, "when he was in Galilee, followed him, and ministered to him; and also many other women who came up with him to Jerusalem" (15:40–41). These women have followed him through the discipleship section. They too are disciples. Two of them, Mary Magdalene and Mary the mother of Joses, see where Jesus was laid (15:47) in the sealed tomb. All the men have failed; maybe in some way these women— the supposedly weaker sex in a patriarchal society—will prove faithful. But don't bet on it.

Mark 14:12–16, 22–26: Sunday after the Most Holy Trinity / The Most Holy Body and Blood of Christ (Corpus Christi)

Sandwiched between the prediction of Judas's betrayal and Peter's denial stands the institution of the Eucharist (14:22–25). In the Synoptic Gospels, the Eucharist is instituted expressly at Passover: it's a Passover meal, Mark writing the word "Passover" three times (14:12, 14, 16). Jesus's disciples ask him about making preparations for the Passover meal (14:12), and Jesus sends two of them to follow a random(?)[13] man with a jar of water to a home and inquire of the owner where the Teacher and his disciples might eat the Passover. There they will find a room ready, and they should, and do, prepare the Passover (14:13–16). The story strikes us as bizarre, but it displays Jesus's sovereign authority: what he says happens.

The Eucharist is a Passover meal in Mark's Gospel, but it's a Passover meal transformed. Here we see again the continuity with Judaism. Jesus takes something from his Jewish heritage and, in his sovereign divine authority, interprets it with reference to himself.

Three items of Mark's presentation of Jesus's Eucharistic Passover merit especial mention. First, although Passover meals require consumption of lamb, Mark mentions no lamb. It's as if Mark (as well as Matthew and Luke in their versions) is suggesting Jesus himself is the Passover lamb.[14] Moreover, Mark's mention of explicit times in his account of Jesus's crucifixion tracks with the times of the *tamid* lamb sacrifice in the Temple: Jesus is crucified at the third Roman hour (9:00 a.m., Mark 15:25); the sky darkens at the sixth hour (12:00 p.m., Mark 15:33); and Jesus dies at the ninth hour (3:00 p.m., Mark 15:34). This corresponds to the daily Temple service.

---

[13] Some scholars suggest this is an indication that Jesus had friends in the city. In the world of Mark's story, however, the passage reflects Jesus's mysterious authority. See footnote 1 of chapter 6 (part II) above.

[14] See Joachim Jeremias, *Die Abendmahlsworte Jesu*, 4th ed. (Göttingen: Vandenhoeck & Ruprecht, 1967), 214. But for a contrary view, see Brant Pitre, *Jesus and the Last Supper* (Grand Rapids, MI: Eerdmans, 2015), 290–292, who argues that the preparations for the Passover in Mark 14 assume a full Passover meal with a lamb, and so Mark emphasizes the bread and wine as Jesus's Body and Blood in the words of institution without denying the presence of other elements.

The Temple opened with the initial *tamid* sacrifice of a lamb about nine in the morning;[15] a second lamb was bound on the altar at noon;[16] and the Temple closed its daily services with the final *tamid* sacrifice of that second lamb around three in the afternoon.[17]

In short, Mark is presenting Jesus's crucifixion in terms of the rhythms of the sacrifice of the Temple's *tamid* lambs, from the Temple's open to close, as if Jesus is the new Temple. Further, if the Jews were praying a version of the classic Eighteen Benedictions at the hours of the opening and closing of the Temple,[18] as many scholars suggest, then they would be praying (among other things) for redemption, for forgiveness of sins, for the coming of the Christ, and for the resurrection of the dead.[19]

Second, the Passover meal is sacrificial. Beyond Mark's tying Jesus's crucifixion to the *tamid* sacrifice, Jesus employs a sacrificial word in his institution of the Precious Blood of the Eucharist. Jesus's Blood is "poured out" or "shed" (*ekchunnō*). The Greek term Mark employs is a Hellenistic derivative of *ekcheō*, which is used for the shedding of blood in sacrificial contexts throughout the Greek Bible.[20]

Third, the Precious Blood of the Eucharist is the sacrifice

---

15 See Exod 29:38–42; Num 28:1–8, and in the Mishnah, m. Tamid 1:2 and 3:2–3, 7.
16 See m. Tamid 4:1
17 See Josephus, *Antiquities* 14.65, and Philo, *On the Special Laws* 1.169.
18 See Genesis Rabbah 68 and, in the Babylonian Talmud, b. Ber. 26b and 33a and b. Meg. 17b, which indicate that Jews prayed everywhere in accord with the offering of the *tamid* lambs. Acts 3:1 seems to reflect this: "Now Peter and John were going up to the temple at the hour of prayer, the ninth hour."
19 See Pitre, *Jesus and the Last Supper*, 325–30.
20 See the LXX of Lev 4:7, 18, 25, 30, 34; Num 35:33; Deut 21:17; Ps 79:10; Ezek 22:3; Joel 4:19; and see Acts 22:20 and Rev 16:6. See also Josephus, *Antiquities* 19.94.

of the "new covenant" (14:24).[21] Jesus here establishes the Christian ritual sacrifice that will replace Temple sacrifices after his crucifixion and after the Temple's destruction.

Yet, continuity remains crucial in the shadow of the Cross: the "new covenant" is rooted in and continues the old. For Catholics, biblical interpretation is a three-stage affair, with the Mass as the realization of salvation history and the anticipation of the eschaton in the present. The Old Testament foreshadows the events of the New, and the sacramental mysteries of the Church make them present. And so the exodus from Egypt grounds the annual Passover, at which Jesus is crucified and institutes his Eucharist, which the Church thereafter celebrates in time. The Eucharist is where salvation history and the risen, eschatological Christ meet in our present.

---

[21] The textual reading "new" has significant manuscript support, and fits well with Mark's polemic against the Temple and the Jewish leadership.

CHAPTER 8

The Grace of God on the Loose
(Mark 16:1–20)

Mark 16 is a dramatic and, for some, maddening end to Mark's wild story. The Gospel itself, in all likelihood, ended at Mark 16:8 with the women fleeing the tomb and keeping silence, thanks to their fear, even though the young man had told them to speak, to go and tell Peter and the other disciples that Jesus goes ahead of them to Galilee. Thus Mark ends on a note of irony. Instead of a divine representative (Jesus throughout the Gospel) adjuring people to silence and secrecy that they then break and speak publicly, here the divine representative (the young man in a white robe sitting on the right side) adjures the women to speak but they keep silent.

That ending is not only fitting but brilliant: Mark dashes readerly hopes that some human being might prove faithful, showing that Jesus alone is finally faithful while inviting his readers by the young man's mention of Galilee in Mark 16:7 to return to the beginning of the Gospel and, thus, in spite of their own failures, to begin following Jesus again.

But that ending has proven unsatisfactory to interpreters ancient and modern. Ancient scribes cobbled longer endings together from stories of Resurrection appearances found in other Gospels and Acts. Many modern scholars cannot bring themselves to believe a Gospel could end on such a weird,

301

anticlimactic note, one even suggesting that what happened was that Mark's Virgin Birth story and Resurrection appearances got lost to history when an ancient codex of Mark lost its first and last pages, as they would have borne the brunt of the wear and tear of being carried around in a satchel.[1]

But Mark ending his Gospel at 16:8 makes literary sense: it fits perfectly with Mark's theme of discipleship failure, his concomitant emphasis on the theology of the cross, and his use of the rhetorical device of irony.[2] Mark's rhetorical strategy is brilliant: instead of spelling it out for his readers and hearers, as didacticism can stultify audiences, he invites his audience into the story, gripping their attention and involvement.

What, then are we to do with the longer endings of Mark?

Christian faith is coherent, and while each Gospel (indeed, each biblical document) has its own particular contours and content, the fact of the biblical canon means that biblical texts get interpreted in the context of the biblical canon. For Catholics, the biblical canon is the result of a long, Spirit-guided, bottom-up process in which the Church discerned and then in its authority determined its contents.

The longer endings of Mark, like the story of the woman caught in adultery in John 7:53–8:11 or the coda to the Lord's Prayer in Matthew 6:13, aren't original to the document. And yet, such passages have found a place in the canon and have functioned as Scripture for Christians for many centuries.

[1] N. Clayton Croy, *The Mutilation of Mark's Gospel* (Nashville, TN: Abingdon, 2003).

[2] The most ancient and significant manuscript witnesses to the text of Mark's Gospel, Vaticanus (B) and Sinaiticus (א), lack the longer ending of Mark 16:9–20. On Mark 16:8 as a fitting end to the Gospel, see J. F. Williams, "Literary Approaches to the End of Mark's Gospel," *Journal of the Evangelical Theological Society* 42 (1999): 21–35, and Andrew T. Lincoln, "The Promise and the Failure: Mark 16:7, 8," *Journal of Biblical Literature* 108 (1989): 283–300.

Thus, there's creative tension between the ideal literary structure of a document and additions that have become canonical.[3] And so we treat of an authoritative version of the longer endings of Mark. When reading, teaching, or preaching Mark's story, then, it's important to maintain the Gospel's ending at 16:8. When reading, teaching, or preaching the longer ending, we might understand and state that it's true in that it represents the broader truth about what Jesus did and said (especially as it draws directly on other canonical texts).

Mark 16:1–7: Easter Vigil

Mark closes chapter 15 by introducing us to a new and sudden character group, women who followed Jesus. We're informed that "There were also women looking on from afar" at Jesus's crucifixion: Mary Magdalene, Mary the mother of James the younger and of Joses, and Salome (15:40). Along with many other women, they "followed" Jesus in Galilee (and so are disciples) and came up to Jerusalem with him (15:41). Indeed, the young man at the empty tomb in Mark 16:7 reminds them of Jesus's promise in 14:28 that he would go forth to Galilee ahead of them after his Resurrection: he says, "There"—in Galilee—"you will see him, *as he told you.*" Mark 16:7 means the women were present on the Mount of Olives with Jesus after the Last Supper (14:26–31) and, thus, in Mark's story, likely at the Last Supper itself (14:22–25).

---

3   Even modern scholarship makes concessions to tradition. Many scholars have thought John's Gospel has five editorial layers, and while no modern scholars think the story of the woman caught in adultery was part of the original text, commentaries treat it in what's become its traditional location (John 7:53–8:11) precisely because the canonical tradition made it part of John. Scholarship may desire to work with autographs—that is, reconstructed original texts—but it is indebted to forms of the texts that have become traditional in the canonical process and works with them.

So these women are disciples of Jesus who followed him on the way of discipleship. Mark raises hopes for his readers that maybe a surprise group of disciples—women at that, who did not have the standing in Jesus's world that they have today—might finally prove somehow faithful.

Mark makes sure to inform his readers that two of them (Mary Magdalene and the Mary the mother of Joses) "saw where [Jesus] was laid" in the sealed tomb (15:47). In fact, 15:40–47 is another Markan sandwich, with Joseph of Arimathea's burial of Jesus (15:42–46) as the B section related in the middle of the two mentions of the women (15:40–41 and 15:47), the A and A' sections. Like all Markan sandwiches, there's a progression even as the two stories interpret each other. The effect of the sandwich is to focus the reader on death: the way of the cross is the end of the way of discipleship. These women followed Jesus from Galilee to Jerusalem, Jesus is dead and buried, sealed in a tomb, and they saw where he was laid. The end.

Or is it? The women Mark mentions in 15:40 wait for the Sabbath to pass, then purchase spices to anoint Jesus's corpse, and then proceed to the tomb (16:1–2). On one hand, they are faithful: they follow Jesus past the point of death. On the other hand, they're seeking a corpse. They believe he is dead. They have no hope for Jesus's life, even though they'll soon be reminded that Jesus had told them to regroup in Galilee (16:7). After all, Mark's already informed us that they were with him in Galilee and came up with him to Jerusalem (15:40–41), implying that they themselves had heard the three Passion predictions on the way, Passion predictions that also predicted Jesus's Resurrection: "And he began to teach them that the Son of man must suffer many things . . . and after three days rise again" (8:31).

But they've forgotten: even in their genuine act of piety

they're seeking a corpse. And they were looking on at the crucifixion "from afar," not going all the way with Jesus to the cross, much like Peter went as far as Caiaphas's courtyard but no farther. And they expect a sealed tomb with a body inside, for they ask each other, "Who will roll away the stone for us from the door of the tomb?" (16:3).

And so, they and Mark's readers are in for a big surprise. They go to the tomb "when the sun had risen" (16:2b), which is a play on words—Greek *hēlios* for sun and *huios* for Son— in suggesting what it sounds like in English: the rising sun is a natural symbol of resurrection, like waking from sleep,[4] so early Christians often prayed and worshipped facing east, the direction of the rising sun. And it's likely Mark's initial readers and hearers[5] would have appreciated the *hēlios–huios* wordplay.

When they arrive at the tomb, there's a surprise: the large stone has already been rolled away (16:4). That's weird enough, but then they encounter not an angel but a "young man," a *neaniskos* (16:5), the same anonymous young man who deserted Jesus with all the other disciples in Gethesemane (14:51–52). He's "sitting on the right side." "Right" in the Bible and Western rhetoric is a positive sign. We speak of human and constitutional "rights," not lefts, and lefthanders know that the world is simply aligned against them, from scissors to silverware.[6] And in the Bible, the right hand is the good hand, as in Isaiah the LORD promises to uphold the Israelites with his "right hand" (Is 41:10, 13) and leads Cyrus the

---

[4] On sleep as a metaphor for death, see Mark 5:39b, 1 Cor 15:51, and Eph 5:14.

[5] Of course, most early Christians were illiterate and would have encountered the Gospel of Mark aurally as it was read to them orally, perhaps in its entirety. See footnote 13 in chapter 1 of part I above on St. Justin Martyr's witness to lengthy Gospel readings in the liturgy.

[6] Indeed, the English word "sinister" derives from the Latin *sinister, -stra, -strum*, which means left.

Persian, his instrument, to deliver them from Babylon with his "right hand" (45:1). The LORD declares that his "right hand spread out the heavens" (Isa 48:13) and swears by his "right hand" (Isa 62:8). In Matthew's Gospel, the sheep are on the right and the goats on the left (Matt 25:33). And in the creeds, we confess that the risen and ascended Jesus sits at the right hand of the Father. Mark's Gospel too reflects this: James and John ask to sit at Jesus's "right hand" in glory (9:38); Jesus tells those interrogating him that they will see the Son of man "sitting at the right hand of Power" (14:62); and the longer ending relates that the ascended Jesus "sat down at the right hand of God" (16:19).

The young man is also wearing now not a mere linen garment, a *sindōn*, but a white robe, a *stolē*. "White" also signifies positively in the Western rhetorical tradition, and in the New Testament in particular.[7] Of particular interest are the usages of the word in Revelation, especially as Mark's empty tomb concerns eschatology, in which the saints in heaven wear white robes (see Rev 6:11; 7:9, 7:13–14; 22:14). The young man's white robe is an eschatological resurrection symbol.

So, the literary signals of "right" and "white" tell readers the young man is to be trusted, that he represents the divine perspective, and thus speaks here from the divine perspective. Beyond that, he's been forgiven his failure, his apostasy. Even though he abandoned Jesus in Gethsemane and ran away naked without his linen garment—does that symbolize the surrender of his baptismal identity, as catechumens-*cum*-baptizands would be clothed in such a garment?—he now wears the white resurrection robe of the saints.

---

7 See, for instance, Matt 28:3; Mark 9:3; John 20:12, Acts 1:10; and Revelations 1:14; 2:17; 3:4–5, 18; 4:4; 6:2, 11; 7:9, 13, 14; 14:14; 19:11, 14.

Now, the Resurrection is not merely the restoration, but even the transformation of Eden.[8] Therefore, the young man is also symbolic of the restoration and transformation of Adam, of humanity. One good interpretation of Jesus's satanic testing in Mark 1:12–13 is that in besting Satan, he there restores Eden. Now, the young man in Gethsemane is nameless, only a "young man," perhaps suggesting all humanity, and thus Adam, who, in his creation before sin, would be young, as aging is a consequence of sin. The young man in Mark's Gospel flees the Garden of Gethsemane, as Adam hid from God (Gen 3:8) and departed the Garden of Eden (Gen 3:24).

Most telling is that the young man in Mark's Gospel is naked, *gumnos*, just as Adam was naked, *gumnos* (Gen 3:10–11). In Gethsemane, then, we would have an Adam–Christ contrast: Jesus, the New Adam, obeys his Father, while the young man recalls the sin of the first Adam in disobeying the LORD God his Father. And so, when the young man appears at the empty tomb wearing not merely the linen garment he left behind in Gethsemane but now a white robe, we have a signal of the Resurrection's transformation of Eden. Humanity isn't simply restored to its prelapsarian state, but transformed into resurrection life.[9]

The women are "amazed" (16:5b), never a good sign in Mark's Gospel. And so he tells them: "Do not be amazed; you seek Jesus of Nazareth, who was crucified. He has risen, he is

---

8 Adam and Eve were, in many ways, mortal at creation; while possessing sanctifying grace, they had not yet eaten of the tree of life, and their bodies do not display the characteristics of Jesus's Resurrection body or the "spiritual body" that Paul discusses in 1 Corinthians 15. Thus, it's improper to say that, in Christianity, *Endzeit* restores *Urzeit*, that the eschaton is simply a restoration of Eden.

9 See Rom 6:1–14. Resurrection life begins with Baptism, as the *Catechism of the Catholic Church* makes plain: "the 'plunge' into the water symbolizes the catechumen's burial into Christ's death, from which he rises up by resurrection with him, as 'a new creature'" (*CCC* §1214).

not here; see the place where they laid him" (16:6). And then he gives them a dominical, divine command:

> But go, tell his disciples and Peter that he is going before you to Galilee; there you will see him, as he told you. (16:7)

The disciples all fled in Gethsemane, as did he; and now they've been restored, as has he. The young man stands in parallel with them. And he says, "Go, tell his disciples *and Peter*"—Peter, whose denial is told with such bitter pathos, is singled out, as if the young man is saying, "Don't forget about Peter!" Forgiveness. Grace. Restoration. Crucifixion and Resurrection can do that for him. For you. For me.

If the women obey and go to Galilee, they will "see" Jesus there. They will be in Jesus's physical proximity and, now, encounter him as the risen Christ. They will "see" him: his ultimate identity as the crucified and risen Lord God will be revealed to them—if they go to Galilee and encounter him there.

But Mark has provided plenty of clues that the women will not prove faithful. They witnessed the crucifixion "from afar" (15:40), suggesting distance from Jesus's presence. They come to the tomb to anoint the rotting corpse inside. And, as they were present for the prediction of Peter's denial in 14:27–31, Jesus thus prophesied also of them, "You will all fall away" (14:27).

And so finally, in the last verse of Mark's original Gospel, they do. They fail. They fall away. A prophecy of Jesus again proves true, encouraging the reader's faith in him. Instead of going to Galilee, "they went out and fled from the tomb; for trembling and astonishment had come upon them; and they said nothing to any one, for they were afraid" (16:8).

Mark 16:1–7: Easter Vigil

Astonishment. Fear. Silence. Irony. What more perfect ending to Mark's Gospel could there be?

Irony: Throughout the Gospel, many whom Jesus has healed have been commanded to silence, but they spoke and spread the news anyway. Now these women are commanded to speak, and they remain silent. And irony in service of a theological point of massive significance: only Jesus is finally faithful—and the God who raised him from the dead.

Is that the end? Is Mark showing us that the mission is thwarted? Some scholars have gone so far as to suggest, in effect, that Mark's theme of discipleship failure is meant to throw the disciples totally overboard, to cut them off from Jesus forever, to distance Jesus's movement from them, daring to go where even Gnostics feared to tread.[10]

No. The young man invited them to go to Galilee, reminding them of Jesus's very command in Mark 14:28. Mission after the Resurrection was to begin again in Galilee, where Jesus's ministry began. And that's the key: Mark's Gospel is not written for its characters, but for its readers. The young man's words invite readers to return to Galilee, to begin reading again at Mark 1:14–20, to repent and believe the Gospel and follow Jesus immediately, like the two pairs of brothers he called by the seashore, to become fishers of men now, in our day.

And it's not at all that Mark thinks his readers can do better than the disciples, that they can succeed where the disciples failed. That's the height of hubris, as if we could do better than those Apostles who were in Jesus's very presence, who themselves had some real success in exorcising and healing (6:13). Have we? We fail too—even canonized saints sinned, that's why they went to confession—and yet, we, like they, are

---

[10] See Theodore J. Weeden, "The Heresy that Necessitated Mark's Gospel," in *The Interpretation of Mark*, ed. William Telford, Studies in New Testament Interpretation (Edinburgh, UK: Bloomsbury T&T Clark, 2000), 89–104.

invited to begin again and again, ever embracing the call of the cross, hoping for our resurrection.

Men and women will fail, but God will not. And for Mark, God is the Holy Trinity, Father, Son, and Holy Spirit. God is not merely some static triune substance above the skies, an object of intellectual assent and theological reflection. For Mark, *God is on the loose.*[11] At the Baptism of Our Lord, the Holy Spirit busted out of heaven through the tear in the cosmic fabric. At the crucifixion of Our Lord, the Father busted out of the Temple's Holy of Holies through the tear in the veil's fabric. And, at the Resurrection of Our Lord, the Son busted out of the tomb, raised by the Father in the power of the Spirit.

God is on the loose, running around the earth, the Persons of the Trinity seeking out those who would follow Jesus on the way of discipleship, who would walk the way of the cross, and achieve its end: their resurrection.

Mark 16:9–15: Saturday in the Octave of Easter

Mark 16:8 seems a weird way to end a Gospel, and so scribes in the early Church concocted triumphant endings to Mark out of material from the other Gospels and Acts, giving us Mark 16:9–20. Although the longer ending isn't original, being so radically different in vocabulary, style, tone, and content, it's canonical. Is there a way to read it in line with Mark's story?

Yes. For all the doubt, denial, and despair in the story, Mark's Gospel is ultimately a story of triumph. Jesus triumphs

---

[11] My phrase here depends on Donald Juel, *A Master of Surprise: Mark Interpreted* (Minneapolis, MN: Augsburg, 2002), 35–36, wherein Juel makes reference to the Holy Spirit's descent through the tear in the heavens (1:10) and the tearing of the Temple veil (15:38): "God, unwilling to be confined to sacred spaces, is on the loose in our own realm." See also ibid., 113, with reference to the Resurrection (16:6): "Jesus is out of the tomb, on the loose."

over sin, death, hell, and the devil, from his exorcisms and healings to his crucifixion and Resurrection. The final word of Mark isn't really the women's failure, but the Resurrection. Whatever the women don't do, God raised Jesus from the dead. And the longer ending reflects that reality, the reality of the Resurrection, as well as the final eternal enthronement and exaltation of Jesus, Son of man and Son of God, in the Ascension.

What has become the canonical longer ending involves scribal summaries of material found in other Gospels. The lectionary selection of Mark 16:9–15 for Easter Saturday presents three Resurrection appearances, each punctuated by Mark with mention of unbelief. The first appearance, to Mary Magdalene, is a summary of Lukan material. In Mark 16:9–11, we are told that Jesus appeared to Mary Magdalene, from whom he had cast out seven demons, and that Mary then went to tell his disciples, but they refused to believe it. Luke reports that the Magdalene had been exorcised of seven demons (Luke 8:2), and that Mary Magdalene, with other women, reported the empty tomb and the message of the two angelic men there to the disciples, but they refused to believe them (Luke 24:10–11).

The second appearance, in Mark 16:12–13, is the briefest summary of Luke's account of the two despairing disciples' encounter with the risen Jesus on the road to Emmaus (Luke 24:13–35), but Mark states that the disciples didn't believe, unlike the denouement in the Lukan account.

The third appearance, in Mark 16:14, is a summary of John 20:19–23, wherein the risen Jesus more or less walks through a wall and appears to the frightened disciples to wish them peace and institute the Sacrament of Reconciliation. Mark 16:14 relates that, before giving them his evangelical commission, Jesus "upbraided them for their unbelief and hardness of heart" because they rejected the Resurrection reports of the Magdalene and the two unnamed disciples.

Although the passage is scribal, readers perceive here connection to Markan themes. Those who bear witness to the Resurrection stand outside the Twelve (or Eleven, now that Judas is gone, Mark 16:14), and the Eleven, as in the Gospel of Mark proper, display rank unbelief and are rebuked by Jesus for it. Like the broader Gospel, then, the Resurrection is a reality in spite of human frailty, and frail men are the vehicles God has chosen to spread the Gospel.

Thus, it's significant that Jesus appears to the Eleven while they are "at table" (16:14). It suggests the Eucharistic communion of the Church under apostolic authority, however frail apostles may be. Nevertheless, they themselves now get to return to the substance of Jesus's original call at Galilee: "Go into all the world and preach the gospel to the whole creation" (16:15).

Mark 16:15–20: Ascension of the Lord / Feast of St. Mark, Evangelist / Conversion of St. Paul the Apostle (16:15–18)

The lectionary now presents Mark 16:15–20 for the Ascension. In 16:15, Jesus has issued an evangelical commission, and now, in 16:16, he insists that belief in him means Baptism as a necessary matter of salvation. For historic Christianity, Catholic or otherwise, faith and sacraments are never opposed. While some Christians separate them, seeing sacraments as exterior works opposed to faith as intellectual assent and an interior attitude, Christian faith is oriented to a living person, the risen and ascended Jesus Christ. The question then becomes: how do we relate to the risen and ascended Jesus Christ in whom we have faith?

Some Christians would answer, "by faith alone": That we relate to Jesus in our hearts somehow. But the historic and more robust answer is that we relate to Jesus also through our bodies, and that means sacraments. The sacraments mediate the most personal relationship with Jesus possible. The Sacrament of Baptism unites us with him metaphysically, ontologically (see Rom 6:1–4), and we and Christ live in each other (see Gal 2:20). In the Eucharist, we eat him. That's about as personal of a relationship as one can get.

Jesus now announces that signs will accompany believers on their evangelistic mission: exorcism, speaking in tongues, handling serpents, and drinking poison without harm (16:17–18). Exorcism and tongues are found throughout the New Testament, and impotent snakebites are found in Acts 28:3–6 and Luke 10:19. Drinking poison is not.

Two items merit discussion. First, for Mark, faith leads to signs like healing and exorcism; signs do not lead to faith. And yet, here in the longer ending, they do. On the other hand, we have seen throughout Mark that Jesus's healings and exorcisms are not always done secretly: often Jesus's healings generate glorification of God (2:12) and wonder (1:27), but also hostility (3:6). They also generate discipleship, as in the case of Bartimaeus (10:46–52). Perhaps here it's best to say that the signs accompany believers in their mission because they do in fact believe first; they're believers. And those who witness their signs will respond in varied ways as they have done throughout Mark's Gospel.

Second, the signs aren't random, but rather indicate Jesus's continuing liberation of the cosmos from sin, death, hell, and the devil in the time of the Church. Indeed, Jesus tells his disciples in Mark 16:15 to preach the Gospel *to the whole creation*. Salvation isn't merely saved souls flitting to heaven when individuals die; it's the restoration and transformation of the whole created order, heaven and earth, visible and invisible.[12] When Mark's Jesus exorcises and heals, he's not simply providing temporal relief to the afflicted. These mighty signs reveal that Jesus is liberating the cosmos from its bondage to sin, death, hell, and the devil.

Further, there are allegorical elements at play here. The word for "serpent" in Mark 16:18a is *ophis*, the same word used in Genesis 3 in the LXX for the satanic viper that threw the whole human race into sin (and indeed, all of creation, as Adam was fashioned from the very stuff of earth, and Eve from him, Gen 2:7, 21–22). The Church, in its mission, triumphs over the satanic serpent.

What's more, the reference to drinking deadly things in Mark 16:18 may refer not simply to common poison. Not so many decades after the writing of Mark's Gospel, St. Ignatius of Antioch advises the Trallians to "abstain from herbage of a different kind" from Jesus Christ—namely "heresy" (*Trall.* 6).[13] For, heretics "mix up Jesus Christ with their own poison, speaking things which are unworthy of credit, like those who administer a deadly drug in sweet wine" (ibid.). For Catholics, then, salvation is found not in the poison of heresy but in the sweet wine of the Eucharist, in which we drink in the Truth himself.

Above all, the signs that accompany the Church on its mission flow from Jesus and he can exercise absolute sov-

---

[12] See Romans 8:19–23: "For the creation waits with eager longing for the revealing of the sons of God; for the creation was subjected to futility, not of its own will but by the will of him who subjected it in hope; because the creation itself will be set free from its bondage to decay and obtain the glorious liberty of the children of God. We know that the whole creation has been groaning in travail together until now; and not only the creation, but we ourselves, who have the first fruits of the Spirit, groan inwardly as we wait for adoption as sons, the redemption of our bodies."

[13] Ignatius, *Letter to the Trallians* 6, in ANF, 1:194–95; see the discussion in James R. Edwards, *The Gospel According to Mark* (Pillar New Testament Commentary; Grand Rapids, MI: Eerdmans, 2001), 507.

ereign authority not only because it was given to him, nor simply because of his own divine identity, but also because of his total embrace of the cross. That's the key: the Church flourishes and succeeds in mission to the extent that it suffers the cross and, so, unites itself to Jesus, and thus to his own authority and person.

Jesus is now ascended, as the crucified and risen Christ has been "taken up to heaven" and taken his rightful place "at the right hand of God" (16:19). The ascended Jesus Christ powers the Church's mission, for after his Ascension, the disciples "went forth and preached everywhere, while the Lord worked with them and confirmed the message by the signs that attended it. Amen" (16:20). Amen indeed! Mission is powered by the crucified, risen, and ascended Jesus Christ.

Why? Although often neglected, the Ascension is a most important component of Christology. It's not an afterthought or appendix. Rather, it completes the circle of the Son of God's life, from preexistence through Incarnation to Cross and Resurrection, returning the Son to the total divine life of God in the Trinity from whence he came, but now with a body.

From his position in heaven at the right hand of the Father, Jesus Christ the Son can now be everywhere. The Ascension grounds the doctrine of ubiquity. From heaven, Jesus Christ can direct and power the Church's mission, which the flow of Mark 16:19–20 suggests. And from heaven, Jesus Christ's risen, resurrected Body can come down upon a million altars as the Church carries forth its greatest sign, the Eucharist.

PART III:

Resources for
Further Study

Of the making of many books there is no end, and so the literature on Mark's Gospel is endless. The books, commentaries, and articles below would be good initial resources for those committed to teaching and preaching Mark well.

On Preaching

Arthurs, Jeffrey. *Preaching with Variety: How to Recreate the Dynamics of Biblical Genres.* Grand Rapids, MI: Kregel, 2007.

Arthurs's work teaches preachers how best to interpret and proclaim the six major genres of the Bible. It includes two chapters on preaching narrative and a chapter on preaching parables. Thus, it's an indispensable resource for preaching Mark's Gospel well.

Genig, Joshua. *Viva Vox: Rediscovering the Sacramentality of the Word Through the Annunciation.* Minneapolis, MN: Fortress, 2015.

Genig, a convert to Orthodoxy from Missouri Synod Lutheranism, does in his book what the title says. His work draws on the Annunciation in service of a robust theology and praxis for homiletics. Drawing deeply on the sacramental implications of the Annunciation, he wishes to move preaching away from the simple dispensing of doctrine and toward the facilitation of a sacramental encounter with Jesus Christ, the incarnate Word in the written word of Scripture.

Lowry, Eugene L. *The Homiletical Plot: The Sermon as Narrative Art Form.* Louisville, KY: Westminster John Knox, 2000.

Lowry here presents a primer on preaching in a narrative mode so that sermons or homilies have a plot that captivates congregations, as humans are narrative by nature.

Wright, John W. *Telling God's Story: Narrative Preaching for Christian Formation.* Downers Grove, IL: InterVarsity, 2007.

The particular strength of Wright's book is that it deals not only with the biblical narrative but also with contemporary narratives regnant in our therapeutic culture that place an individual's felt happiness at the center. Wright sees a conflict between the biblical narrative that should give shape to Christians' lives and the counternarratives most Western Christians in fact live by. As such, Wright aims at a form of preaching that situates the stories of congregants and families inside God's story of salvation history and forms them as God's people first.

Commentaries

Edwards, James R. *The Gospel According to Mark.* Pillar New Testament Commentary. Grand Rapids, MI: Eerdmans, 2001.

Perhaps the one commentary on Mark's Gospel for working homilists to own—erudite, theological, accessible. Dr. Edwards is an evangelical, ecumenical Presbyterian. The commentary is more historically oriented than an examination of Mark's story, but Edwards pays sufficient attention to Mark's intratextual dynamics.

Healy, Mary. *The Gospel According to Mark*. Catholic Commentary on Sacred Scripture 1. Grand Rapids, MI: Baker Academic, 2008.

Dr. Healy, a professor at Sacred Heart Major Seminary in Detroit, provides us with a serviceable, efficient commentary committed to an orthodox Catholic perspective.

Marcus, Joel. *Mark 1–8: A New Translation with Introduction and Commentary*. Anchor Yale Bible Commentaries 27. New York: Doubleday, 2000.

———. *Mark 8–16: A New Translation with Introduction and Commentary*. Anchor Yale Bible Commentaries 27a. New York: Doubleday, 2009.

Dr. Marcus teaches at Duke Divinity School. His perspective is thoroughly historical-critical, so these two volumes are the one commentary to have for consideration of historical-critical questions and socio-cultural background. His perspective is different from most historical critics on many critical questions (for instance, he argues for a Syrian, not a Roman, provenance for Mark's Gospel), increasing the value of his work.

Books/Monographs

Best, Ernest. *Mark: The Gospel as Story.* Edinburgh, UK: T&T Clark International, 1988.

> Best approaches Mark as a coherent work of literature situated chiefly within the matrix of the Old Testament that should be read as a narrative. Like Juel's *Master of Surprise,* (see below) his book is not a commentary, but an exploration of scenes, characters, and themes.

Fowler, Robert M. *Let the Reader Understand: Reader-Response Criticism and the Gospel of Mark.* Harrisburg, PA: Trinity Press International, 2001.

> Fowler's work is a responsible exercise in reader-response criticism, which holds as an axiom that meaning is the product of an encounter between socio-culturally situated readers and particular texts. Thus, meaning is never determinate, but fluid and context-dependent. The book contains crucial insights and serves as a worthy counter to the still regnant historical-critical paradigm.

Juel, Donald. *A Master of Surprise: Mark Interpreted.* Reprint. Minneapolis, MN: Augsburg Fortress, 2002.

———. *The Gospel of Mark.* Interpreting Biblical Texts. Nashville, TN: Abingdon, 1999.

> The late Dr. Juel was a Lutheran professor of Scripture at Luther Seminary and Princeton Theological Seminary. He uses literary insights to get at Mark's literary and theological dynamics. If you read one thing on this list,

make it *Master of Surprise*. The second work, *The Gospel of Mark*, is accessible as well and presents further insights not present in *Master of Surprise*.

Kingsbury, Jack Dean. *The Christology of Mark's Gospel*. Philadelphia, PA: Fortress, 1983.

Kingsbury is a pioneer in narrative approaches to the Gospels. In this work, he situates the significant titles of Jesus that Mark's Gospel presents in their narrative context. He finds that much talk of the "messianic secret" in Mark's Gospel has been misguided, for the true secret known to Mark's Jesus and Mark's readers is his identity as Son of God. The work remains profitable for preachers because it not only models biblical scholarship done in a narrative key but also presents a compelling picture of the Markan Jesus.

Powell, Mark Allan. *What Is Narrative Criticism?* Guides to Biblical Scholarship New Testament Series. Minneapolis, MN: Fortress, 1991.

This little work is the most handy book-length crash course on narrative approaches to the Gospels available, and clergy formed by the historical-critical paradigm—and that's most clergy even today—who wish to develop skills in narrative interpretation would do well to read this book.

Rhoads, David, Joanna Dewey, and Donald Michie. *Mark as Story: An Introduction to the Narrative of a Gospel*. 3rd ed. Minneapolis, MN: Fortress, 2012.

Rhoads, a New Testament scholar, and the late Donald Michie, a professor of English, collaborated and first published *Mark as Story* in 1982. It is fair to say that the book began a steady revolution in Markan studies and Gospel studies more broadly. It approaches Mark's Gospel as a coherent narrative, introduces readers to narrative interpretation, and contains chapters on the narrator, settings, plot, characters, audience, and the ethics of reading. A must-have for preachers desiring to get the most out of Mark's Gospel and deliver it to their congregations.

Articles and Essays

The first two articles below deal with the phenomenon of Markan intercalation, so important for understanding Mark's literary dynamics. Edwards focuses in a more traditional way on threefold sandwiches in particular, while I draw on literary theory to focus on a particular fourfold intercalation, Peter's denial of Jesus and Jesus's confession of his identity before the high priest. The final two essays below deal with how narrative approaches might generate meaning (the Struthers Malbon piece) and the very structure of Mark's story (the Moloney piece).

Edwards, James R. "Markan Sandwiches: The Significance of Interpolations in Markan Narratives." *Novum Testamentum* 31 (1989): 193–216.

Abstract: Readers of the Gospel of Mark are familiar with the Second Evangelist's convention of breaking up a story or pericope by inserting a second, seemingly unrelated, story into the middle of it. A good example occurs in chapter 5, where Jairus, a ruler of the synagogue, importunes Jesus to heal his daughter (vv. 21–24). A woman with a hemorrhage interrupts Jesus en route to Jairus's house (vv. 25–34), and only after recording the woman's healing does Mark resume with the raising of Jairus's daughter, who had died in the meantime (vv. 35–43). The literary technique has a theological purpose: the sandwiches emphasize the major motifs of the Gospel, especially the meaning of faith, discipleship, bearing witness, and the dangers of apostasy. Moreover, the middle story nearly always provides the key to the theological purpose of the sandwich.

Huizenga, Leroy A. "The Confession of Jesus and the Curses of Peter: A Narrative-Christological Approach to the Text-Critical Problem of Mark 14:62." *Novum Testamentum* 53 (2011): 244–266.

Abstract: Joel Marcus has recently revived the view that the longer reading of Jesus's words in Mark 14:62 is original, as the shorter reading threatens Markan priority, given Jesus's enigmatic, ambivalent response in Matthew 26:64. Marcus and all other commentators have conducted the debate on traditional text-critical and redaction-critical grounds. In response, employing a disciplined and historical approach to narrative criticism, my article (1) contends on narrative and Christological grounds that the shorter reading of Jesus's words in Mark 14:62 is original and (2) explores how narrative criticism contributes to textual criticism.

Struthers Malbon, Elizabeth. "Narrative Criticism: How Does the Story Mean?" In *Mark and Method: New Approaches in Biblical Studies*, 29–58. Edited by Janice Capel Anderson and Stephen E. Moore. Minneapolis, MN: Fortress, 2008.

Struthers Malbon offers a chapter-length introduction to the theory and terms involved in interpreting Mark's Gospel as a story, and so her contribution makes for an efficient introduction to narrative criticism of the Gospels. She covers basics such as the difference between story and discourse, concepts such as the implied author and the implied reader, characterization, spatial and temporal settings, the distinction between plot and narrative world, and narrative rhetoric.

Moloney, Francis J. "The Markan Story." *Word & World* 26 (2006): 5–13.

Moloney offers a solid overview of the structure and import of Mark's story and discusses some important terms and concepts of literary theory along the way. Particularly helpful is his pointing out of certain textual markers that do not simply reveal Mark's own outline but also model how one ought to read Gospels and other ancient narrative literature. As regards Mark's Gospel, he writes explicitly against Bultmann's idea that Mark as author was an incompetent who recorded an incoherent mishmash of traditions, contending that Mark in fact "had a clear plan and a definite theological intention," that "Mark tells a striking story that calls us into its message" (p. 5).